"A passion for deep, responsible, and faithful t
a hallmark of Grant Osborne's ministry in both the academy and church. His
writings have long been in use by scholars. In these commentaries on Colossians
and Philemon he gifts to all of us a reliable, meaty exposition in everyday language. Those studying the Bible personally and in groups, as well as pastors and
teachers, have here a good resource. It is rooted in scholarship, for the church,
and gets straight to the point. This is serious thinking, plainly written."

—Jon C. Laansma, Associate Professor of Greek and New Testament,
Wheaton College and Graduate School

"Grant Osborne is ideally suited to write a series of concise commentaries on
the New Testament. His exegetical and hermeneutical skills are well known,
and anyone who has had the privilege of being in his classes also knows his
pastoral heart and wisdom. This commentary is ideal for pastors and Bible
study leaders as it pays close attention to the text without getting lost in technical details. Osborne expounds the text faithfully, asking what God was
saying through Paul to the Colossians and to Philemon and what that means
for us today. This will be a wonderful resource for preachers and Bible study
leaders, and for help in daily Bible reading."

—Ray Van Neste, Professor of Biblical Studies, Director of the Ryan Center for
Biblical Studies, Union University

"Grant Osborne is an eminent New Testament scholar and warm-hearted professor who loves the word of God. Through decades of effective teaching at
Trinity Evangelical Divinity School and church ministry around the world,
he has demonstrated an ability to guide his readers in a careful understanding of the Bible. This accessible new commentary on Colossians and Philemon
helps readers understand the text clearly and accurately. But it also draws
us to consider the implications of the text, providing key insights on faithful application and preaching that reflect a lifetime of ministry experience.
This unique combination of scholarship and practical experience makes this
volume an invaluable resource for all students of God's word, and especially
those who are called to preach and teach."

—H. Wayne Johnson, Associate Academic Dean and associate professor of
pastoral theology, Trinity Evangelical Divinity School

"For many years it has been my privilege to serve with Dr. Osborne as a fellow elder in our church and to observe him preaching and teaching the New
Testament to enthralled laypeople. This commentary (series) provides exactly
what our church has appreciated again and again: his winsome ability to step
down the current of high-voltage scholarship in ways that illuminate the biblical
text for ordinary Christians, and energize them to light their world for Christ!"

—Todd Habegger, Senior Pastor, Village Church of Gurnee (IL)

Praise for the Osborne New Testament Commentaries

"The Osborne New Testament Commentaries draw from the deep well of a lifetime of serious study and teaching. They present significant interpretive insights in a highly accessible, spiritually nurturing format. This is a tremendous resource that will serve a new generation of Bible readers well for years to come. Highly recommended!"

—Andreas J. Köstenberger, Founder of Biblical Foundations™
(biblicalfoundations.org), Senior Research Professor of New Testament &
Biblical Theology, Southeastern Baptist Theological Seminary

"Grant Osborne has spent his entire professional career teaching and writing about good principles for the interpretation of Scripture and then modeling them in his own scholarship, not least in commentaries on numerous New Testament books. The Osborne New Testament Commentaries, therefore, are a welcome new series by a veteran New Testament scholar determined to spend as much time as God gives him in his retirement years distilling the conclusions of the finest of scholarship without bogging down the reader in detailed interaction with all the various perspectives that have been suggested. If all the volumes are as good as this inaugural work on Revelation, the series will become a most welcome resource for the busy pastor or teacher."

—Craig L. Blomberg, Distinguished Professor of New Testament,
Denver Seminary

"Like many others in the church and academy, I have greatly benefitted from the writings of Grant Osborne over the course of my professional career. Grant has a gift for summarizing the salient points in a passage and making clear what he thinks the text means—as well as making it relevant and applicable to believers at all levels of biblical maturity. I especially commend the usefulness of these verse by verse commentaries for pastors and lay leaders."

—Stanley E. Porter, President, Dean, and Professor of New Testament,
Roy A. Hope Chair in Christian Worldview, McMaster Divinity College,
Hamilton, Ontario, Canada

"For years I have found Grant Osborne's commentaries to be reliable and thoughtful guides for those wanting to better understand the New Testament. Indeed, Osborne has mastered the art of writing sound, helpful, and readable commentaries and I am confident that this new series will continue the level of excellence that we have come to expect from him. How exciting to think that pastors, students, and laity will all be able to benefit for years to come from the wise and insightful interpretation provided by Professor Osborne in this new series. The Osborne New Testament Commentaries will be a great gift for the people of God."

—David S. Dockery, President, Trinity International University

COLOSSIANS & PHILEMON

Verse by Verse

OSBORNE · NEW TESTAMENT COMMENTARIES

COLOSSIANS & PHILEMON

Verse by Verse

GRANT R. OSBORNE

LEXHAM PRESS

Colossians & Philemon: Verse by Verse
Osborne New Testament Commentaries

Copyright 2016 Grant R. Osborne

Lexham Press, 1313 Commercial St., Bellingham, WA 98225
LexhamPress.com

Print ISBN 9781577997368
Digital ISBN 9781577997375

Lexham Editorial Team: Abby Salinger, David Bomar, Elliot Ritzema, Justin Marr, Scott Hausman
Cover Design: Christine Gerhart
Back Cover Design: Brittany Schrock
Typesetting: ProjectLuz.com

CONTENTS

Series Preface   ix

COLOSSIANS

Introduction to Colossians   3

1:1–14   Greeting and Prologue: The Power of the Gospel   16
         in the Church

1:15–2:23 The Preeminence of Christ in   32
         Christian Doctrine

3:1–4:1 The Preeminence of Christ in Christian Living   89

4:2–18   Concluding Thoughts   129

PHILEMON

Introduction to Philemon   147

Letter opening   157

1–7   The Love and Faith of Philemon   157

8–20   Letter body   165

21–25   Letter Closing   179

Glossary   183

Bibliography   185

Subject and Author Index   187

Index of Scripture and Other Ancient Literature   198

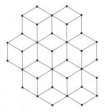

SERIES PREFACE

There are two authors of every biblical book: the human author who penned the words, and the divine Author who revealed and inspired every word. While God did not dictate the words to the biblical writers, he did guide their minds so that they wrote their own words under the influence of the Holy Spirit. If Christians really believed what they said when they called the Bible "the word of God," a lot more would be engaged in serious Bible study. As divine revelation, the Bible deserves, indeed demands, to be studied deeply.

This means that when we study the Bible, we should not be satisfied with a cursory reading in which we insert our own meanings into the text. Instead, we must always ask what God intended to say in every passage. But Bible study should not be a tedious duty we have to perform. It is a sacred privilege and a joy. The deep meaning of any text is a buried treasure; all the riches are waiting under the surface. If we learned there was gold deep under our backyard, nothing would stop us from getting the tools we needed to dig it out. Similarly, in serious Bible study all the treasures and riches of God are waiting to be dug up for our benefit.

This series of commentaries on the New Testament is intended to supply these tools and help the Christian understand more deeply the God-intended meaning of the Bible. Each volume walks the reader verse-by-verse through a book with the goal of opening up for us what God led Matthew or Paul or John to say to their readers. My goal in this series is to make sense of the historical and literary background of these ancient works, to supply the information that will enable the modern reader to understand exactly what the biblical writers were saying to their first-century audience. I want to remove the complexity of most modern commentaries and provide an easy-to-read explanation of the text.

But it is not enough to know what the books of the New Testament meant back then; we need help in determining how each text applies to our lives today. It is one thing to see what Paul was saying his readers in Rome or Philippi, and quite another thing to see the significance of his words for us. So at key points in the commentary, I will attempt to help the reader discover areas in our modern lives that the text is addressing.

I envision three main uses for this series:

1. *Devotional Scripture reading.* Many Christians read rapidly through the Bible for devotions in a one-year program. That is extremely helpful to gain a broad overview of the Bible's story. But I strongly encourage another kind of devotional reading—namely, to study deeply a single segment of the biblical text and try to understand it. These commentaries are designed to enable that. The commentary is based on the NIV and explains the meaning of the verses, enabling the modern reader to read a few pages at a time and pray over the message.

2. *Church Bible studies.* I have written these commentaries also to serve as guides for group Bible studies. Many Bible studies today consist of people coming together and sharing what they think the text is saying. There are strengths in such an approach, but also weaknesses. The problem

is that God inspired these scriptural passages so that the church would understand and obey *what he intended the text to say*. Without some guidance into the meaning of the text, we are prone to commit heresy. At the very least, the leaders of the Bible study need to have a commentary so they can guide the discussion in the direction God intended. In my own church Bible studies, I have often had the class read a simple exposition of the text so they can all discuss the God-given message, and that is what I hope to provide here.

3. *Sermon aids.* These commentaries are also intended to help pastors faithfully exposit the text in a sermon. Busy pastors often have too little time to study complex thousand-page commentaries on biblical passages. As a result, it is easy to spend little time in Bible study and thereby to have a shallow sermon on Sunday. As I write this series, I am drawing on my own experience as a pastor and interim pastor, asking myself what I would want to include in a sermon.

Overall, my goal in these commentaries is simple: I would like them to be interesting and exciting adventures into New Testament texts. My hope is that readers will discover the riches of God that lay behind every passage in his divine word. I hope every reader will fall in love with God's word as I have and begin a similar lifelong fascination with these eternal truths!

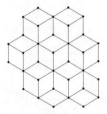

COLOSSIANS

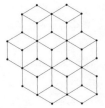

INTRODUCTION TO COLOSSIANS

AUTHORSHIP AND DATE

The letter claims to have been written by Paul, the apostle of Christ (1:1), and this claim was accepted until modern times, when a growing number of scholars began to dispute this and label the letter **pseudonymous** (falsely ascribed). They argued that Colossians has a different style from Paul's main letters (Galatians, Romans, 1 and 2 Corinthians) and that its theology is advanced, especially in terms of its high **Christology** and what they refer to as "over-realized **eschatology**" (the view that God's promises for the future have already come to pass). In fact, some have gone so far as to call Colossians a later and lesser copy of Ephesians.

However, none of this is necessary. As seen in 1 Corinthians 8:6 ("one God ... one Lord, Jesus Christ") and Romans 8:34, 38, Paul has a strong doctrine of Christ as one with the Father, and he has penned powerful christological hymns in Romans 1:3-4; 10:9-20; and Philippians 2:6-11. Certainly Paul reaches new heights with the claims of 1:15-20, but the Christology here builds on what he has said before. Moreover, his style is in keeping with the rest of the Prison Letters (Ephesians, Philippians, Philemon) and is not dissimilar to that of his other letters. None of us has a writing style that remains the same in all situations and contexts. Based on the criteria used by some scholars, my own writings could have been penned by four to five different people!

The opening and closing of the letter, the use of phrases like "in Christ" or "Lord Jesus Christ" or "the old self," and the strong ethical exhortation and use of vice codes—all are in keeping with Paul's style elsewhere. It is true that Colossians contains more than the usual emphasis on the realized side of eschatology—like the "seek and think the things above" section of 3:1-2—but this passage takes place in the context of Christ's return; consider 3:4 ("when Christ ... appears"; see also 1:20, 22, 28). The eschatology of this letter is inaugurated, with a proper tension between the already and the not yet—the present and future fulfillment of God's promises to his people. In short, there are insufficient reasons for doubting Paul's authorship of this letter.

Among interpreters who favor Paul as the author, all agree that this letter was written during a time of imprisonment—but which one? There are three such periods recorded in Acts: in Philippi (16:19-34), Caesarea (23:23-26:32), and Rome (28:11-31). In addition, it is likely that Paul was in prison briefly in Ephesus at the end of the third missionary journey (Acts 19:35-41; 1 Cor 15:32). Both the Philippian and Ephesian imprisonments were too brief to be likely for the Prison Letters (see below), so the choice is between Caesarea and Rome. The circumstances behind the Caesarean incarceration, with Paul languishing while the governor, Felix, was waiting for a bribe and the Jerusalem leaders were lobbying for Paul's execution, do not fit the production of these letters. Furthermore, Caesarea was too small to have become the missionary center for Paul and his team, and it is not mentioned in any of the letters, while Rome appears frequently. A Roman imprisonment is definitely the most likely.

Paul was taken to Rome in AD 60 and was on trial there for two years, until AD 62. During that time he wrote four letters known as "the Prison Letters"—Colossians, Philemon, Ephesians, and

Philippians, in that order. We know that Philippians was the last based on the comments in this letter regarding the end of Paul's trial (1:20-23; 2:23-24). When we compare the sister letters of Colossians and Ephesians, we conclude that Ephesians was most likely written later and that it expands on ideas set forth in Colossians, as opposed to the opposite scenario, which would mean that Colossians abbreviates Ephesians. This comparison is similar to that between Matthew and Mark; the consensus is that Mark, the shorter of the two Gospels, was written first and later expanded in Matthew. Colossians and Philemon, then, were evidently written sometime around the end of AD 61 and sent with Tychicus and Onesimus (4:7-9) to Colossae and Laodicea, with Ephesians being penned three to six months later and Philippians just prior to Paul's release. While some think Paul was not released but was executed at the end of this first imprisonment, Philippians reflects that he expected to be released (1:23-26; 2:24). If Paul wrote 1-2 Timothy and Titus—and I strongly believe he did—we may conclude that he was released and went back to Philippi and Asia Minor. If this is the case, he would have been executed at the end of his second imprisonment (2 Tim 4:6-8) during Nero's persecution of AD 64-65.

CIRCUMSTANCES AND CITY

At the end of the third missionary journey, in AD 57, Paul traveled with a delegation of leaders from the churches in the Roman provinces of Macedonia and Asia (Acts 20:4) to take the collection for the poor in Palestine to Jerusalem. He stopped at Miletus (the port city of Ephesus) and called for the elders from Ephesus to meet him for a "farewell address." On that occasion he called for them to faithfully oversee God's flock and delivered a prophetic warning regarding the future onset of false teachers who would come from both outside (20:29) and inside (20:30) the congregation, calling them "savage wolves" who would "not spare the flock."

Judging from Paul's letter to Colossae four years later, his prophecy was fulfilled as the wolves appeared in that city. In Paul's sister letter to the Ephesians, these wolves are mentioned only at 4:14 (the "cunning and crafty schemers"); apparently they had not yet arrived at Ephesus. However, within two years of the writing of Ephesians, Paul was forced to send Timothy to try to counter these heretics, who were gaining more and more influence in the area (1 and 2 Timothy). As far as we know, Timothy failed to stem the tide, but we have no further reports until the early 80s in 1–3 John (which most interpreters believe were written to the believers in Ephesus). In those letters the heretics seem to be even more entrenched. The one recorded victory does not take place until AD 95, as seen in the letter to Ephesus in Revelation (Rev 2:1–7) in which the Ephesian leaders expose and triumph over "the Nicolaitan heresy." So Colossae seems to be the point of entry for a dangerous set of teachings that would threaten the church for 30-plus years. Of course, we do not know the relationship among the heresies reflected in these various letters; they could either be interrelated or separate movements. We do know that they took place in the same region over a three decade period, so some interconnection is at least a possibility.

Colossae, one of three leading cities (with Laodicea and Hierapolis) in the Lycus Valley, lay on the major Roman road running east from Ephesus through Asia Minor. It had been one of the wealthiest and most powerful cities in the region, commercially important due to its wool industry. However, in the third century BC Colossae began to lose its influence, and by the first century it was eclipsed by both the other cities. Close to the time of Paul's letter a major earthquake had severely damaged Laodicea and Colossae (in AD 60–61); the former town rebuilt itself, while Colossae languished. So Paul wrote to Colossae not because of the importance of the city but because of the danger posed by the false teachers.

An interesting historical fact helps us understand the situation. In the third century BC Antiochus III (father of Antiochus

IV, whose "abomination of desolation" in 167 BC had led to the Maccabean revolt) settled some 2,000 Jewish families in the region of the Lycus Valley, leading to a mixture of Jewish, **Hellenistic**, and eventually Christian influences. The three movements apparently amalgamated to some extent, borrowing practices and beliefs from one another and thereby creating a syncretistic situation that seems to have fueled the heretical movement Paul was countering in Colossians.

The church at Colossae was founded during the third missionary journey, in which Paul spent over two years in Ephesus and might have sent evangelists into the whole province, with the result that "all the Jews and Greeks who lived in the province of Asia heard the word of the Lord" (Acts 19:10). However, we have no hard evidence that Paul himself ever accompanied any of those evangelistic teams to visit Colossae. The founding pastor of the church in Colossae was Epaphras (1:7-8; 4:12-13), who apparently led the mission to the Lycus Valley and its three leading cities. He came from Colossae, was converted under Paul in Ephesus, and returned to his home area with the gospel. Nearly all the converts were Gentiles, as the descriptions of their past denote a pagan background (1:21, 27; 2:13), yet many of the teachings reflect a Jewish background (2:16-18).

THE COLOSSIAN HERESY

We know nothing about this movement apart from what Paul has stated in this letter. Clearly it is false teaching, for he warns his readers against deception (2:4) that can "take them captive through hollow and deceptive philosophy" built on "human tradition"(2:8). The Jewish aspects are clear and dominant, with the mention of food laws, festivals, purity regulations (2:16, 18, 21), and circumcision (2:11). Gentile elements are also evident, however, as in the "harsh treatment of the body" (2:23) and emphasis on the cosmic powers (2:15, 18). It is frequently noted that the cult centered on visions (2:18b, literally "entering into what they have seen") and angel worship (2:18a, "worship of angels"). Its adherents conceived of angels having mediated the law at Sinai (Heb 2:2)—a tradition that is not mentioned in the OT, though angels are stressed in connection with Sinai and the exodus (Exod 23:20–22; Deut 33:2; Ps 68:17), and Second Temple Jewish texts portray angels as having brought the law (Jubilees 1:27; 2:1; and Josephus' *Antiquities of the Jews*, 15:163). Paul argues that these are, in reality, fallen angels (the "elemental spirits" of 2:8, 20), commenting on a form of demon worship in which ascetic rules and practices both enhanced the vision state and placated the angel-beings.

All of this was wedded to a type of proto-**gnostic** Hellenistic philosophy that centered on knowledge as salvation and focused on speculative philosophical musings. The result was a syncretistic new religious movement that was Christian in name only. Paul's solution lies in the true doctrines of the Lord Jesus Christ as supreme over his creation and of his atoning sacrifice on the cross as the only path to salvation. Colossae was contending with a primarily christological heresy, and Paul's point is that the fullness of life with God can be attained only through Christ and that wisdom and knowledge can be found not in fabricated human philosophy but only in him. Thus the movement's legalism is based on false premises and its ascetic practices devoid of any value. This religion and its so-called understanding are both fleshly and antithetical to God and to true religion.

STRUCTURE AND OUTLINE

There can be no question that Paul was a gifted writer, employing rhetorical style and organization to render his letters artistic successes with a powerful effect on readers. A good example of this can be found in the opening and closing portions of his letters. In one sense they follow letter-writing conventions of the first century, with the author-recipient-greeting-thanksgiving-prayer format of the openings and the greetings-instructions-farewell structure of the closings. However, Paul goes beyond mere form to transform both openings and closings into strong rhetorical and theological devices.

Modern outlines go only so far in helping us understand the literary argumentation employed by Paul, though their value and purpose is to enable today's audience to follow the strategy and logic behind Paul's developing message. The outline that follows attempts to supply the structural pattern of Paul's argumentation:

I. Greeting and prologue: The power of the gospel in the church, 1:1–14
   A. Greeting to the church, 1:1–2
   B. Thanksgiving for the growth of the gospel among the Colossians, 1:3–8
      1. The basis: Their faith and love grounded in hope, 1:3–5a
      2. The result: The spread of the gospel, 1:5b–6
      3. The ministry of Epaphras, 1:7–8
   C. Prayer for the knowledge to live a life pleasing to the Lord, 1:9–14
      1. The knowledge to walk worthily, 1:9–10a
      2. The means by which we can walk worthily, 1:10b–12a
      3. The work of the Father within the believer, 1:12b–14

II. The preeminence of Christ in Christian doctrine, 1:15–2:23
   A. Christ's supremacy in creation, redemption, and the church, 1:15–23
      1. Christ's supremacy in creation and redemption, 1:15–20
         a. The exalted Christ and creation, 1:15–17
            1) Christ as the image of God, 1:15a
            2) Christ as the firstborn over creation, 1:15b
            3) Christ as the sphere, instrument, and goal of all creation, 1:16
            4) Christ as the sustaining force in creation, 1:17

b. The exalted Christ and redemption, 1:18-20
  1) Christ as the head of the body, 1:18a
  2) The supremacy of Christ over "all things," 1:18b
  3) The fullness of the Godhead residing in Christ, 1:19
  4) The purpose of Christ's coming: Reconciliation and peace, 1:20
2. The meaning and effects of reconciliation for the church, 1:21-23
  a. The believers' past: Alienated from God, 1:21
  b. The believers' present: Reconciled and made holy, 1:22
  c. The believers' future: Steadfast in the faith, 1:23
B. Paul's gospel ministry, 1:24-2:5
  1. Paul's struggle in proclaiming Christ's mystery, 1:24-29
    a. Paul's suffering for the sake of the church, 1:24-25a
    b. Paul's commission to proclaim the mystery, 1:25b-27
    c. Paul's ministry of proclamation, 1:28-29
  2. Paul's struggle for the Colossians, 2:1-5
    a. Paul defines his struggle, 2:1
    b. The goal: United under God's mystery, Christ, 2:2-3
    c. Warning against the false teachers, 2:4-5
C. Confronting the false teachings, 2:6-23
  1. Challenge to be anchored in Christ, 2:6-7
  2. Warning against the deceptive teachings of the heretics, 2:8
  3. The meaning of true Christianity, 2:9-15
    a. The fullness in Christ and the church, 2:9-10
    b. The first description of the Christian: Died and raised in Christ, 2:11-12

c. The second description of the Christian: Forgiveness and the cancellation of debt, 2:13–15
4. Warnings against submitting to rituals and ascetic practices, 2:16–23
   a. Warning against dietary restrictions and calendar observances, 2:16–17
   b. Warning against misuse of visions, 2:18–19
   c. Warning against asceticism and legalism, 2:20–23

III. The preeminence of Christ in Christian living, 3:1–4:1
  A. A life focused on the things above, 3:1–4
    1. The resurrection life, 3:1–2
    2. The new life as hidden with Christ in God, 3:3
    3. Our future life in glory, 3:4
  B. Remove the filthy clothes of the fleshly life, 3:5–11
    1. The old life of sin, 3:5–8
      a. The command to put off sin, 3:5
      b. The result of sin: The wrath of God, 3:6–7
      c. The command to get rid of sin, 3:8
    2. The new life of unity in Christ, 3:9–11
  C. Life in the new community, 3:12–17
    1. Clothe yourselves with Christian virtues, 3:12–14
      a. The new clothing in Christ, 3:12
      b. Forgiveness and love in the new community, 3:13–14
    2. The centrality of the Lord Jesus in the new community, 3:15–17
      a. Christ's peace must reign, 3:15
      b. Christ's truth must indwell and produce worship, 3:16
      c. All of our actions must be done in the name of Christ, 3:17
  D. Honoring Christ in the household, 3:18–4:1
    1. Wives and husbands, 3:18–19
    2. Children and parents, 3:20–21

3. Slaves and masters, 3:22–4:1
   a. Obedience and faithfulness of slaves, 3:22–25
     1) Sincerity and reverence, 3:22
     2) Work for the Lord and his inheritance, 3:23–24a
     3) Jesus as Lord and Judge, 3:24b–25
   b. The fairness of masters, 4:1

IV. Concluding thoughts, 4:2–18
   A. Prayer and discernment, 4:2–6
     1. Call for prayer and vigilance, 4:2
     2. Prayer for Paul's gospel ministry, 4:3–4
     3. Challenge for the Colossians' interaction with outsiders, 4:5–6
   B. Final greetings and instructions, 4:7–18
     1. The messengers who bear the letter, 4:7–9
     2. Greetings from Paul's associates, 4:10–14
     3. Further greetings and instructions, 4:15–17
     4. Paul's signature and benediction, 4:18

THE THEOLOGY OF THE LETTER

CHRISTOLOGY

There can be no doubt that the primary theme in this letter is the lordship of Christ. While we lack details about the beliefs of the false teachers, we know that they had a deficient Christology. Their emphasis on visions and so-called **gnosis** (knowledge) likely replaced in their minds the centrality of Christ. From the start of the letter, then, Paul emphasizes "the Lord Jesus Christ" (1:3) and the necessity of living "a life worthy of the Lord" (1:10).

The core passage of the letter is the Christ-hymn of 1:15–20, where Jesus is proclaimed as "God of very God" (the image of Godhead), the supreme agent over his own creation, including both the heavenly and the earthly, the spirit-world and the physical world of humanity. All things are under his rule, and he both supervises his creation and will bring it to completion. In short, he is fully God, as all God's "fullness dwells in him" (1:19).

Christ is fully victorious—the victory having been won by his blood on the cross, resulting in reconciliation and peace for humankind (1:21, 22). Paul's ministry is a proclamation of the gospel defined as the "mystery" of Christ, "the hope of glory" (1:27). Jesus alone, not visions or ascetic rites, is the source of wisdom and knowledge (2:2-4); the fullness of life takes place only "in him" who is "the fullness of Deity" (2:6, 9-10). Forgiveness of sins, the cancellation of the IOU, comes via the cross (2:13-14), not through the speculations of the false teachers. Moreover, the cosmic powers have been defeated and disarmed by his resurrection and exaltation (2:8, 15, 20). We no longer live in and for the things of earth; since we have died and been raised with him (2:12; 3:1-2), we live under his lordship, and in him we have already been glorified (3:3-4) as a foretaste of his triumphant return (3:4).

THE CHURCH

The primary recipient of the work and words of the Lord Jesus is the people of God. When people become Christians, they are "in Christ"—a special emphasis in the Prison Letters that connotes at the outset union with Christ in conjunction with becoming part of his body, the church. Christ as Lord of all is the "head" of the body (1:18), and the believers are the members of that body, reconciled to God by his blood (1:20, 22). The church is the product of the new creation, the inaugurated rule of Christ in which a new spiritual reality has entered this world and been mediated through a new people of God who proclaim the new "mystery," Christ. Paul suffers "for the sake of his body" (1:24) and discloses the "mystery" of salvation in Christ "to the Lord's people" (1:26), who in turn proclaim it to the world.

Christ's cosmic rule over all his creation centers especially on his followers, with whom he shares his "glory" (3:4). The theological reality of the church as the redeemed people of God must be reflected in their everyday practice—the subject of 3:1–4:1. The members of the body of Christ have died to the old humanity and must put on the new humanity (3:9–10), which is made visible in new behavior patterns and Christian virtues. Finally, as mediator of the new creation, the church has a mission of spreading these truths to outsiders and taking every opportunity to provide answers to all who ask (4:5–6).

THE COSMIC POWERS

Christ's role as the agent of creation includes not just the physical universe but spiritual reality and spirit-beings as well. His Lordship over *all* creation implies both the good and the fallen angels—"whether thrones or powers or rulers or authorities, all things have been created through him and for him" (1:16). Paul uses this cosmic reality to challenge and correct the false teachers, who contended that Jesus alone was insufficient to defeat the cosmic powers and that visions and ascetic practices were necessary to do so.

The heretics claimed to be worshiping the angels who mediated the law at Sinai, but Paul corrects this false assumption, insisting that demonic forces, whom he refers to as "principalities and powers" and as "elemental spirits" (2:8, 20), have taken possession of these false teachers and directed their terrible teachings. These cosmic powers, Paul contends, were disarmed and defeated at the cross and resurrection (2:15). This assertion reflects Jesus' programmatic statement in Mark 3:27, where God's Son depicts himself as the "stronger man" who enters Satan's fortress, binds him, and plunders his kingdom. The forces of evil have been finally and utterly defeated, and Christ's followers are meant to live in victory.

ESCHATOLOGY

There are two categories of themes in the doctrine of "last things": *final* eschatology, centering on the events that will end human history and usher in eternity (the "not yet"); and *realized* eschatology, centering on the present fulfillment of God's end-time promises (the "already"). Most recognize that Paul in Colossians is emphasizing the latter. In 2:12 and 3:1 the believer is said to have already experienced a spiritual resurrection and begun a new life in Christ. The "hope stored up in heaven" (1:5) is realized in the "glorious riches" (1:27) of present salvation, and believers have already been "made alive" in Christ (2:13). However, this does not mean there is no final eschatology in the letter. In 3:4 the final glory of the saints will take place "when Christ appears," at which time faithful Christians will receive their "inheritance" (3:24). There also is emphasis on the final judgment (the "wrath of God" in 3:6), when those who have done wrong will be "repaid" for their sins (3:25). Many believe that the idea of "presenting" the believers "holy" (1:22) and "mature" (1:28) refers to the final presentation of them to God at the **eschaton**. In short, Colossians exhibits an inaugurated eschatology with the healthy New Testament tension between the "already" and the "not yet."

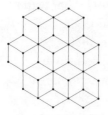

GREETING AND PROLOGUE
THE POWER OF THE GOSPEL IN THE CHURCH
(1:1–14)

Ancient **Hellenistic** and Jewish letters typically began with the author, the recipient, and a basic blessing, followed by a brief thanksgiving and a prayer wish for the recipients. Paul borrowed this form for his letters and modified it by expanding the thanksgiving and prayer sections into an introduction to a letter's contents and themes. The theological depth of Paul's introductions is astounding. In Colossians he emphasizes faith, hope, and love as the necessary results of the gospel, building to an incredible declaration on the significance of Christ. Much of the material in the introduction (1:3-14) and the **christological** passage (vv. 15-23) leads up to Paul's correction of the Colossian heretics in 2:6-23.

PAUL GREETS THE CHURCH (1:1-2)

As stated above, Paul verses 1-14 follows an ancient letter form—already used centuries earlier by Nebuchadnezzar in Daniel 4:1: "King Nebuchadnezzar, to the nations and peoples of every language, who live in all the earth: May you prosper greatly!" Paul employs the Hellenistic version of his own name rather than the Jewish "Saul" (Acts 7:58; 9:1), since that is how he was known in the Gentile churches. In the majority of his letters (except for Philippians, Philemon, and the Thessalonian letters) he identifies himself as "an apostle of Jesus Christ," stressing his election to the office: Paul was "sent by" Jesus Christ (*apostolos* means "a sent one") and chosen by "the will of God." In using "apostle" Paul reveals his desire for the Colossians to recognize his special authority, equal to that of the Twelve, as he opposes the false teachers and establishes the true doctrine that should guide the church. With Christ as the sender and God's will as the basis for his office, Paul is virtually declaring that the Triune Godhead stands behind his authority.

The co-author of this letter is "Timothy our brother," a young coworker (Rom 16:21) who had joined Paul from his home in Lystra (Acts 16:1–3) and become his main assistant, accompanying him even during his Roman imprisonment. Timothy may well have been the secretary who penned this letter in Paul's behalf (note 4:18, where Paul adds Timothy's name to the letter). He was a dedicated, loving individual often lauded by Paul (1 Cor 4:17; Phil 2:19–24) and called here a genuine "brother" in the faith, connoting not only a fellow Christian but also an associate in Paul's ministry.

The recipient is the church at Colossae, a town ten miles east of Laodicea and the least important of the three cities in the Lycus Valley (with Hierapolis). It was known for its wool industry, though Laodicea was far more significant in terms of its banking and trade (see Rev 3:14–22). Still, Colossae evidently had significant influence among the churches in the province of Asia and was important enough to receive one of Paul's letters. Paul calls the members of the Colossian church "holy ones" and "faithful brothers and sisters." The first of these descriptions (meaning "saints") is common in Paul's letters; the connotation of those who are "holy" or "set apart" from the world for God is part of its meaning. The believers are "saints" in terms of their inclusion within the messianic community of Christ and "holy" in view of their lifestyle. They are also "faithful" in terms of their commitment to obey the ethical and spiritual teachings of Christ. All of this centers on their position "in

Christ," referring to their union with Christ and their membership within his body—the church in dynamic fellowship under his lordship.

Paul's greeting combines language commonly found in Hellenistic letters ("grace/greetings") with Jewish letters (*shalōm*, or "peace"). He Christianizes both concepts and turns them into **eschatological** promises, in effect stating, "What you have been hoping for in your very greetings—divine grace and peace—is now being offered to you in Christ Jesus." It is *only* in Christ that people can find favor with God and the peace that passes all understanding.

PAUL GIVES THANKS FOR THE GROWTH OF THE GOSPEL AMONG THE COLOSSIANS (1:3-8)

THE BASIS: THEIR FAITH AND LOVE GROUNDED IN HOPE (1:3-5A)

Paul's typical thanksgiving, here applied to the Colossians, comes as the result of reports he and his associates have received about the church (from Epaphras and others, vv. 7-8). The language ("We always thank God") reflects that Paul's team conducted regular prayer and praise sessions that often centered on the situation at Colossae. Paul stresses that thanksgiving to God is to be a continual feature of the Christian life and should infuse everything the believer does (2 Cor 1:11; Eph 5:20; Col 3:17). Note that the thanksgiving he calls for is corporate, as opposed to merely individual—an integral part of the praise and worship experience in church life. As we experience God's guidance and empowering presence, we are led naturally to thanksgiving and praise for all he has done.

The focus of the thanksgiving is not horizontal, to other Christians, but vertical, to God—who is presented as "the Father of our Lord Jesus Christ." This phrasing is more elaborate than Paul's more common "to God" (1 Cor 1:4; 1 Thess 1:2) or "my God" (Phil 1:3; Phlm 4), emphasizing Jesus as the Son of God, his Father, and as "Lord" of all. Paul's thanks is directed to both the Father and the Son. The added "when we pray for you" seems redundant at first but emphasizes the frequency of the prayers Paul and his team lift to God on behalf of the churches in his charge. The life of the church dare never become insular, focused solely or primarily on local needs. For a church to fulfill its God-given purpose it must be missional, focused on God's work through God's eyes—concerned for the worldwide spread of the gospel and for the situations of churches elsewhere.

The basis for Paul's thankful heart is the report he has received from Epaphras (1:7) of the Colossians' spiritual state (v. 4). Note the familiar Christian triad of "faith, love, and hope," seen in 1 Corinthians 13:13 (also Gal 5:5–6; Eph 4:2–5; and 1 Thess 1:3; 5:8). The believers' "faith in Christ Jesus" is saving faith (belief in Christ that brings salvation, as seen in Rom 10:9) and more—that daily, absolute trust in Christ in which we acknowledge that he is Lord over everything we do. Our position "in" Christ becomes the sphere within which our faith infuses our daily activities.

The vertical (faith in Christ) must empower and result in the horizontal (love for the saints). Once we as believers learn to focus on Christ through faith, that Christ-centeredness can only result in our emulating his love for "all God's people" (Greek: "saints"). Paul's emphasis is not just on the fact that they are saints but reflective of the definition of "saints" as "holy ones." The believers' love is natural in that they share an intimate bond with all those who have been "set apart" from the world for God. As a group they do not belong to this world; as citizens of heaven (Phil 3:20) they are "aliens and foreigners" on earth (1 Pet 2:11; cf. 1 Pet 1:1, 17). This new family they have joined is typified by communal, mutual, reciprocal love.

This faith leading to love "springs from hope" (1:5a) because hope provides the basis for both the vertical faith and the horizontal love. In 1 Peter 1:3 we read that a "living hope" is the natural result of the new birth, with hope becoming the dynamic force that transforms our approach to life. Although oriented toward the future, that hope is neither ephemeral nor uncertain. It provides an anchor that secures the future with the knowledge that the sovereign Lord is in charge (1 Pet 1:5, "kept by the power of God for a salvation ready to be revealed in the last time").

THE RESULT: THE SPREAD OF THE GOSPEL (1:5B-6)

This hope that anchors the Christian life is "stored up for [us] in heaven." The verb here, with its nuance of "kept in readiness" or "kept safe," speaks of absolute security. Our secure location is "in heaven"; God (the implied subject) is at this very moment guaranteeing the future for his people—a future banked in heaven. More than a future-oriented outlook, this ultimate hope functions as a present force in which the uncertain future becomes an already existing reality, as in the definition of faith in Hebrews 11:1: "Now faith is confidence in what we *hope for* and assurance about what we *do not see.*" In Christian hope I am more certain about my ultimate future than I am about my complicated present! Many interpreters believe that Paul's statement about hope stored up in heaven is intended to correct a key error of the false teachers, who follow a realized form of Christianity devoid of future hope. Without a future dimension such a belief system ceases to be Christianity.

This emphasis on the secure nature of the believers' future hope is at the heart of the Christian message; the Colossians first "heard" it when they received "the true message of the gospel" (literally, "the word of truth, namely the gospel") when the church was founded by Epaphras and others (1:7-8). Clearly hope is an essential component of gospel proclamation and of Christian "truth." This is an essential aspect of Paul's refutation of the "false" teachers: By ignoring the future hope of the believer, they had deviated from true Christianity. Ultimate truth is encapsulated in God's "word" and must be holistic. There cannot be a side of "truth" that is realized without its being shaped by the future hope that anchors it in God's final plans.[1]

---

1. "Realized eschatology" is a theological concept that emphasizes the present work of Christ in the world today as he prepares for the end of history. For more on **eschatology**, see the glossary.

Having established the components of the gospel, Paul in verse 6 turns to its dynamic power in the world. His point that the gospel has "come to" his listeners conveys that it is now among them. The emphasis is on the presence and power of its message in their midst. Paul moves from past to present, from the gospel's triumphant procession through "the whole world" to its powerful effect on Colossae to the news of its ongoing effect on the Colossian church based on the joyous report of Epaphras.

Paul begins with the "worldwide" spread of the gospel. His stress on "the whole world" is not hyperbole; a few years earlier Paul had written that "from Jerusalem all the way around to Illyricum, I have fully proclaimed the gospel of Christ" (Rom 15:19). Paul had overseen the spread of the gospel in virtually every town and village in the eastern half of the Roman Empire. His desire had been to spend the rest of his life in the western half of the empire from Rome to Spain, "where Christ was not known" (Rom 15:20). Indeed it was a worldwide movement, and Paul was rejoicing over the fact that the Colossian church was part of that universal thrust of the gospel message.

Moreover, the good news was "bearing fruit and growing," imagery echoing the creation account in Genesis 1:22, 28 ("Be fruitful and increase ... fill the earth"). Paul considered it the mission of the church to be part of a "new creation," a spiritual re-creation of humankind in the image of God (see also John 1:3-4). Fruit bearing is an important image for the expansion of the church, first to the unbelieving world and then to Christians as they "grow" in Christ (John 15:4, 8). Paul applies this powerful process of growth to the Colossians by adding, "as it has been doing among you."

This growth of the mission has been made possible as the believers have begun to "understand truly the grace of God" (literally, "know the grace of God in truth"). In the rest of chapters 1-2 Paul will apply frequent emphasis to "knowledge" and "understanding," due at least in part to the influence of the false teachers. On a more basic level, it is essential for all believers to realize that spiritual growth cannot take place unless they "understand" the deep Christian "truths." The Greek word here for "understand" is *epiginōskō*. I used to think of this kind of understanding as a more directed, intense "knowledge," but recent studies have shown that in the Koine Greek period of Paul's day the term had virtually the same force as that of *ginōskō*, or "knowing." Paul is saying that the Colossian believers, having already been immersed in "the word of truth" (1:5), are now growing in it, though they need a deeper knowledge and experience of "God's grace" in their lives. We can never have enough gospel truth in our lives, and it's impossible to fully plumb the depths of the Word. I have been teaching and preaching for almost fifty years and wish I had another fifty in which to explore the incredible truths that still await my comprehension!

The Ministry of Epaphras (1:7–8)

Epaphras is likely short for Epaphroditus, possibly the same person mentioned in Philippians 2:25 and 4:18. He is mentioned again in 4:12–13 and in Philemon 23 is called Paul's "fellow prisoner," meaning either that he is with Paul in prison or (perhaps more likely) that he and Paul are both "prisoners of Christ." Epaphras, an associate of Paul, probably founded the church at Colossae during the third missionary journey, when teams were dispatched throughout the province of Asia to evangelize its cities (Acts 19:10). He appears to have been in charge of all the churches in the Lycus Valley region (4:12–13) and was Paul's source of information about the Colossian church.

Paul calls Epaphras "our dear fellow servant" (Greek: "beloved fellow slave"; also v. 12), implying a close personal friendship between the two men, along with their mutual and entire dependence upon Christ as Lord and Master. Epaphras, likely one of Paul's primary associates (along with Timothy), was a "faithful minister (*diakonos*) of Christ," stressing his office as founding pastor at Colossae and his trustworthiness in adjudicating his duties there. The *diakonoi* were preaching and teaching leaders in the church, and Epaphras was an outstanding model of a successful "minister."

Epaphras not only took the gospel to the Colossians but was also a faithful messenger in reporting the progress of this church back to Paul and the team. As such he ministered in two ways—for Paul to the Colossians and for the Colossians to Paul. Epaphras' report about the believers' love points back to verse 4 and the news Paul had received about "the love they have (for all the saints)." This love-bond in the Colossian church will be revisited (2:2; 3:14) and was a prime characteristic of these people. The means "by" (Greek: *en*) which this love is manifested is "the Spirit." It is the Holy Spirit who forges unity and love in the community and provides the enabling power to surmount the human ego and "value others above [ourselves]" (Phil 2:3).

PAUL PRAYS FOR THE KNOWLEDGE TO LIVE A LIFE PLEASING TO THE LORD (1:9–14)

THE KNOWLEDGE TO WALK WORTHILY (1:9–10A)

Paul and his team participated in regular prayer times (v. 3), to the extent that they "never stopped praying" and "continually asked God" to intervene in the Colossian church (v. 9). From the moment Epaphras gave his report and the team "heard" of the situation at Colossae, Paul and his associates interceded for their needs.

As verse 9 conveys, Paul's central petition is that God would grant the Colossians "knowledge of his will." Note how strongly Paul expresses this: He asks not merely that God will give the believers a bit of wisdom, but that he will "fill them to overflowing" with profound understanding of the divine will for their lives. Note also that God, not church tradition, was to be the source of this knowledge. Too often our views are forged more strongly by the latest popular preacher than by the Word of God. The idea of fullness occurs often in this letter (1:19, 24–25; 2:2–3, 9–10; 4:12) and probably stems in part from a false claim of the heretics that their teaching brought true "fullness." Here the point is full knowledge, a robust doctrinal understanding that can enable one to realize God's "will" in daily conduct. The heretics had their own **gnosis**, but it was a false "knowledge" based on speculation and lies rather than on the truths of God.

The instrument of this God-centered knowledge is "all wisdom and understanding." The adjective "spiritual," certainly a reference to the Holy Spirit, is rightly translated in the NIV "that the Spirit gives," referring back to 1:8 ("in the Spirit"). Once again it is the Spirit who endows the believer with the "wisdom" and "understanding" necessary to discern God's truth and live accordingly. Descriptions of the Spirit imparting these aspects of mental and spiritual acumen are found often in the Old Testament (e.g., Exod 31:3; 35:31 [of the craftsmen building the tabernacle]; Deut 34:9 [Joshua filled with the "spirit of wisdom"]), and most notably in Isa 11:2, where the "Spirit of wisdom and understanding" will rest on the "shoot of Jesse," the messianic "Branch"). In both Testaments, the possession or exercise of wisdom equates to living in God's world on the basis of God's will—turning knowledge into practice and doing it God's way. All those in ministry today should seek the Spirit-imparted wisdom to guide their people in a quest for understanding and living out the deep truths of the Word.

The goal of such knowledge is to "live a life (Greek: 'walk') worthy of the Lord" (1:10). Effective Bible study is always practical; the purpose of biblical understanding is to change lives and enable people to discern God's will for their daily conduct. To "walk worthy of the Lord" refers to a lifestyle that reflects God in every way, that asks in every decision "What would God have me do?" The Lord of the universe decides what counts as righteous behavior, and we are to make Christ the Lord of our life in the small things as well as the consequential.

The purpose is to "please him in every way," a restatement of "walk worthily" that adds the nuance of bringing God pleasure by living according to his will. A basic question at every stage of life should be "Whom do I seek to please—myself, my friends,

or God?" The idea of pleasing God appears frequently in the letters of Paul (Rom 8:8; 12:1–2; 1 Cor 7:32; 1 Thess 2:4, 15), who here
adds "in every way" to stress the all-encompassing nature of
this quest: It is wide-sweeping, demanding absolute obedience
in every area of life.

THE MEANS BY WHICH WE CAN WALK WORTHILY (1:10B–12A)

Paul uses four participial clauses to define how this God-
oriented lifestyle works. The first two reiterate verse 6, which
pointed out that the gospel was "bearing fruit and growing"
around the world. Paul now applies that image to the spiritual
growth of individual believers.

1. The God-pleasing life is one of "bearing fruit in every
   good work." Fruitfulness in the New Testament means
   both winning souls for the Lord and growing spiritually, as evidenced by manifesting the "fruit of the Spirit"
   (Gal 5:22–23). This is a subset under the second category, with the fruit being good works. God had done his
   work among the believers, producing a wonderful fruit-
   harvest of souls in Colossae; now they are to produce a
   similar harvest of good works for God. Paul may have had
   in mind the harvest parables of Jesus, especially that of
   the Sower and the thirty-, sixty-, and one-hundredfold
   yield of the "good soil" (Mark 4:8). As stated in Hebrews
   10:24, we as Christians are to "consider how we may spur
   one another toward love and good deeds"—to exemplify
   in explicit acts of kindness the same love that typified the
   Colossians in verse 4.

2. To please God Christians also need to be "growing in the
   knowledge of God." This means getting to know God in a
   deeper, more intimate way. Knowing God was a lifelong
   pursuit for Paul, initially as a rabbi-in-training and much
   more after his Damascus road experience. In Philippians
   3:10 he expresses that "to know [Christ]" is the starting
   point for all Christian understanding; he is referring not

to mere academic knowledge but to a life-altering, personal coming-to-understanding that infuses every area of our life. Everything Paul did contributed to his process of coming to know the Triune Godhead, and he was never satisfied—continuously seeking growth in this area throughout his life.

3. Paul realized that he could live a "worthy" life only by being "strengthened with all power according to his glorious might." Note the terms he uses here—"strength," "power," and "might." Clearly Paul realized the utter inadequacy for believers of trying to grow in Christ through our own meager efforts. All three terms refer to God's "mighty power" that alone can "strengthen" us. This echoes Isaiah 40:31: "Those who wait upon the LORD will gain a new strength." Isaiah 40:30 had just cited the great athletes/soldiers of the prophet's day: These "youths" would grow "weary" and "stumble" despite their impressive strength (think of the game-losing fumble or the ninth-inning strikeout). Yet whenever we're ready to collapse in our own weakness and despair, we can turn to the Lord and receive not a renewal of our own strength but an influx of God's inexhaustible power that will enable us to "soar on wings like eagles"!

This is the point in 1:11 as well. Almighty God pours his strength into us "with all power"—with the omnipotence that infuses us with his limitless endurance even in our utter exhaustion (as Peter expresses in 1 Pet 1:5, we are in our exigency "kept by the power of God"). The basis for the outworking of this divine power made available in our lives is "his glorious might." The Greek word for "glorious" could be read either as a noun, referring to the mighty strength provided by the **Shekinah** glory of God (i.e., the Glory "dwelling" in our midst), or as an adjective, portraying God's might as majestic and marvelous. Both options are viable, but I think "glorious might" fits the context slightly better.

The purpose of this infusion of divine strength is "that you may have great endurance and patience." The Greek term for "great" is *pas*, "all," which leads to the translation "all the endurance and patience you need" (NLT). Combined with the previous statement, this reading provides assurance that God empowers us with an incredible ability to persevere through all the difficulties of life. The terms "endurance" and "patience" are near synonyms. The first connotes perseverance amid trying circumstances, while the second conveys the attitude of "longsuffering" that enables us to endure patiently. "Patience" is in this sense the attitude, "endurance" the resultant "action."

4. The result of these three—bearing fruit, growing, and being strengthened—is "joyous thanksgiving" poured out "to the Father." The phrase "with joy" could hark back to 1:11, "enduring with joy," or to verse 12, "joyful thanks." Both readings make sense, but the first three clauses each contain a verb-phrase ("bearing fruit in every good work," "growing in knowledge," and "strengthened with all power"), and it is likely that this one does as well: "giving thanks with joy." Paul in verse 3 expresses his gratitude to God for the church in Colossae, and his elaboration extends that thanksgiving to all the difficulties of life that must be "endured." Hebrews 12:11 concedes that "no discipline (affliction) seems pleasant at the time, but painful." Yet we as Christians are called to rejoice even in the midst of trials (Jas 1:2; 1 Pet 1:6), not because of our suffering but because of the great God who stands beside and watches over us. In the short term there is pain, but in the long run we know that "God works all things for the good" (Rom 8:28) and that the Spirit is interceding for us with

"deeper groanings" than we are lifting up to God (Rom 8:26). With that knowledge we rejoice in thanksgiving.

THE WORK OF THE FATHER WITHIN THE BELIEVER (1:12B–14)

The underlying impetus for our thanksgiving and patience in the vicissitudes of life is our knowledge of all God has done for us. Paul in this section cites the doctrine of salvation to demonstrate God's powerful work in the believer, beginning with the salvation experience and its results. It is clear that the basis for God's "qualifying" the saints is the blood of Christ that atones for our sins and leads to forgiveness and justification. Paul makes this evident several times in Colossians (1:20, 22; 2:10–12, 13–14). There is an interesting interplay between "we" in verses 9 and 13 and "you" in verses 10–12. The "you" refers to the inclusion of the Gentiles in Colossae among God's people, while the "we" is the combined church, consisting of both Jews and Gentiles, emphasizing that all of humanity is the focus of Christ's redemptive act.

The purpose of Jesus' redemptive work is that his followers may "share in the inheritance of the saints." This echoes Genesis 13:14–17 and the promise to Abraham that he and his progeny will inherit the promised land, a promise reiterated to Israel in Deuteronomy 32:9 and Joshua 19:9. This is part of the new-exodus motif in the New Testament, the notion that the church as the new Israel will fulfill God's promise to the people of Israel that they will one day "share" an "inheritance." This inheritance will be realized "in the kingdom of light" (Greek: "in the light"). The idea of a "promised land" as the earthly inheritance of God's people segues in the New Testament into a heavenly inheritance of "the kingdom of light"—eternal life in heaven. Believers no longer belong to the world but are already now "children of light" (John 12:36; 1 Thess 5:5).

Light/darkness dualism is present in 1:12–13; Paul adds that Christ has "rescued us from the dominion of darkness" (v. 13) and qualified us to inherit "the kingdom of light" (v. 12). There is an A-B-A pattern in these two verses, as the kingdom of light in verse 12 is reiterated as "the kingdom of his beloved Son" in verse 13. Note the language of "delivered ... transferred" (NIV: "rescued ... brought into"). Once again this alludes to the Israelites in the exodus, who were delivered from the Egyptians, "redeemed" (see my comments on v. 14, below) from slavery, and "brought into" the promised land and freedom (Exod 6:6; 14:30; Deut 7:8).

We as saints have been "rescued" from "the dominion of darkness," with sin pictured as a dark realm under the rule of "the god of this world" (2 Cor 4:4), Satan. Darkness has taken control of the world of unbelievers, and its tyrannical rule has destroyed countless lives. There is no hope apart from Christ, who died on the cross in order to deliver those in darkness, redeem them from their sins, and transfer them into "the kingdom of light" (1:12).

The light/darkness dualism as a metaphor for salvation was common in both Judaism and the early church (it is a major theme in the Gospel of John), and Paul here pictures two kingdoms at war with each other for the souls of humanity (see Rom 6 for a similar portrayal). In the "armor of God" passage in Ephesians 6:10–17 Paul portrays the struggle of the believer as a fight "against the powers of darkness and against the spiritual forces of evil" (Eph 6:12).

The new believers are transferred into a new realm, "the kingdom of his beloved Son." This is the domain of "light" from 1:12, and now we see that it belongs to the Son of God, whose sacrificial death has made it possible for us to inhabit this eternal kingdom. Since the Son is equated with the Father, the deity of Christ is part of the thrust of this passage (the same point is made in Paul's sister letter in Eph 5:5). As in Colossians 1:15–20, Christ's exalted status and divine authority make him Judge over the church. He reigns over the "dominion of darkness," of which the false teachers are a part. This emphasis on his exalted status prepares for the christological hymn of verses 15–20 and provides the material and impetus for combating the false teachers in 2:6–23. The title "beloved Son" stems from

God's affirmation of Jesus at his baptism: "You are my beloved Son; with you I am well pleased" (Mark 1:11).

There is a definite *inaugurated* aspect to this kingdom, meaning that it is already present in the life of every Christian who becomes a citizen of heaven (Phil 3:20), even though it will not be fully realized until the eternal kingdom has arrived.[2] There may also be an allusion here to David's covenant of 2 Samuel 7:11–16, where God promised his servant an eternal kingdom, saying, "I will establish the throne of his kingdom forever. I will be his father, and he will be my son. ... My love will never be taken away from him." This covenant promise could be fulfilled only in the Davidic Messiah, as David's descendants threw away their birthright due to sin.

The new-exodus imagery is completed with the note that in Christ "we have redemption" (1:14), with the present-tense verb stressing the continuous power of his redemptive act to change lives. The idea of God "redeeming" his people finds continuous emphasis in the exodus accounts (see passages above) and in Isaiah (Isa 43:1; 48:20; 51:11; 52:9). In the New Testament Christ's sacrificial death is portrayed as a "ransom" payment that "frees" people from the power of sin and makes them children of God.

Paul specifies the result of Christ's redemptive work on the cross: the "forgiveness of sins." In the Greco-Roman world "redemption" referred to a "ransom" payment that freed people from bondage/slavery, and here Paul is discussing bondage to the enslaving power of sin (as in "domain of darkness," 1:13). This imagery presents conversion as a kind of "independence day" made possible by the cross. Paul depicts sin in Romans 6 as an invading army from the realm of darkness that seeks to conquer us and become our "master" (Rom 6:14). The believer must unite with Christ in his death (Rom 6:5) and "die

---

2. "Inaugurated eschatology" emphasizes the "already and not yet." The last days have already begun but have not yet been consummated at the return of Christ. For more on **eschatology**, see the glossary.

to sin" (Rom 6:11); the redemptive work of Christ thereby liberates the enslaved sinner and leads to forgiveness of sins. Paul will restate this in 2:13, 20 as a correction to the false teachers' ascetic religion; not religious ritual but Christ's life-producing death on the cross results in forgiveness. This passage sets the stage for the incredible hymn to Christ, the exalted Creator God.

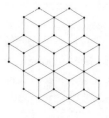

THE PREEMINENCE OF CHRIST IN CHRISTIAN DOCTRINE

(1:15–2:23)

P aul has set the scene in his introductory paragraph (vv. 1–14), in which he has greeted the saints of Colossae, thanked God for them, and prayed for them. Three themes stand out and will be further developed in the letter: (1) the spiritual depth and faithful walk of the believers there; (2) the power of the gospel, both throughout the world and in Colossae; and (3) the centrality of the person and work of Christ for both creation and the church. This third motif is the focus of verses 15–23. Paul is saying that the exalted Christ provides the foundation for both the original creation and the new creation of the people of God. There are two parts to this passage: the **christological** hymn (vv. 15–20) and the effects of the exalted Christ on the church, resulting in reconciliation and sanctification (vv. 21–23).

CHRIST IS SUPREME IN CREATION, REDEMPTION, AND THE CHURCH (1:15–23)

CHRIST'S SUPREMACY IN CREATION AND REDEMPTION (1:15–20)

The majority of scholars agree that this is an early Christian hymn either borrowed by Paul or created by him for this passage. It is slightly more likely that Paul wrote the hymn, since every part of it resonates with his familiar themes. There has been a good deal of discussion in recent decades regarding what constitutes an early Christian hymn. Let me point to some of the relevant features found in this passage: (1) the use of relative clauses ("who") at key points (vv. 15, 18); (2) parallelism of lines; (3) the presentation of deep theological truths (**Christology, soteriology**); (4) teaching that goes beyond the needs of the context and takes on a life of its own; and (5) similarities in style and substance to other passages that have been identified as New Testament hymns (Rom 1:3-4; Phil 2:6-11; 1 Tim 3:16).

The background of this hymn is critical for understanding it. It is generally agreed that Paul has here combined creation material from Genesis 1-2 with wisdom themes—and indeed creation theology plays a major role in Old Testament wisdom material. Several scholars believe that Paul wrote this hymn as a meditation on the creation story in Genesis 1, infusing it with wisdom ideas. Jesus is the Wisdom of God and, at the same time, both the instrument through whom creation was effected and the One who sustains or holds together the created order. Numerous wisdom motifs can be found here—the image of God, visible/invisible, firstborn/supreme, created/creation, holding together, beginning, and fullness. Yet Paul goes further to identify these themes with the Jesus of history. How utterly astounding for Wisdom to be embodied in a historical figure who was at once both God and man! Jesus is Wisdom and yet much more than Wisdom: He is God, redeemer, and reconciler, the initiator and goal of both creation and salvation.

The structure of this hymn is rather widely debated. Due to the complexity of the material there are a myriad of ways in which it can be organized. One popular method is to see **chiasm** behind it, meaning that there is a central idea with a reversal of order leading up to it:

A — 1:15-16
  B — 1:17a
    C — 1:17b
  B' — 1:18a
A' — 1:18b-20

This way of organizing the hymn has proven popular, for the central idea is "in him all things hold together." The problem I have with this is the sheer size of the A and A' sections compared to the other parts. The middle section (vv. 17a–18a), though it works with the scheme, covers only a quarter of the material.

A more linear outline, with perhaps three options, depends on how one views the hymn's thematic construction:

(1) If "who is" is the determining factor, then
    A = 1:15–18a
    B = 1:18b–20

(2) If we divide the first section (1:15–18a) into two parts, then
    A = 1:15–16
    B = 1:17–18a
    C = 1:18b–20

(3) If "firstborn" is the deciding factor, then
    A = 1:15–17
    B = 1:18–20

I prefer the third approach on thematic grounds. Verses 15–17 center on Jesus' supremacy in creation, while verses 18–20 focus on his supremacy in redemption. In my opinion this organizational structure makes the most sense of this beautiful and meaningful hymn.

The exalted Christ and creation (1:15–17)

CHRIST AS THE IMAGE OF GOD (1:15A). It makes perfect sense that the hymn begins with the Father-Son relationship. John 4:24 states that "God is spirit," meaning not just that he is non-corporeal but even more that he is a spiritual being who must be worshiped "in spirit and truth." As "invisible," God cannot be approached in any way other than spiritually; there is a double meaning here, in that true worship is both "spiritual" and "by the Spirit." No one has ever been able to "see God" (Exod 33:18–23; John 1:18), and no one is permitted to represent the "spirit-God" in any physical form (Exod 20:4; Ps 106:20; 115:3–8; Rom 1:23), as this would constitute idolatry. As spirit, God is omnipresent and is to be worshiped "in the Spirit."

Yet Jesus is the God-man, the "Word made flesh" who as deity "dwells among us" (John 1:14). As "the one and only God who is himself God," he "has made [God] known" (John 1:18). In other words, to look on the face of Jesus is to look on the face of God! This is what Paul means when he calls Jesus "the image of the invisible God." In the incarnate Jesus, the "God of very God" (as the Nicene Creed affirms) has taken on human form. The notion of "image" alludes to the creation story in Genesis 1:26–27 ("God created mankind in his own image"), and some think this hymn as a whole is a midrash (a Jewish exposition intended to explain a biblical text) on the Genesis account (though in my opinion this overstates the case). God created humanity in his image, meaning that humankind represents him among the created beings. However, due to sin, that image was marred. Jesus has taken upon himself that image and has thus made it possible for people to know God. He is the last Adam, and he has overcome the sins of the first Adam (Rom 5:12–21), thereby returning the image to God's people.

The main point is that Jesus as divinity, as a member of the Triune Godhead, has made the invisible God visible in his person. He has revealed God and made him known (John 1:18) as never before. Several passages reiterate this truth. In Romans 8:29 we read that God has predestined believers to "be conformed to the image of his Son," meaning that we are to become increasingly more like Christ. First Corinthians 15:45–49 states that, via spiritual worship, "the image of the earthly man" is transformed into "the image of the heavenly man" (Jesus). The more Christlike we become the more the "image of God" is returned to us. Second Corinthians 4:4 speaks of "the light of the gospel that displays the glory of Christ, who is the image of God," and Hebrews 1:3 refers to Jesus as "the radiance of God's glory and the exact representation of his being." Throughout the New Testament Jesus is presented not only as divine but as the perfect replica of God in all reality.

It is generally agreed that this identification reflects the role of Jesus as the divine Wisdom, which Proverbs 8:22 declares to have been present at creation. Jesus as Wisdom channels God's people into both seeing and knowing God, so that we as saints can truly experience and walk with him.

CHRIST AS THE FIRSTBORN OVER CREATION (1:15B). Paul turns his attention from Christ's relation to the Father to his relation to creation. The idea of "firstborn" can be taken as temporal (meaning the first to be born) or can represent status (the foremost or most important of a group). Jesus is not presented here as the "first" of God's created beings to have been "born"; it is clear that he is not a created being, for his preexistence is presupposed throughout Scripture. Rather, Jesus is presented as the Creator, the instrument of God's creation. The Old Testament uses the term "firstborn" in the sense of status. In Psalm 89:27 King David is called "firstborn" as a designation of his status as "the most exalted of the kings of the earth" (also Ps 2:7), and in Exodus 4:22 God calls Israel "my firstborn son" in the sense of the Israelites being his covenant people (see also Jer 31:9). In these instances "firstborn" connotes preeminence and supremacy. In Hebrews 1:6 the term becomes a title (see also Rom 8:29; Rev 1:5) emphasizing Christ's preeminence within the created order (specifically in relation to the angels) as the God-man. In Hebrews 12:23 his followers join him as "firstborn."

The supremacy of Christ "over all creation" becomes a title for the section that follows, depicting him as the instrument and goal of creation. This does not mean that Jesus was a *part of* creation ("firstborn among all creation"), for clearly in 1:16 he is Creator rather than created. The point, which will be elaborated in the rest of the hymn, is that Christ is Lord of the universe and that every part of creation finds its value and meaning in him. There is a wisdom emphasis here, in that creation theology was an essential aspect of the wisdom tradition; however, Paul's statement goes beyond that tradition, for Proverbs 8:22 identifies Wisdom as the first to have been created, while Paul affirms Christ as the agent through whom creation itself came into being.

CHRIST AS THE SPHERE, INSTRUMENT, AND GOAL OF ALL CREATION (1:16). The reason (*gar*, "for") Christ is supreme over all created things is that he himself, in conjunction with his Father, is the Creator of all things. We are told that creation took place "in (Greek: *en*) him," which could mean that Christ was the means ("by him"), the instrument ("through him"), or the sphere ("in him") for creation. Since other Greek prepositions that denote instrument and goal ("through him and for him") are found at the end of this verse, it is likely the latter option (sphere) that is intended here. This is an all-embracing concept, with God as the implied subject of the divine passive "were created" and Christ as the locus of the creation act. In an inclusive sense, sphere may be seen to incorporate both instrument and goal, embracing every aspect of creation; this is similar to the "in Christ" motif with relation to all believers. Everything ("all things") in creation, as well as everything the believer possesses, has been accomplished "in Christ," and it is in union with him that both creation and salvation are made possible. God and Christ have acted together to produce life—both physical life in creation and eternal life in salvation.

The place of Christ in creation is often explored in the New Testament. In John 1:3 we learn that "without him nothing was made," and in Romans 11:36 Christ is presented as the source, instrument, and goal of "all things." In 1 Corinthians 8:6 Christ is described as the One "through whom all things came," and Hebrews 1:3 describes him as the One "through whom he made the universe." Paul's opening declaration in 1:16 ("For in him all things were created") could be said to encompass all the others. Some have proposed that Paul may be drawing from Stoic thought regarding Mother Nature as the all-embracing source of creation, but the parallels are much closer to the thought patterns of Judaism, especially in terms of the wisdom ideas. The superiority of Christ, then, is anchored in the reality of Genesis 1 and the creation account.

The rest of verse 16 functions as a commentary on "all things," using four word-pairs. The first is "things in heaven and on earth," probably an allusion to Genesis 1:1 ("In the beginning God created the heavens and the earth"). This goes beyond Hebrews 1:3 ("made the universe"), for "in heaven" here refers not to the sky and the stars but to the home of God and the angels. The second word-pair is "visible and invisible," forming a chiasm with the first word-pair (heaven = invisible; earth = visible). Both this material world and the unseen world of God were created by him with Christ. As we will see in 2:8–15, the false teachers at Colossae were preoccupied with asceticism and the cosmic powers. The absence of focus on the centrality of Christ's earthly life and work was having tragic consequences. A truly biblical theology must embrace the harmony between the earthly and the heavenly.

The third and fourth word-pairs belong together, with all of them related to celestial beings, both good and bad angels. Most likely they all relate to the "invisible" things above, the heavenly world. Another possibility is that all four word-pairs refer to ruling angels. Scripture seemingly presupposes three classes of angels in the higher orders, though it tells us little about them—seraphim (Isa 6:2, 6), cherubim (Ezek 10:1–3, 6–9), and archangels (1 Thess 4:16; Jude 9). The seraphim and cherubim appear to be elite throne-room attendants, with the cherubim holding up the throne of God, as depicted in the golden statuettes atop the ark of the covenant (Exod 25:18–20). Yahweh is portrayed as riding the cherubim, soaring "on the wings of the wind" (Ps 18:10, corresponding to 2 Sam 22:11). Michael is the only archangel named (Jude 9), and in Daniel 10:13, 21 he is called "one of the chief princes" of the heavenly realm. (Seven archangels are named in 1 Enoch 20:1–7 [an ancient text not included in the Hebrew Bible]).

The "thrones" here relate to those of the twenty-four "elders" in Revelation 4:4, most likely referring to the heavenly council, with God sitting at its center (1 Kgs 22:19; Dan 7:9-10; 2 Enoch 20:1 [another ancient writing not included in the Bible]). The other three terms all relate to this ruling class of angels. "Powers/dominions" (Greek: *kyriotēs*), often translated "lordship," speaks of ruling authority, while the final word-pair, "powers or authorities," is frequently translated "principalities and powers." This pairing is used by Paul to signify the cosmic powers arrayed in opposition to Christ (1 Cor 15:24; Eph 1:21; 3:10; 6:12). Paul's point is that Christ in not only supreme over these spirit beings but created them in the first place and thus has complete authority over them.

CHRIST AS THE SUSTAINING FORCE IN CREATION (1:17). Paul culminates his point by restating and expanding his declaration from the beginning of verse 16: "all things have been created through him and for him." Note the three prepositions in this verse: Christ is the sphere (*en*, "in"), the instrument (*dia*, "through"), and the goal (*eis*, "for") of all creation. As the agent through whom creation took place, Christ was the means by which God enacted Genesis 1-2. While Christ as the sphere and instrument of creation has parallels in Wisdom literature (Ps 104:24; Prov 3:19), that is not the case with Christ as the goal of creation. Note 1 Corinthians 15:24, which refers to the time of the **eschaton**/end when Christ, in whom all creation is summed up, will "hand over" all of creation to his Father. Christ, who created this world, now sustains it (see the discussion of verse 17 to follow) and at the end of history will return it to his Father. In all of this Christ will "reconcile" creation (1:20, below) to its originally intended state and bring about the "new heavens and new earth" (Rev 21:1-22:5).

Paul concludes this section (1:15-17) by reiterating Jesus' supremacy over "all things," adding that he also "sustains" or "holds together" the creation (v. 17). The first clause adds a fourth preposition to those in verse 16: *pro*, which can designate either or both time ("before") and rank ("above"). In this statement it probably incorporates both ideas. This preposition is ordinarily temporal in the New Testament—likely the case in this verse. As such, it proclaims Christ's pre-existence, stating that he existed "before" creation took place. This is another declaration of his deity, as only God could exist before the universe was brought into being. It is generally agreed that this also indicates Christ's status, affirming his primacy and superiority over ("above") the world he has created. So Christ both precedes his creation and has precedence over it—a restatement of the earlier claim that he is "firstborn over creation" (v. 15).

A sixth statement (looking again at verse 17) concludes the first half of the hymn—the meditation on Christ and creation. Paul has already affirmed that Christ has primacy over creation, constituting the sphere within which it occurred, the means by which it took place, the goal it aspires to achieve, and the prior force that made it possible. Now Paul proclaims that Christ is the sustaining power that holds creation together (see also Heb 1:3, "sustaining all things by his powerful word"). The phrase "in him," as in 1:16, likely contains the force of both instrument ("by him") and sphere ("in him"). The whole universe ("all things") finds its unity and coherence in Christ. He provides the force and the energy that keeps it together, for the sin that humankind introduced into all of creation has made it so frustrated that it tends at all times toward dissolution (Rom 8:18–22).

The exalted Christ and redemption (1:18–20)

CHRIST AS THE HEAD OF THE BODY (1:18A). The second half of the hymn begins with the headship of Christ, continuing the theme of supremacy but now centering on his "body, the church." The Christ who has priority over creation also has priority over the church, and the Christ who sustains a fallen creation also provides redemption for fallen humanity. The church is itself a "new creation," and in it, as Christ's creation and gift to the world, lies the hope of humankind for redemption and purpose. The idea of headship focuses on three things: (1) authority, with Christ sovereign over his church; (2) control, as Christ leads the church in the direction God would have it go; and (3) the force that holds the body together and supplies it with the energy that allows it to grow (see Eph 4:15-16). Christ is at once the church's power and its provider, the One on which it is utterly dependent for its very life. The Greeks believed that the head provided the life force that keeps the body together and nourishes it. Paul is building on this metaphor.

As he frequently does, Paul identifies the "body" with the church (Rom 12:4-8; 1 Cor 12:12-27; Eph 4:15-16). One of his favorite images for the church is the body-life metaphor. Christ is the head, directing and leading the church, and every believer is a "member" of the body, given spiritual gifts by God that enable him or her to function for the benefit of the body. When every member does their part the body moves properly, fulfills its God-given role, and grows. As Paul says in Romans 12:5, "in Christ we, though many, form one body, and each member belongs to all the others." The ability to perform our God-given function and "build up" the body/church stems from the presence and strength provided by the head.

The emphasis here is on the corporate body of the church and its importance to the plan of God for this world. In our culture of rugged individualism, it is crucial to understand the importance of the church as a corporate group. No Christian is meant to function independently, and nearly all of Scripture's commands for Christian living are plural—that is, they are given to the whole body of Christ so that the church can work at these issues together, rather than as isolated individuals. Christ as the head guides the church, as a group and as individuals, to live according to the will of the Father.

THE SUPREMACY OF CHRIST OVER "ALL THINGS" (1:18B). Paul returns to the issue of God's creation in Christ, repeating the crucial point of Christ's primacy. The head of the church is also supreme over everything in the cosmos. Paul's labeling of

Jesus as "the beginning" could well be an allusion to the creation account (Gen 1:1, "In the beginning") and affirms Christ's primacy once again as the Creator who is pre-existent over his creation. This thrust is also wed to the previous acclamation of Christ as head of the church, melding the notions of his preeminence over the original creation and the new creation. In Jesus' death and resurrection a re-creation of the cosmos has been initiated via redeemed humanity and the church. So Jesus "begins" a new era, culminating the old and inaugurating the age of salvation. He both "rules" (*archē* means both "beginning" and "ruler, prince") over this new realm and has primacy over it.

Paul's attribution of Jesus as initiator, founder, and ruler of the new creation is extended in his affirmation of Christ as the "firstborn from the dead," a celebration of his resurrection and exaltation to the right hand of God. We have already seen in 1:15 Christ's status/rank as pre-eminent "over all creation." Now we are told of his preeminence over both the new creation and the church. Christ, as the "first to be raised from the dead," anchors the new creation in terms of its redemptive power for humanity. His death and resurrection made the new age possible and became the central event of history—his resurrection "from the dead" rendered him "the firstfruits of those who have fallen asleep," making possible eternal life for the redeemed. The Jesus who is ruler over all creation also rules over the redemption he has established for fallen humanity.

Paul reiterates the reason: "so that in everything he might have the supremacy." Every word in this phrase restates the main themes of the hymn. "In everything" sums up "over all creation" (v. 15) as well as "all things" (twice each in vv. 16–17). Clearly Christ is pictured as the basis for and ruler over every aspect of both the original creation and the new creation. This also is communicated in Paul's acclamation of Christ as "supreme" over all things, as seen in the "firstborn" of verses 15 and 18, in the "before all things" of verse 17, and in the "headship" of verse 18a. Christ is sovereign over every aspect of creation, and especially over the new creation in which God's salvation is uppermost.

THE FULLNESS OF THE GODHEAD RESIDING IN CHRIST (1:19). Everything stated in the hymn regarding the supremacy of Christ comes to fruition here, as Paul states absolutely that Jesus is fully God ("God of very God," as expressed in the Nicene Creed). The basis for Christ's status, as explained in verse 18 (causal *hoti*, "for"), is the fullness of God centered in Christ. We can make sense of this declaration in several ways. The implied subject could be God ("God was pleased that all his fullness might dwell in Christ") or Christ ("Christ was pleased that all God's fullness might dwell in himself"). While both of these readings are possible, a third option seems to make the most sense: allowing "fullness" to be the subject ("In him all God's fullness was pleased to dwell"). This last rendering fits the similar statement in 2:9: "in Christ all the fullness of the deity lives in bodily form." In the final analysis, however, all three readings have essentially the same meaning. "All the fullness," as a virtual title for God, can be translated "God in all his fullness." This assertion constitutes one of the strongest statements in the New Testament affirming the deity of Christ. Christ is not just "a god" or "a part of the Godhead." He is fully God, quintessential deity in all its fullness.

This complete deity "was pleased to dwell" in Christ. God draws intense pleasure from his trinitarian essence. Each of the three parts of his "Godness" is "pleased" with the other aspects of his one being. There are questions about the exact connotation of the infinitive here rendered with the English "to dwell." It would be natural to link the phrase "was pleased to dwell" with God's declaration of his pleasure at Jesus' baptism: "You are my son, whom I love; with you I am well pleased" (Mark 1:11). But that would be adoptionism, the belief that Jesus was chosen *as God* only at his baptism. It would be more instructive here to focus on a connection with

Jesus' incarnation—asserting that Christ at his conception was already fully God.

However, this Christ-hymn also stresses Jesus' pre-existence (see my comments on 1:15b), and Paul provides no hint that he is thinking chronologically. The Son has always been one with the Father, and the emphasis here is on the all-embracing "fullness" of authority and power that has existed in Christ from eternity past. Still, since "pleased to dwell" is linked with God's divine choice, there is undeniably some connection to the incarnation, through which God in his fullness chose to dwell bodily in the God-man, Christ (as in 2:9).

THE PURPOSE OF CHRIST'S COMING: RECONCILIATION AND PEACE (1:20). God chose to send his Son for the elect purpose of reconciling all creation, and in particular fallen humanity, to himself, and Christ became the instrument ("through him") for achieving this purpose. Obviously, the means by which this was accomplished was Christ's sacrificial death on the cross. The atoning effects of his blood sacrifice became the ransom payment that redeemed humankind from sin and led to God justifying repentant sinners, forgiving them, cleansing them from sin, and adopting them as his children (Rom 3:21–26; 8:14–17).

"Reconciliation" (Rom 5:10–11; 1 Cor 7:11; 2 Cor 5:18–20; Eph 2:16) defines the social side of salvation, speaking of establishing a relationship between two parties formerly at enmity. Reconciliation is the natural result of justification; we were estranged from and enemies of God (Rom 5:8), but in love he reached out and brought us to himself. God the Father accepted Christ's ransom payment as a substitute for us and credited his blood payment to our account. This led to forgiveness of sins, and God as the righteous Judge declared us to be righteous on the basis of that sacrificial death. The result is the establishment of a new relationship with him, as he becomes our Father and we join his family as co-heirs with Christ. Reconciliation is both legal and personal. We have been redeemed, justified, and reconciled with the Triune Godhead. It is not we who have initiated and achieved this reconciliation but God the Father and Christ the Son who have made this possible.

The emphasis here is not just on our new relationship with God but also on the new order in creation, as "all things" are made right with God and Christ. The scope is cosmic as well as personal. This point is debated, as several commentators believe that reconciliation is strictly personal and therefore cannot be accomplished on behalf of the inanimate creation. The implication is that only human (earthly) and angelic (heavenly) beings can be "reconciled." It is clear, however, that "all things" in verse 20 is taken from verses 16 and 17, where "all things" refers to the whole of creation, animate and inanimate. Paul often personifies creation as a living entity (Rom 8:18–22), and he does so here, as well.

Thus Paul is reiterating 1:16 as he explains that "things on earth" and "things in heaven" have been brought into harmony with their Creator. In Romans 8:18–22, Paul states that all of creation has been made "subject to frustration" by the sin people brought into the world and by the resultant dislocation with God—which affects not only ourselves, but also God's non-human creation, earthly and heavenly. All of nature is subject to decay and death and longs to be released. God is in the process of removing alienation—not only of us but of the whole creation—and of reconciling "all things" to Christ. There is an inaugurated sense to this; creation has joined us in right relationship with the Godhead but awaits with us its full restitution at the eschaton/end of this fallen world.

Paul specifies the means by which reconciliation has been made possible as Christ's "blood shed on the cross." As noted above, this is a reference to the atoning sacrifice of Christ that is alone sufficient to pay for our sins and produce forgiveness and reconciliation with God. "Peace" is both the means and the result of reconciliation. The blood of Christ has produced a new peace with God that has led to reconciliation. At the same time it constitutes the meaning of reconciliation, the state of ever-lasting peace with God.

"Making peace" has a multifaceted meaning here: (1) The primary thrust is the new "peace-full" relationship with God in which the enmity caused by sin is gone. (2) There may be an implied contrast with *Pax Romana* (the Roman Peace), a façade perpetrated by the conqueror's sword. Whereas Rome "pacified" its vassals by imperialistic power, Jesus, as "the servant of Yahweh," accomplished peace through his atoning death on the cross. (3) This new peace entails not only reconciliation with creation and forgiven sinners but also the "pacification" of the cosmic powers. The death of Christ not only has removed the charges arrayed against us (2:14), but also has "disarmed" the principalities and powers in opposition to God (v. 15). This process has begun: Satan knows he has been defeated (Rev 12:12), and the saints already have been granted authority over the demons (Mark 3:15; 6:7). Yet the full victory will not come until the events initiated by Christ's return (Rev 19:20; 20:10, 14).

All of God's creation will be pacified and reconciled, and full harmony will be restored among things "in heaven and on earth and under the earth," as Paul expresses in Philippians 2:10. This incredible reconciliation with the Creator of every aspect of his creation could be achieved only by Christ on the cross, for there is nothing sinful humanity could have done to effect such peace on so cosmic a scale. Christ alone has paid the price, bringing universal salvation to God's world.

THE MEANING AND EFFECTS OF RECONCILIATION FOR THE CHURCH (1:21–23)

Paul turns from the theoretical (Christology) to the practical, elucidating the implications and effects of the hymn for the Colossians. He has centered in verses 15–20 on the person and work of Jesus the Christ. Now he shifts to the spiritual situation of the Colossian believers, following a past-present-future format. He begins by defining their situation before they committed to Christ (past) and then shifts to the difference that the death of Jesus has made to their situation (present). After describing their current stance with God, he challenges them to remain firm in their faith (future).

The believers' past: Alienated from God (1:21)

The abrupt beginning (Greek: "And you") points to the letter's recipients at Colossae. Paul has been speaking globally but wants them to realize that everything he has said applies to them. Reconciliation by definition concerns two or more groups that have been alienated or estranged from each other—a precise depiction of the Colossians' situation before the gospel reached them. The disparity between past and present is clear in the language: "at one time … but now."

Note Paul's three descriptors of the unbelievers. (1) They were in a continuous state of "alienation," implying the complete absence of any contact with God. The parallel in Ephesians 2:12 shows that the intention here is both personal and relational: They had been "excluded from citizenship in Israel and foreigners to the covenants of promise"—estranged from God because of sin and from Israel because they were Gentiles. As a result, they had no hope and no future. (2) They had been "enemies" of God—"hostile" in their "mind," implying a studied animosity and antagonism toward God in their mindset. As Paul says in Romans 1:21, "their thinking became futile, and their foolish hearts were darkened" (see also Eph 4:18). (3) As a person's thought life invariably finds an outlet in action, so their "deeds" have been "evil." The Colossians' behavior has demonstrated their enmity against God and the evil cast of their thinking. John 3:19 expresses the situation well: "Light has come into the world, but people loved darkness instead of light because their deeds were evil." In a similar vein Paul refers in Romans 13:12 and Ephesians 5:11 to "the deeds of darkness."

The believers' present: Reconciled and made holy (1:22)

The wondrous work of Christ has solved the tragic situation of the Colossians' godless past. Due to their total depravity, the people of this world could not traverse the enmity gap between themselves and God, so a loving, merciful God sent his Son to bridge the gap for us through his sacrificial death on the cross. By placing our sins under his blood, Christ made atonement, and the result was reconciliation (as Paul spells out in v. 20). "Now" (v. 22), based on that pivotal event in human history, our present situation is radically different, typified by a new relationship with God. Paul likely added the emphasis on Christ's "physical (Greek: 'fleshly') body" to clarify that it was the incarnate Jesus who died. God sent his Son to become the God-man Jesus Christ and to suffer physical death on the cross so that we could find salvation and be reconciled to him. It is possible also that Paul was voicing a further correction of the Colossian heretics, who had a **docetic** understanding of Christ's life and death—the notion that Jesus' body had not been quite real, that he had not suffered a physical death per se.

The purpose of Christ's reconciliatory work was "to present [us] holy in his sight, without blemish and free from accusation." Paul utilizes sacrificial imagery here—"present," "without blemish," "blameless"—to add force to this statement. The verb is used often in the **Septuagint** for "presenting" a sacrifice to God; it also came to be used for God's people "presenting" themselves to him (Deut 21:5; Dan 7:13). Paul uses this verb in Romans 12:1, urging his readers to "present your bodies as a living sacrifice" (see also 1:28, below). This makes sense in light of the emphasis in verse 20 on Jesus' sacrificial death, which Paul considers a model for the Christian life of sacrifice for God. This depicts the believer standing before the throne of God and presenting her life to him for approval.

The goal is threefold: that God, as he tests an individual's life, may find it to be holy, without defect, and without blame. "Holy" is used both of the sacrifices (Num 18:8–9; Ezek 42:13) and of the altar (Lev 10:12), which belong entirely to God; "without blemish" refers to a sacrifice that has no defects and is thereby worthy of being offered to the Lord (Lev 4:3, 23; Num 29:2, 13); and "blameless," though not stemming from sacrificial imagery, is a judicial and moral term, referring to a person whose conduct is "without reproach"—an individual of good standing in the community. In this context, "blameless" refers both to a person's present walk with God and to the final judgment, when the individual's whole life lies open to God (1 Cor 1:8). Jesus provides the perfect model, and God's people at all times seek to attain Christ-likeness—"the whole measure of the fullness of Christ" (Eph 4:13). God attributes Christ's sacrificial death to our account, and we at all times seek to emulate his perfect life in our daily conduct.

The believers' future: Steadfast in the faith (1:23)

In light of Christ's atoning death, the reconciliation with God that resulted, and the believer's accountability before God, Paul challenges the Colossians to persevere in their walk with God. There is a critical condition ("if indeed, provided that") to be met if they are to be presented before God as holy and blameless (v. 22). Some interpreters wrongly take this as an expression of confidence that the believers will indeed stand firm. More likely, however, the conditional aspect is stronger, making their future presentation to God dependent on their firm stance for him. The emphasis is on the absolute necessity ("you must") of their compliance to this charge. Paul is confident of them (see 2:5) but still demands that they take their Christian obligations seriously.

The present tense "continue" or "remain" commands ongoing perseverance in faithfulness to the Christian life. "Your faith" (perhaps better rendered "the faith," as in the ESV) refers to the Christian faith in an objective sense—the teachings they received about Christ—rather than the Colossians' subjective trust in God. They must remain committed to the truths of the gospel, and their resolve must be "established and firm." These are construction metaphors related to the strength of a building's foundation. Looking at their life as God's house (1 Cor 3:10–15), they must make certain they are secure, firmly established in Christ. He is the foundation (1 Cor 3:11; Eph 2:20) in whom each follower must be securely grounded. There could be a further word-picture here, for this language also suggests God's creative activity of "laying the foundations of the earth" (Ps 102:25; Isa 51:11; Heb 1:10). With the creation imagery so dominant in 1:15–20, Paul demands that God's new creation find a firm foundation in him as well.

The danger is that we might allow life's circumstances and troubles to "move" or "shift" us away from that commitment. The building metaphor continues, this time depicting an earthquake "shifting" a building from its foundation and moving it away to its destruction. For believers to allow the world to shake them from their moorings in Christ would mean to lose "the hope of the gospel," which alone can be the source of true hope; to be "removed" from that source is to lose one's only valid "hope" for the future. This kind of hope, far from being ephemeral or fleeting, is grounded in the assurances of the gospel.

This is a hope the Colossians have "heard" in Epaphras' "proclamation" of the gospel described in verses 5 and 7. Both in the spread of the Christian faith throughout the Roman world and in God's witness to himself in creation (Rom 1:20), this gospel hope has been "proclaimed to every creature under heaven." Alternatively, this could be rendered "in all creation under heaven"—a reading I prefer due to the use of *ktisis* for "creation" throughout 1:15–20; the point becomes stronger translated this way. As the gospel is being proclaimed in every part of the world, this is a universal "hope" that will bring all of creation back into harmony with its Creator. This goes beyond the restitution of fallen humanity to God, constituting the fulfillment of the longing of all creation to be returned to its original state (Rom 8:18–22).

Paul wants us to know that his entire sense of ministry flows from this astounding truth. He has dedicated the rest of his life to participation in this universal proclamation. As he expresses in Romans 15:20, "It has always been my ambition to preach the gospel where Christ was not known." Paul was at heart a "minister" (NIV: "servant") of the gospel—a calling that defined his self-awareness. He will develop this theme in the next section of the letter (1:24–2:5).

PAUL'S PROCLAIMS HIS GOSPEL MINISTRY (1:24–2:5)

Paul has already spoken of the gospel ministry among the Colossians (1:5) and of the work of Epaphras in establishing the church in Colossae (v. 7). After Paul's marvelous hymn exalting the person and work of Christ (vv. 15-20) and his summary of the salvation resulting from Christ's work (vv. 21-23), he joyously proclaims his own gospel ministry and servanthood in 1:24–2:5. This section builds on Paul's declaration of salvation (vv. 21-23) and explores his personal role in Christ's ongoing work to the world and, in particular, to the Colossian church. Paul echoes 2 Corinthians 3-5 as he meditates on the meaning of his apostolic work for Christ and the church.

The emphasis in this section is on the difficulty of Paul's ministry. The two sections begin with "suffering" (1:24) and "agony/contending" (2:1), and throughout Paul emphasizes his dependence on Christ to provide strength for his strenuous gospel proclamation to the Gentiles. In Christ he has a "powerful energy" (1:29) as he "agonizes" in his effort (2:1) to both encourage the Colossians (2:2) and help them to mature in Christ (1:28).

This part of the letter contains two sections: (1) Paul's struggle in proclaiming Christ's mystery (1:24-29) and (2) his striving to enhance the believers' knowledge of divine truth (2:1-5). In the first section he centers on his ministry in the church as a whole, while in the second he zeroes in on the Colossians. Paul's purpose is not simply to remind his readers of the great sacrifices he has made for the ministry but, even more, to remind them of the overriding importance of the gospel, the "mystery" of Christ, and of their part in it. This prepares for the next section (2:6-23), in which Paul will oppose the false doctrines of the heretics. The Colossians must comprehend the profound truths of the Christian faith and be able to recognize when "teachers" depart from it. This is an important reminder for us as well, living as we do in a shallow age when all too many churches are not proclaiming the gospel or theological doctrines of the faith. We must do our part to bring biblical depth back into our churches!

PAUL'S STRUGGLE IN PROCLAIMING CHRIST'S MYSTERY (1:24–29)

Paul's suffering for the sake of the church (1:24–25a)

We must remember that this is a Prison Letter and that Paul is imprisoned in an apartment in Rome waiting to learn whether he is to live or die for the sake of Christ (Acts 28:16–20; Phil 1:21–23). He "suffers" while on trial for his life, though he also could have in mind here the hardships he has endured for the sake of the gospel (2 Cor 11:21–29). Amazingly, Paul's response is one of "rejoicing" in his ministry—a reality that frames the section (1:24; 2:5). Joy and suffering, far from being polar opposites, indeed are central to a Christian understanding of trials endured in the name of Christ (Jas 1:2; 1 Pet 1:6). The basis for Paul's joy is that his suffering is "for you"—based on his gospel proclamation to the Colossians. Many interpreters struggle with this statement because, as far as we know, Paul never visited Colossae; the church there had been founded by his team (see 1:7). He may be regarding the Colossians as beneficiaries of the hardships he endured as the "apostle to the Gentiles" (Rom 11:13; Gal 2:8).

The second half of the verse is one of the more difficult statements in the New Testament to understand. What might Paul be implying in his declaration that "I fill up in my flesh what is still lacking in regard to Christ's afflictions"? Is he suggesting that our Lord didn't suffer enough and needed Paul to make up the deficit? This cannot be the case. Paul's statement here is based on a little known but important doctrine for the early church known as "the messianic woes." In every segment of Judaism and the early church it was believed that, before the Messiah would return at the end of history, there would be a series of "birth pangs"—serious afflictions that would befall God's people (see, e.g., Dan 12:1; 4 Ezra 13:16-19 [in the Apocrypha]; Mark 3:20 and their parallels in 2 Thess 2:11-12; Rev 6:9, 13:7). This idea builds on a Jewish teaching that God had established a certain amount of suffering and martyrdom to be experienced by his messianic community, and that when the full amount is reached the culmination of history will ensue (4 Ezra 4:35-37; 1 Enoch 47:1-4 [another apocryphal book]). These afflictions that will help bring about the eschaton (the end) have been labeled "the messianic woes" (Mark 13:8 calls them "birth pains"). Paul's reference, then, to "the afflictions of Christ" is not limited to Jesus' messianic sufferings, but includes as well the suffering endured by his messianic community (which in Philippians 3:10 he calls "the fellowship of his sufferings"; see also Gal 4:19). For this reason, the phrase "afflictions of Christ" might be better translated "messianic afflictions" or "messianic woes." An important aspect of this doctrine is found in Revelation 6:11, where God promises his martyred saints that he will vindicate their blood but asks them to wait "until the full number of ... their brothers and sisters [are] killed."

When Paul says his sufferings are filling up "what is still lacking in regard to Christ's afflictions," all of this is in mind. Every difficulty he endures (along with the suffering we face, too) is helping to bring about the return of Christ. It isn't that Christ somehow has not suffered enough and looks to us to help him reach the quota, but rather that we all are called on by God to suffer in his name (John 16:33; Acts 14:22; Rom 8:17), and the final result will be God's victory over evil. Paul's point is that he undergoes every hardship specifically "for the sake of his body, which is the church" (on body-life imagery, see 1:18). This phrase at the end of verse 24 is the third time Paul expresses his actions for the sake of believers, after verse 9 ("praying for you") and earlier in verse 24 ("suffering for you"). In this instance Paul does not specify the Colossians but cites the church as a whole as the reason for his ministry of suffering.

He surrenders his life and comfort for the sake of the gospel so that the "church" may be built up and grow.

Christ is the head of the church (v. 18), and Paul is its servant (v. 23). The servanthood emphasis of verse 25a grows naturally from the themes of verses 18 and 23. As in verse 23, the Greek word *diakonos* in verse 25 means both "servant" and "minister." As "servant," Paul subordinates himself to the needs of his congregations—both those he planted himself and those he adopted, such as the church in Colossae. As "minister," he proclaims the gospel and strengthens the believers. Paul's mission is defined both by the gospel and by the lost world (see v. 6).

Paul's commission to proclaim the mystery (1:25b-27)

The basis (*kata*) for Paul's servanthood is "the commission God gave" him. Paul considers himself a "steward" whom God "commissioned" to fulfill a role in his kingdom. Paul is an administrator "of grace" (Eph 3:2) called into the apostolic office, and God expects him to act as an overseer (Titus 1:7) in the ministry assigned to him. Paul explains that ministry here as the commission to preach the gospel both to the lost and to members of the church. Both groups are specifically in mind here, as Paul is to present the gospel to those Colossians who are already Christians and to proclaim it to the Gentile non-Christians in their midst. This sacred calling he received on the Damascus road (Acts 9:15-16; 26:17-18) is God's plan, not Paul's idea, and he has the privilege and joy of being God's chosen channel of this great "mystery" for the world. Paul is not the creative agent but the chosen minister who is allowed to explain this world-changing plan to the Colossians and enlist their participation in it.

In doing this (1:25) Paul will be "fulfilling the word of God" (NIV: "present to you the word of God in its fullness"). He uses the same term he did in verse 24 for "filling up" what was lacking in Christ's afflictions. There are at least four ways we can understand the meaning here: Paul's desire (1) to "fulfill" or bring to completion his calling to preach; (2) to "fully proclaim" the Word (NASB); (3) to make its mysteries "fully known" to others (ESV, NIV, NRSV); or (4) to preach "the entire message" of the gospel (NLT). In light of the parallel in verse 24 and the sense here, the first rendering seems to make the most sense. Paul has been commissioned by God to "fulfill" or complete his apostolic office in bringing God's plan of salvation to the world. He is "filling" his sacred office in keeping with the mission he clearly delineates in Romans 15:19 to "fully proclaim the gospel of Christ," referring to the powerful, Spirit-led proclamation of the Word throughout the world.

The contents of the commission are described here as "the mystery that has been hidden ... but is now disclosed." "Mystery" was a major apocalyptic term that became important in Judaism from the time of Daniel and his use of the Hebrew *raz* (nine times in Daniel 2:18–47) for a divinely revealed truth that had previously been hidden ("for ages and generations," probably referring to time) but was now being "disclosed to the Lord's people" (the meaning of *raz*) concerning God's future plan that has been inaugurated with the coming of Christ and the kingdom of God (1 Cor 2:6, 7). *Apokalypsis* is the Greek term for the "revelation" of a truth that God had "hidden," (the verb *kalyptō*, meaning "to cover" or "to hide," is the root of *apokalypsis*), and *mystērion* describes the content of that newly revealed truth. This is the age of revelation, and the saints are the recipients not only of God's great acts in history but also of his disclosure of truths regarding the new age of salvation and the inauguration of the last days.

Paul goes on to expand (1:27) his description of those to whom God is revealing these "mysteries." In verse 1 we read that he has been called to be an apostle "by the will (*thelēma*) of God," and here he asserts that God "wills/has chosen" (*thelō*) to reveal these incredible truths to his people. The verb "make known" is another way of saying "reveal" or "make visible," in this case to the church. It is possible to translate this phrase as "through whom God chose to make known his riches among the Gentiles," thereby turning it into a mission statement, with the Colossians sent out to the nations to spread the gospel. This understanding is not as likely, for the context centers on God's revelation of his mystery to the Colossians rather than on their involvement in the Gentile mission.

Paul proceeds to define the "mystery" in this instance. It is indeed the spread of the gospel to the Gentiles, of whom the Colossian Christians are a part (rather than being agents of spreading the gospel, they are its recipients). Paul calls this "the glorious riches of this mystery"; "riches" is his favorite term for the blessings God pours into the lives of his people (used seven times in Ephesians and Colossians). Ephesians 1:7–8 speaks of "the riches of God's grace that he lavished on us" as a depiction of God "making known to us the mystery of his will." There the mystery is redemption in Christ. Then in Ephesians 1:18 Paul describes the **eschatological** hope of believers as "the riches of his glorious inheritance among the saints." This idea of the eternal "wealth" that belongs to the saints is enhanced by "glory," a term connoting the **Shekinah** glory of God dwelling among his people; Paul goes on to speak of the "glories" that belong to them as a result. This association enhances the "richness" of the metaphor by showing how eternally "glorious" our inheritance really is.

Paul speaks of the mystery in various ways, as being our redemption, our hope, our future inheritance, and the unity between Jew and Gentile as the new Israel. But all of this is summed up here in the archetypal image: The "mystery" is essentially "Christ in you, the hope of glory." This will be restated in 2:2, "that they may know the mystery of God, namely Christ." Here the emphasis is twofold: the coming of Christ, the incarnate Son of God, and the arrival of "Christ in you," meaning the coming of the Christ to bring the Gentiles into the people of God. The proof of this inclusion of the Gentiles into the church is the Colossians themselves ("in you"), and the result is the presence of "hope," the realization that in Christ the future is sure and salvation is guaranteed. Structurally, the terms "Christ" and "hope" are set in apposition to each other, suggesting that Christ virtually defines hope and that this hope is **eschatological**, centered on the "glory" that is to come at the **parousia** of Christ. So in this verse we have both "glorious riches" (present) and "hope of glory" (future). The glory of God defines both what we are and what we will be, and it is indeed a "living hope" (1 Pet 1:3).

Paul's ministry of proclamation (1:28-29)

God has commissioned Paul to be the channel through which he pours out the riches of his mystery, Christ, to the Gentile world. Paul answers that call in these two verses, beginning with the natural response, "He is the one we proclaim." Note that Paul acknowledges his ministry team, with "we" including Epaphras (1:7-8) and the others who have ministered the gospel in the province of Asia. Paul's point is that every Christian is part of the proclamation of the gospel to humanity. Each and every one of us is included. The verb "proclaim" is the first of three (along with "admonish" and "teach") by which Paul defines the ministry of preaching here. There are many other terms that commonly describe this ministry to both Christian and non-Christian; these include "witness," "evangelize," "announce," and "exhort." The presentation of God's truths are at the heart of the Christian call in every way, and Paul in all of his letters highlights the teaching and preaching ministry of the church. Any church that fails to disseminate doctrinal truth is not biblical, and shallow preaching is a major problem of the church in our day. Pastors and teachers alike need to be vigilant with regard to the apostle's warning in 2 Timothy 2:15: "Do your best to present yourself to God as one approved, a worker who does not need to be ashamed and who correctly handles the word of truth." How many of us will stand before God in shame at the final judgment?

Paul further depicts the proclamation ministry in 1:28 as "admonishing" and "teaching." His language is similar to that of 2 Timothy 3:16, where he declares that "all Scripture is God-breathed and is useful for teaching, rebuking, correcting, and training in righteousness." One could say that admonition constitutes the second and third (rebuking, correcting) of these functions, while teaching is reflected in the first and fourth (teaching, training). As Hebrews 4:12 reminds us, "The Word of God is alive and active, sharper than any double-edged sword." The purpose of the church's teaching ministry is to expose the needs of every person, convict individuals of the need to change, and present a plan to guide them in doing so. The church must proclaim the good news of Christ and his indwelling Spirit, so that it can help the individual to root out the bad and forge a healthy life of fruitfulness for God.

Key here is the "wisdom" with which believers are to wield the sword of the Word. In 1:9 Paul prayed that the Colossians would have knowledge with "all the wisdom and understanding that the Spirit gives," and here in verse 28 he asks for the result—that they teach "with all wisdom." Notice that in both cases they need "all the wisdom" God will give them. As I pointed out in the discussion of verse 9, wisdom is the Spirit-endowed mindset that goes beyond simply understanding the Word to living it out practically. Three times in verse 28 the Greek text refers to "every person" (many English translations condense to only two references). Every believer needs this in-depth experience with the Word, and the ministry of the Word must be at the heart of all church life. A tragedy of our time is that it is not!

The goal of such teaching is to "present everyone fully mature in Christ." Again the stress is on every single church member (and probably also those who have not yet believed). As in verse 22 Paul uses the sacrificial image of "presenting" a person as an offering to God. In Romans 12:1 God's people respond to Christ's sacrifice by "presenting" themselves as "living sacrifice[s]," and in ministry we re-enact Christ's sacrifice as we "present" those under our care back to God. The sacrificial lamb was to be "without blemish" (as in 1:22, above). So too the goal of our ministry is to present people "perfect" or "mature" to God (the Greek word *telion* means both). While every believer strives to reach perfection, the image here is more likely of Christian maturity (though the one should work toward the other).

This is the metaphor in the parallel passage of Ephesians 4:12–15, where the purpose of ministry is to "build up" the "body" so that it can "reach/attain" its growth (to adult stature) and "become mature, attaining to the whole measure [of the stature] of the fullness of Christ" (Eph 4:13). There, as here, Paul depicts the Christian life as a child maturing into an adult. The Word of God is the food (as in 1 Pet 2:2–3) that enables the spiritual infant to grow and mature, so the task of the teacher is to prepare gourmet meals in the Word that will lead to the members of the church "craving the spiritual food" of the Word (again, see 1 Pet 2) and growing more mature. The goal is to immerse them in the Word so they can become fully Christlike, united "in Christ" and centered on his will (see 4:12, below, where maturity is described as standing firm in God's will).

The goal of presenting believers to Christ fully mature is the reason Paul "labors" (NIV: "contend") in ministry (1:29). Paul in this paragraph has centered on the two spheres of proper Christian service—evangelizing the lost (v. 27) and helping Christians grow spiritually (v. 28). Both tasks deserve (and demand) all his energy. The Greek verb translated "labors" is present tense, conveying continuous "toil" in the Lord's work. It is a strong verb, connoting one who works to exhaustion, and that certainly describes Paul; even during the siesta time in Ephesus he could be found in the lecture hall of Tyrannus proclaiming Christ (Acts 19:9–10). He was tireless in his work for the Lord.

This language continues as Paul describes his labor as "strenuously contending" ("toiling" or "striving"), using the verb transliterated into English as "agonizing" (Greek: *agōnizomenos*). This is an athletic image, depicting runners straining with every muscle toward the finish line. There is a double meaning in this, as Paul both "strives" and "struggles" in his ministry (recapitulating the suffering theme of 1:24). God calls us to ministries that are interesting and challenging, but rarely smooth and easy.

Paul needs a lot of strength, and he receives it via "all the energy Christ so powerfully works in me." This is similar to the language of Isaiah 40:31, which depicts the person who despite growing "tired and weary" has learned to "wait on the Lord," with the result that they receive not a reinfusion of their own strength but a whole new source of strength as God pours his power into them. Paul states this powerfully (pun intended) using a pair of related terms, saying literally "his energy (Greek: energeian) that energizes me." Then he adds a further point ("in power") to strengthen the effect. When Paul is in agony as he struggles in his ministry, Christ graciously fills him with divine power that far surpasses what any Energizer battery or Powerade drink could ever begin to supply! As Peter expresses it, we are "kept by the power of God" (1 Pet 1:5).

Paul's Struggle for the Colossians (2:1–5)

Paul's discussion of ministry in 1:24–29 is general, worldwide, and intended for the church as a whole. Starting in 2:1, he focuses on the Colossian and Laodicean churches. Laodicea was the major town in the area, ten or eleven miles northwest of Colossae and six miles south of Hierapolis (4:13). Its church was the recipient of one of the seven letters in Revelation 3:14–22, and it was a wealthy town due to trade, banking, and its textile industry. Laodicea also had a large Jewish population. Paul is deeply concerned for the churches of the Lycus Valley, as this letter demonstrates.

Paul defines his struggle (2:1)

The phrase "I want you to know" demonstrates that Paul is anxious to convey his deep concern for the Colossians and how hard he is striving to meet their needs. His pastoral care is evident in his language here. He has never been to Colossae, nor has he met many of the believers from the community, but his love for them is evident. To convey his point he uses the term "agony/

struggle" (agōna) to define the extent to which he is "contending" for them. His intense struggle was all the greater due to his imprisonment in Rome and consequent inability to deal with the believers' situation directly. There likely were four aspects to what he was feeling: (1) his desire to evangelize and spread the gospel in the Lycus Valley; (2) the difficulties occasioned by his capital trial in Rome; (3) his desire to see the Christians in Colossae and Laodicea grow spiritually; and (4) his need to counter the false teachers and their destructive influence in the region. All four aspects are addressed in the letter.

Paul includes two other groups in addition to the Colossians—the Laodiceans and "all who have not met me personally," likely referring to members of the other churches in the Lycus Valley, such as the one in Hierapolis (4:13). The Laodicean church, which actually received a separate letter from Paul (v. 16; obviously a lost letter), was important in its own right (see above). He wants them to realize that, even though he cannot be with them he cares deeply about them and is working intensely on their behalf.

The goal: United under God's mystery, Christ (2:2-3)

Paul relates four purposes/goals of his ministry to the believers: (1) He wants to "encourage" their hearts. The verb here is one of the primary terms Paul uses to convey the teaching/preaching task. In various contexts it can mean "exhort," "comfort," "encourage," "strengthen," or even "admonish" (Heb 3:13). Here in Colossians 2 the context is rich enough to incorporate nearly all of these connotations. All the material on spiritual growth in the previous section contributes to the thrust here; Paul's meaning transcends the emotional aspect of spiritual comfort, centering more on the task of anchoring the believers through instruction in the Christian life. In Scripture the "heart" is not just the emotional side of a person (feelings) but involves as well the inner spiritual life of thought and will.

(2) When believers have been taught and encouraged in Christian truth, they also will be "united in love," with the verb portraying a congregation that is "knit together" or drawn into

a deep fellowship with one another. Some prefer to read this as "instructed" more than "united," but the flow of thought and the basic meaning of the term point to "united" as the better meaning. This concept is developed further in Colossians 2:19 and in Ephesians 4:16, where Paul defines unity as the "body" of Christ "supported and held together" in oneness and thereby "growing" together under God. The thread that "knits" the believers together is love, "the bond of perfection" (Col 3:14; NIV: "binds them together in perfect unity").

(3) The purpose of this "perfect unity" forged in love is to enable believers to attain "the full riches of complete understanding," which as in 1:28 lifts the accumulation of biblical and theological knowledge to the level of divine "riches." This entire section stresses the "rich treasures" of biblical comprehension, a perspective desperately needed in the church today. Paul calls this the "full assurance of understanding," meaning the complete assurance and certain knowledge of God's truths that only true "understanding" can produce. Once we truly comprehend what God has said in his Word, that insight provides a straight path for our feet that leads to deep conviction and clear vision for the church and for our individual lives. When this critical discernment takes hold, no false teaching will be able to make inroads into our church.

(4) This biblical insight and theological understanding will lead us to know "the mystery of God, namely, Christ." Each of these terms has been emphasized earlier in the letter, so Paul is culminating a major theme here. Colossians abounds with words for "knowledge"—including "learning," "understanding," "wisdom," "insight," "make known," and "reveal." In 1:9 Paul prays that God will "fill you with the knowledge of his will," and in 1:10 he adds the prayer that the believers might "[grow] in the knowledge of God." In 1:23 his focus is knowledge of the gospel truths, in 1:25 understanding of "the word of God in its fullness," and in 1:26 (as here in 2:2) knowing and experiencing "the glorious riches of this mystery." In light of the heretics' dissemination of false teaching, knowledge of God's truths was all

the more important. Note that Paul in the third purpose statement, above, has already highlighted the "fullness" and "riches"
of this understanding, on which he builds here.

There is a text-critical problem with the next phrase—
"mystery of God, namely, Christ." Later scribes were con-
fused, and a host of readings appeared in copies. But scholars
are fairly unanimous in believing that the strongest external text-traditions—ancient manuscripts called "Papyrus 46"
(𝔓46; early third century) and "Codex Vaticanus" (early to mid-
fourth century)—favor the reading here, and it best accounts
for the other variants. We have already discussed the meaning
of "mystery" in 1:26-27 as the content of God's hidden truths
now being revealed in these last days. Here the core thrust of
them all is presented: God's mystery is Christ himself. Christ
was "hidden" not in the sense of messianic expectation but in
the fullness of Christ as incarnate Son and Lord of all. All the
other "mysteries," like his atoning sacrifice and the inclusion of
the Gentiles into the people of God, flow out of the quintessential mystery, Christ himself.

In Colossians 2:3 Paul further defines the mystery of Christ.
Interestingly, he concedes that it still contains "hidden" truths,
part of the meaning of "mystery" and "apocalyptic." These
mysteries are in the process of being revealed, as the coming
of Christ has introduced the last days and the kingdom of God
has arrived. They are being made known "in him," a phrase
that virtually governs the christological hymn of the previous
chapter (1:16-17, 19); the kingdom reality and the knowledge it
brings derive from the sphere of Christ. Stored within Christ
are "all the treasures of wisdom and knowledge," identifying
Christ as the sole source of these wondrous gifts. Paul presents wisdom and knowledge under one article, as a single, combined item (see also Prov 2:2-3; Rom 11:33; 1 Cor 12:8). Only in
Christ can we find the knowledge to understand God's truths
and the wisdom to live by them—"treasures" to be prized above
all else. Like all treasures, they are hidden in the sense of being
kept not *from* God's people but *in* Jesus' storehouse. In a similar

passage (Matt 13:52) Jesus describes a kingdom disciple as one who "brings out of his storeroom new treasures as well as old," depicting a wealthy homeowner entering his storeroom with the intention of dispersing precious items to family or friends. There too the image portrays God's truths as a treasure house of wisdom. Christ is God's storehouse, the repository of the heavenly treasures about to be dispersed or revealed to his people.

Warning against the false teachers (2:4–5)

In verse 1 Paul says "I want you to know," and here the phrase "I say this" implies that the warning to follow is part of what Paul wants them to realize. Here we find the first direct mention of the false teachers in the letter, but they have been in mind throughout. The danger was that these seemingly authoritative teachers might "deceive" the Colossians "by fine-sounding arguments." Clearly the ideas they were expounding were evil; the Greek verb here means to "delude" or "lead astray" with falsehood. The means by which they were leading the people astray was "well-crafted reasoning," persuasive arguments that sounded convincing but were sidetracking people into serious error (an idea Paul develops further in verse 8). These false teachings are the polar opposite of the "treasures of wisdom" found in Christ (v. 3).

Paul's dilemma is that he is "absent from [them] in body" (v. 5) while he is in prison facing trial in Rome. He has worked hard in this letter to demonstrate how much he loves the believers and how concerned he is for them, but he cannot be with them. He would love to confront these false teachers directly and expose their dangerous error in person, but he is in Rome. However, he wants the Colossians to realize that he is "with [them] in spirit." Paul elsewhere speaks of being "absent in body" and "present in spirit" (1 Cor 5:3; 1 Thess 2:17). The phrase "present in spirit" could mean that he is with them via the Holy Spirit or that he is with them spiritually through prayer and Christian concern; likely his meaning contains nuances of both. In some way this language might also signify his apostolic presence or authority. God had given him responsibility (stewardship, 1:25) over the church. In that sense Paul is present in their midst, in heart through the Spirit, and in this apostolic letter he is with the believers in authority. So the letter itself signifies "present in spirit."

Still, he "delights to see" (literally, "rejoicing and seeing") that they are not capitulating to the heretics but are growing spiritually. The problem he addresses, though serious, is not devastating. The terms he uses to describe the church in 2:5 ("disciplined" and "firm") are military metaphors. The Greek word for "disciplined," *taxis*, speaks of the disciplined "order" a military camp was supposed to exhibit at all times, as well as the order of battle that was to be maintained by the soldiers. The word for "firm" is *stereōma*, referring to the "firmness" of the battle lines. Paul uses both terms here to describe the strength of this church and its faithfulness to Christ. Rather than being separate ideas, these terms probably express a single thought, centering on the stability and depth of the Colossians' commitment to Christ. Their "firm faith" is a rock solid, Christ-centered ("in Christ") stance. There are no signs at this stage that the church is deviating in its faith due to the influence of the false teachers, and Paul "rejoices to see" this.

PAUL CONFRONTS THE FALSE TEACHINGS (2:6–23)

All interpreters agree that this section brings us to the central core of the letter. There is an A-B-A-B pattern, but the opening pair is quite short and the closing pair fairly lengthy. The believers in Colossae are first challenged to live faithfully (2:6–7) and then warned about the false teachers (v. 8). This pattern is then expanded with a brilliant rehearsal of what it means to be a Christian (vv. 9–15), followed by a lengthy diatribe against the religious rituals and ascetic practices of the heretics (vv. 16–23). Throughout the letter thus far, Paul has frequently commented on the strong faith of the Colossian church (1:3–6, 8, 22; 2:5) while still urging them to work hard at strengthening that faith (1:9–11, 22–23, 28; 2:2–3). Now he applies both aspects to the danger posed by the heretics. This section begins with a further exhortation to be anchored in Christ, drawing together the material on the lordship of Christ (2:6 corresponds to 1:15–20) and on the necessity of a well-grounded faith (2:7 follows up on 1:10–12; 2:3–5).

CHALLENGE TO BE ANCHORED IN CHRIST (2:6–7)

These two verses sum up the letter thus far and launch into its central theme: correction of the false doctrines on the grounds of the accepted truths of the gospel. "So then" points back to what Paul has said in 1:24–2:5 and draws a conclusion, saying in effect, "Since we have seen the meaning of the exalted Christ and the critical importance of a firm faith, let's now consider the implications." Paul begins with a formal introduction, using a technical verb for the transmission of traditional truths ("just as you received"). The best-known example of this pattern is 1 Corinthians 15:3–5: "For what I received (from the Twelve) I passed on to you"—namely, the core creedal truths on the death and resurrection of Jesus. So Paul is referring to the central tenets of the Christian faith passed from community to community to preserve true doctrine. He is reminding his readers of the ultimate importance of the lordship of Christ for Christian belief and life (for examples of "Jesus Christ is Lord" as a creedal tradition, see Rom 10:9; 1 Cor 12:3; Phil 2:11).

"Christ Jesus is Lord" sums up everything Paul has said about Christ in the letter thus far, from "Christ Jesus" as the basis for his apostolic office (1:1) and the believers' new relationship to God as saints (v. 2) to Christ making the kingdom available to God's people by providing redemption (vv. 13–14) to his incredible lordship over creation (vv. 15–17) and redemption (vv. 18–20) to his headship over the church as his body (v. 18) to Christ as the mystery of God (v. 27; 2:3). All of these themes are present in this creedal affirmation. Christ is both Messiah (*ton Christon*, with the article, expresses a title) and Lord of all—the truth that provides the basis for the warning about the false teachers in verse 8.

With the lordship of Christ governing their lives, the Colossians must "continue to walk in him"—that is, to make certain their conduct at all times reflects Christ, reiterating Paul's directive of 1:10 ("walk worthily of the Lord"). Right belief produces right behavior. When believers have received "the word of God in all its fullness" (v. 25) and as a result are "filled with the knowledge of his will" (v. 9), day-by-day decisions will have an entirely different look. As often in Colossians 1, the basis for that conduct will be a life lived "in him"—in union with Christ and as part of his body.

The Greek text includes four participles in this section, recapitulating the four that defined the Christian life in verses 10-12. Paul is deeply concerned for the stability of the Colossian church. He has focused on the "what" of the Christian life in 2:6, and now he tells the "how," using metaphors borrowed from horticulture and architecture: "by being rooted and built up in him." These verbs are divine passives; God is the active force in changing our lives. Paul presents two powerful images, for crops were the basis of life in the ancient world, and the Romans were one of the greatest architectural forces in all of history. Several interpreters have pointed out that the church as God's temple may have inspired the imagery (as in 1 Cor 3:16; 2 Cor 6:16; 1 Pet 2:5), especially since Herod's temple was still in the process of being built at the time Paul wrote. If the Romans rather than the Jews had built it, it would have been one of the seven wonders of the ancient world, for it was every bit the equal of the temple of Artemis in Ephesus. Paul's point is that God's people must be grounded in Christ, erected on a strong foundation, and built up to become God's temple.

A similar image follows, as Paul calls upon the believers to be "established" or "strengthened in the faith." This continues the imagery of a church that is grounded in Christ and stable; stemming from the world of ideas, it depicts a well-grounded insight or established fact. As we have seen earlier (1:23), "the faith" in this passage denotes not subjective trust in Christ but objective belief in the gospel truths of the Christian faith.

This is evidenced in the added "as you were taught," referring to the doctrinal truths the Colossians had learned from Epaphras (v. 7) and "received" in the traditions of the church (2:6).

Finally, Paul enjoins the Colossian believers to be "overflowing with thanksgiving"—his third mention of this directive (after 1:3, 12; see also 3:15–17; 4:2). In the midst of life's difficulties believers are to be aware of the sovereign God, who guides and empowers them. While that does not remove their pain (Heb 12:11), it does provide a new perspective, along with a heightened awareness of God even in "the valley of the shadow of death" (Ps 23:4). This gratitude toward God is corporate, based on the church's sharing in the difficulties of each member and in the worship of the loving Father its people enjoy together.

WARNING AGAINST THE DECEPTIVE TEACHINGS OF THE HERETICS (2:8)

Paul has been preparing for this moment with nearly every point he has made thus far. Now he opens his arguments countering the dangerous ideas being promulgated by certain teachers at Colossae. He begins strongly with "See to it" (or, perhaps better, "Beware!"), a frequent signal prior to his pointing out a serious danger to the church (1 Cor 8:9; 10:12; Gal 5:15). Spiritual vigilance is called for in response to such enemies of God, who often go tolerated and unexposed (as in the letters to Pergamum and Thyatira in Revelation 2:12–29). The heretics' strategy is to "take (you) captive," a military metaphor picturing these teachers as an invading army; this is similar to the imagery of Romans 6, where Paul depicts sin as an invading horde bent on capturing and enslaving people in its depravity. Here in Colossians 2 the Christians run the risk of becoming enslaved to false doctrines and practices. Their need is for Jesus, the divine warrior, to go to battle on their behalf and bind the evil forces (Mark 3:27), as well as for the armor of God for protection from the powers arrayed against them (Eph 6:10–18).

The means by which these heretics capture and enslave is the weapon of "hollow and deceptive philosophy"—literally, "a philosophy characterized by empty deceit." The Greco-Roman world was enamored with "philosophies" of every stripe; the marketplace in any city was likely to feature street-corner philosophers expounding their pet theories. Municipalities went so far as to have these street preachers appear before civic leaders to judge whether they were worthy of speaking (as was the case with Paul before Sergius Paulus and on Mars Hill; Acts 13:17–12; 17:19–34). The heretics' hollow ideas might have appeared reasonable, and even compelling, until one examined them carefully and discovered there was absolutely no substance; the whole system was designed to fool the unwary. We can find an apt analogy in modern advertising, for that is precisely what false teaching is—deceptive marketing meant to trap gullible people looking for a quick fix. How different this is from "the true message of the gospel" (1:5) that delivers "the knowledge of God" (1:10). Contrast this further with Christ, in whom dwells "all the fullness" of the Godhead (1:19).

The problem is that underneath these high-sounding ideas lies only "human tradition." Note the further contrast with 2:6, which traces the true traditions "received" by the Colossian church, teachings that came from God through the apostles. These heretics referred to their shallow teachings as "tradition," but they were of human origin, with nothing in them of God or truth (compare Mark 7:3, 8; 1 Pet 1:18). However, the real source of these ideas is not merely human; they stem from "the elemental spiritual forces (Greek: *stoicheia*) of this world"—from the influence of demonic powers. This provides the very definition of heresy, in that the proponents of these lies are under satanic influence. There are actually several possible understandings for these *stoicheia*, which could be: (1) the "elemental" forces of the world, such as earth, fire, water, and air, suggesting that Paul is warning against becoming enamored with material things, or (2) the elementary teachings for beginning learners (the thrust in Heb 5:12)—perhaps Jewish teachings, as in Galatians 4:3, referring to the Jewish basis of this Colossian cult. However, (3) the majority of commentators today agree that *stoicheia* refers to the "elemental spirits," the demonic powers alluded to often in Colossians and Ephesians (Col 1:13, 16; 2:10, 15, 18; Eph 1:21; 3:10; 6:10–12). The teachings of these heretics do indeed constitute "the devil's schemes" (Eph 6:11), and the purveyors of such pervasive falsehoods are virtually demon-possessed.

These ideas, stemming as they do from human and demonic origin, are not "according to Christ." Clearly the false teachers are portrayed as unbelievers who are deliberately modeling their teachings on half-truths intended to deceive and having no connection whatsoever to Christ. All of the christological content we have seen thus far in this letter is included by Paul partly for the purpose of unmasking and exposing the terrible error in the false teachers' "philosophy." Christ created and sustains his world, and they have misrepresented the true meaning of life in his creation. We need to realize that there are far more cults and false teachings today than in Paul's time, and we need to be even more vigilant to identify half-truths and outright lies coming from modern pulpits.

The Meaning of True Christianity (2:9–15)

The fullness in Christ and the church (2:9–10)

Paul now provides the antidote to the disease of this false movement by rehearsing the true origin and meaning of the Christian faith. It begins with the reality of the personhood of Christ, who in himself contains "the fullness of the Deity." The teachings of the heretics are "empty"; the "fullness" resides in Christ. I have already explored in 1:19 the fullness of God dwelling in Christ; to reiterate, Jesus is completely "God of very God," and in him all the essence of God resides. The idea of deity "dwelling" on earth was called the **Shekinah** (from the Hebrew *shakan*, "to dwell"), and in the Old Testament this referred to the temple, and especially to the Holy of Holies where God dwelled (Ps 68:16; 87:1-2). In this sense Jesus is the incarnate Shekinah (see John 1:14).

"Dwells bodily" has been understood in several ways, including: (1) the elemental forces of creation in a "cosmic body" residing in Christ (a theory not otherwise scripturally supported); (2) the divine powers dwelling "in essence" or "really" in Christ (viable, but not strong enough); (3) the presence of God manifesting itself through the "body of Christ," the church (but the thought here is **christological**, not **ecclesiological**); and (4) the full deity of the Godhead being incarnated "in bodily form" (this traditional interpretation is certainly the correct one). There is some truth in the second view, in terms of the contrast between the false teachers' insistence that God in Jesus is a mere shadow paralleling the law and Paul's declaration that he is "actually" God. But there is certainly an incarnational emphasis here.

The idea of "fullness" continues (2:10) with the movement from the noun (*plērōma*), referring to Christ, to the verb (*peplērōmenoi*), expressing the result for the church. In Christ resides the "fullness" of deity, and the people of God are in turn "filled in him." It is not in esoteric doctrinal speculations that the saints can find truth but in the person of Jesus, in whom they can be "completed" (another meaning of the verb *peplērōmenoi*). Note all the action words in the context of Colossians 2 thus far. The faithful are encouraged, united, filled with knowledge, firm in the faith, rooted, built up, established, thankful, and filled with God in Christ. In light of the concrete reality believers have in Christ, why would anyone be satisfied with speculative ideas lacking content?

This is especially true when one realizes that the heretics are filled with demonic lies, while Christ is "the head over every power and authority." Some have interpreted these "powers" as secular human authorities, like kings and generals, but clearly this term (as earlier in the letter) refers to the cosmic powers, the fallen angels. Christ is the "head" of the church (1:18) and supreme over creation, including the angelic forces, as its Creator (1:16). As such, he retains absolute authority over the demonic hordes. There is no dualism, with God and Satan as equal forces vying for power. Nor are Satan and Christ equal commanders under God; Jesus is in sovereign control. Later, in 2:15, we will see that the evil powers have already been disarmed and utterly defeated by Christ, and in Mark 3:15 and Mark 6:7 Christ grants his followers authority over demons. That includes the false teachers, the followers of the demonic powers.

The first description of the Christian: Buried and raised with Christ (2:11–12)

Building on verse 10, Paul spells out via two extended metaphors (vv. 11–12, 13–15) what it means to be a true follower of Christ, experiencing his fullness. He centers on circumcision (v. 11) and baptism (v. 12). Circumcision, as the covenant rite that signified the Israelites as the people of God (Gen 17:10–14; Exod 4:25; Lev 12:3), served as an "identity marker" to distinguish a Jew from a Gentile. It is difficult to know why Paul uses the image here. Perhaps circumcision was part of the required rituals of the false teachers; had this been the case, however, we would have expected Paul to discuss it negatively in 2:16–23, which he does not. It is also possible that for the early church baptism was thought to be the replacement for circumcision as the initial covenant rite for Christians, but there is no hint of such a substitution anywhere else in the New Testament, rendering this explanation unlikely. Paul probably mentions circumcision here simply as a good image for the incorporation of a believer into the church.

Circumcision was the physical act of removing the foreskin to designate a man as one of God's people; the Old Testament frequently calls for "circumcision of the heart," because the external act divorced from right conduct was unacceptable to God (Deut 10:16; 30:6; Jer 4:4). In the context of Paul's letter this becomes a metaphor for spiritual salvation, "a circumcision not performed by human hands," meaning a heart change. This word-picture had its origin in diatribes against idols that *were* "made by hands" (Isa 31:7; 46:6; Dan 5:23). In both Testaments "not performed by human hands" refers to something that is not of human origin and so clarifies the important point that linking salvation to believers' physical actions would be anchoring it in a human/idolatrous system.

Paul unpacks this idea in the second half of 2:11, using two *en* phrases to convey the means "by" which true salvation/ circumcision of converts takes place. Literally, the Greek reads "in the putting off of the fleshly body, in the circumcision of Christ." Both phrases stem from the imagery of circumcision, and both are debated. Does Paul's word-picture connect Christ's circumcision with his death on the cross ("Christ put off his fleshly body, namely in his own circumcision [on the cross]") or to our own circumcision of the heart ("you stripped off your fleshly body in Christian circumcision")? Both readings make sense in this context, and it is difficult to determine Paul's intent.

The **christological** interpretation looks at Christ surrendering his life (stripping it away) as a circumcision, a metaphor for his death on the cross. The **soteriological** interpretation, on the other hand, looks at the believer joining Christ in dying to sin as a spiritual circumcision—perhaps a reference to baptism as Christian circumcision. Overall, I prefer the soteriological interpretation in this context of salvation, but I don't think Paul means for baptism to be seen as the new circumcision. Instead, it anchors the point of verse 11a—circumcision of the heart as a metaphor for salvation. In the Old Testament circumcision was a physical act signifying that the Israelite was a member of the covenant community, whereas in the New Testament it is a spiritual metaphor for heart conversion, signifying that the person is a member of the new covenant community.

Paul turns to the analogy of baptism (v. 12), using the same approach as in Romans 6:3–5. When believers are baptized they are immersed under the water, signifying that they are "buried with [Christ] through baptism into death" and "united with him in a death like his." Emerging from the water signifies that believers are "united with him in a resurrection like his." The imagery here is exactly like that of Romans 6, especially in the opening "having been buried with him in baptism." This is a temporal participle—*"when* you were buried with him," a reference to conversion. Paul's statement here is often mistaken for a mere metaphor, as the convert dies in a way similar to Christ and is raised in a way similar to Christ. In reality the believer *actually* dies with Christ and is *actually* raised with him to new life—a true religious experience.

As in Romans 6 the new convert dies to sin and gains power over it. The old self is nullified and becomes an external force, trying to invade and regain its mastery. So after dying with Christ to sin, it is natural that "in Christ" the believer is also "raised with him" to a new existence. Scholars debate whether the pronoun should be translated "in which," referring to baptism, or "in whom," referring to Christ. Taking it as a reference to baptism does avoid a clumsy double reference to Christ (i.e., "In him you were raised with him"), but I agree with those who see the strong christological sense of the verse and Paul's frequent use of "in whom/him" (e.g., 1:16, 17, 19; 2:3, 6, 7, 9, 10, 11) as favoring "in whom" here. It is only "in Christ" that anyone can attain eternal life, and the emphasis is on this idea rather than on baptism, which is an analogy rather than the focus of the verse.

The instrument through which the saints can participate in Christ's resurrection is "faith in the working of God, who raised him from the dead." This is the same term (*energeia*) as in 1:29, where it is translated "the energy Christ so powerfully works in me." Paul uses the same metaphor in Ephesians 1:19-20 when he speaks of "the incomparably great power ... the same as the mighty strength he exerted when he raised Christ from the dead." The point here, as in Ephesians 1, is the incredible power of God that both raised Christ from the dead and raises us up to newness of life. It was proven with Christ and experienced at conversion, and it is available to all who are "kept by the power of God for a salvation ready to be revealed in the last time" (1 Pet 1:5). The resurrection power is not simply experienced one time, at conversion, but is an ever-available strength meant to be experienced on a daily basis. The resurrection life is a present reality and not just a past act.

The second description of the Christian:
Forgiveness and the cancellation of debt (2:13–15)
In verses 11–15 Paul is at his creative best, providing unique word-pictures of what conversion entails. The first set of analogies (vv. 11–12) centered on the death and resurrection of Christ as reenacted in the conversion experience. Now, with a second set of analogies (vv. 13–15), Paul provides further astounding material on the meaning of our salvation. These verses add the experience of forgiveness and the defeat of the cosmic powers that took place at the cross and resurrection.

The picture begins with Paul reiterating the gospel message of sin and salvation (see Eph 2:1–3), describing the Colossians (emphatic "you") as at one time "dead in your sins and in the uncircumcision of your flesh." The "in" could be causal ("because of your sins"), and the Greek word often rendered as "sins" more precisely means "trespasses," a strong term emphasizing the conscious rebellion that leads people to turn against God so that they stand guilty before him. The reference to "uncircumcision" looks back to the imagery of verse 11 and highlights that the Colossian believers were uncircumcised Gentiles who had been outside the covenant (as also in Eph 2:11–12). As a result they had been "dead" spiritually, separated from God and any hope of eternal life.

Due to the grace and mercy of God this state of sin and death has been discontinued. God has "made you alive with Christ," referring back to the "buried with him" / "raised with him" language of 2:12. These former "walking dead" are now alive—not just alive with respect to earthly existence but part of a new creation. Theirs is a never-ending life based entirely on the reality that they have come back to life "with Christ"; Christ's resurrection is the firstfruits guaranteeing our present and future eternal life. Those who deserve eternal condemnation now share the new life of Christ and will be joint-heirs with him in the heavenly reward (Rom 8:17).

As a result of Christ's death and resurrection being attributed to "our" account (note the switch from "you" to "us" to include all believers), God "forgave us all our sins." Forgiveness must take place before God can "make us alive," because sin is an abomination that must be destroyed by God. Christ had to become the atoning sacrifice, providing redemption by paying the ransom payment, purchasing us for God, procuring our freedom from the enslaving power of sin, and thereby bringing about our forgiveness from sin. Note that "all our sins" are forgiven. If even one sin remained, God would have to consign us to eternal damnation. Paul's next two statements explore the meaning and extent of forgiveness.

Divine forgiveness implies the "cancellation" not only of the guilt but of any record of the sin ever having been committed (2:14). This is a potent metaphor, for it looks at sin as "debt," as in the Lord's Prayer at Matthew 6:12 ("forgive us our debts"). It considers sin a "debt" owed to God, incurred by our throwing away the relationship with God that he has freely given us. The NIV's "charge of our legal indebtedness" translates the Greek term for "written decree," with its imagery of a commercial transaction—an IOU or certificate of debt. The debt incurred is written down in the heavenly ledger, with a future accounting as the inevitable conclusion.

There is a doubly negative emphasis here, for the written record is "against us," and its "regulations" are "opposed to us" (NIV: "condemned us"). There also could be a nod to the Torah in the note on "regulations" here. If so, the payment of the debt and the twofold "against us" would invoke the idea of the covenant curses that were to fall upon those who "trespassed" against God's laws. The sacrificial death of Christ applied to our account has caused those debts recorded in the heavenly

IOU to be "cancelled" or, perhaps better, "erased"—a powerful word-picture for the forgiveness of our sins!

Paul utilizes a second metaphor for forgiveness: Christ has taken our sin away by "nailing it to the cross." This picture, which clarifies *how* our certificate of debt has been cancelled, is a brilliant image, reflecting a key detail of Jesus' crucifixion. His cross would have included an upper vertical extension, typically used only when it was necessary to nail the legal sentence above the head of the condemned prisoner. The "decree" nailed above Jesus was "Jesus of Nazareth, the King of the Jews" (John 19:19). In Colossians 2:14 Paul is saying that, along with the charge against Jesus, another document was nailed there: "Grant Osborne, sinner, in debt for the sins of ... ." As Jesus triumphed over death, he triumphed over my sins as well. His blood paid my debts, and I received forgiveness, meaning that my sins have been cancelled, erased, removed.

Jesus' death is at the core of 2:13-14, and his resurrection is the driving force behind verse 15. The victory over death was won at the cross, and the victory over the cosmic powers was announced at the resurrection. Battle imagery has often been cited in this section. The false teachers, under the control of demonic forces, have invaded the lives of God's people in Colossae, seeking to "take them captive" (v. 8) and enslave them. But Christ has defeated the evil forces and here is seen to have "disarmed" the demons, carrying them off in his triumphant procession through the heavens at his resurrection/exaltation. The word "disarmed" also can be translated "stripped off," setting up an interesting play on words with verse 11. There the same term (*apekduō*) was used to describe the believers "stripping off" their body of sin at their conversion; here Christ has "stripped" the evil powers of their weapons and authority in this world. God certainly is the one acting here, as he is the subject throughout this section. But at the same time, God and his Son are acting together.

Let's follow the events of that fateful Friday. As he neared death on the cross, Jesus announced "It is finished" (John

19:30), followed by "Father, into your hands I commit my spirit" (Luke 23:46). At that moment he went home to his Father. As he left his body, Scripture tells us that he did two things: First, "he went and made proclamation to the imprisoned spirits" (1 Pet 3:19), which commentators almost unanimously see as the announcement that he had won the victory on the cross. Second, as stated here, he and his Father "disarmed" the demonic powers and led them on his victory procession through the heavens on his way to the Father, at whose right hand he was to sit while preparing to return for his post-resurrection appearances.

This imagery is similar to that of Mark 3:27, where Christ depicted himself "binding" Satan, rendering him powerless, in Satan's own stronghold. Here is one of the great turnarounds in all of history: The One who came "in the form of a slave" and died the most humiliating death imaginable (Phil 2:7-8) has now been exalted, has been given "the name above every name" (Phil 2:9-10), and has stripped the demonic realm of its power (also Eph 1:20-21).

The subjugation of the "powers (literally, 'rulers') and authorities" by God is pictured as a Roman triumph (as also in 2 Cor 2:14-16). After a victory the conquering general, wearing the *toga picta* (a purple emperor's robe with gold ornaments), would ride through the streets of Rome in a war chariot drawn by four horses. Marching behind in chains was the defeated army as captives, with the generals to be executed and the soldiers sold into slavery. Thus many interpreters translate this clause in 2:15 "made public display, leading them as captives in his triumphal procession." Christ is exalted and demonstrates his glory publically for all the heavens to see by stripping the satanic forces of their power and leading them captive behind his victory chariot on his way through the heavens. Paul's point is that both the evil powers and their minions, the false teachers, have been defeated, and Christ's followers experience the spoils of that victory. The Colossian Christians should be defeating the Colossian syncretistic cult. The tenets of that movement are explored next in verses 16-23.

PAUL WARNS AGAINST SUBMITTING TO
RITUALS AND ASCETIC PRACTICES (2:16-23)

We are now in the final section of verses 6-23, detailing the anti-dote for the Colossian heresy. Paul has already provided two brief introductory sections, the first regarding the Christian life (vv. 6-7) and the second a warning against deceptive teachings (v. 8). He follows this by two expansions of these opening gambits—first in a description of true Christianity (vv. 9-15, expanding vv. 6-7) and now in a warning about erroneous practices (vv. 16-23, expanding v. 8). In light of the victory of Christ over the demonic forces and their heretical followers, the true believers of Colossae should not allow evil practices to influence their church. This section has three parts: (1) a warning against the heretics' Jewish-based rituals (dietary and cal-endar-based observances), verses 16-17; (2) a warning against their visionary experiences, verses 18-19; and (3) a warning against their ascetic and legalistic practices, verses 20-23. Yet this section has a positive flavor as well. The defeat of the evil powers means that the saints are liberated from subjugation to their "fleshly" and ascetic rules and free to worship Christ directly.

WARNING AGAINST DIETARY RESTRICTIONS
AND CALENDAR OBSERVANCES (2:16-17)

The heretical teachers were pressuring the Christians of Colossae to surrender and follow the rituals mandated by the cultic system they had instituted. They had set up an obligatory set of required practices and were "judging" those who failed to comply, possibly with fines or other punishments but definitely with social pressure. Paul discusses two categories of practices. The first is dietary—"what you eat or drink"—but moving beyond Jewish food laws, since those centered on eating rather than drinking. So the heretics' program may reflect pagan as well as Jewish practices (the Nazirite vow prohibited strong drink, Num 6:3-4). Likely the adherents of these teachers were obliged to follow a selectively rigid lifestyle, probably more during times of fasting or vows than on a regular basis.

The second category of practices was calendar-based, with three specifics mentioned: religious festivals, new moon celebrations, and Sabbath rules. This list is a traditional grouping, found as well in 1 Chr 23:31; Isa 66:23; Ezek 46:1; and other passages). Jews held seven feasts (Passover, unleavened bread, first fruits, Pentecost, trumpets, Day of Atonement, and tabernacles), and the new moon was celebrated on the first of every month with trumpets and burnt offerings (Num 10:10; 1 Sam 20:5, 18; 1 Chr 23:31). Paul's comments here do not imply that he was opposed to observing the feasts, but rather that he did not want the believers (particularly Gentile converts) bound by the legalistic regulations that often accompanied them, as was the case with the false teachers. The issue is similar to that covered in Romans 14:1–15:13, where the "strong" viewed themselves as free from requirements such as food laws (Rom 14:2–4) or Sabbath observance (Rom 14:5–6).

Both types of religious restrictions are wrong, for they replace true worship with false, and heavenly worship with the occult (the "elemental spirits" in 2:8, 20). Paul labels such Jewish religious practices "a shadow of things to come." The term "shadow" was used in both **Hellenistic** (e.g., Plato) and Jewish contexts to convey a contrast between the insubstantial and the real. Hebrews 8:5 calls the temple a "copy and shadow of what is in heaven," and Hebrews 10:1 calls the law "a shadow of the good things that are coming." Here the term implies that the Old Testament regulations "foreshadowed" the new covenant reality, that the "things to come" are not the events of Christ's return but of the New Testament age, which would fulfill the Old Testament feasts and regulations. To require such practices now, after Christ has come, is to pour new wine into old wineskins, as Jesus remarked in Mark 2:21–22. The false teachers are destroying the newness Christ has intended for true worship. The old rituals were not meant to be destroyed but to be completed in Christ; they were transitory, and to continue them constituted an abomination.

There is also a christological error in the heretics' system, for "the reality is found in Christ," not in the continuance of practices that God has willed to be fulfilled or completed in Christ ("Christ is the culmination [end] of the law," Rom 10:4). However, since Paul uses *sōma* ("body") in 2:17 rather than the more common *eikōn* ("image"), several commentators interpret this as "the body of Christ," so that the church as incorporated into Christ becomes the thrust. If that were the case, Paul would be saying that the church as "in Christ" is the reality, pointing forward to the head/body emphasis in verse 19. While interesting and possible, this explanation is unlikely. The emphasis here is more **christological** than **ecclesiological**, favoring the translation "the reality (*sōma*, substance) is found in Christ." The primary heresy of the false teachers is the denigration of Christ to the status of one of the elemental spirits. As in Colossians 1:15–20, Christ is supreme, God himself, the Lord of all. As such, he is the only basis for our salvation.

WARNING AGAINST MISUSE OF VISIONS (2:18–19)

A second warning ensues, centering on ascetic self-humiliation and angel-worship and connected to visionary experiences (v. 18). In verse 16 the heretics have been "judging" those who refused to adhere to their legalistic restrictions. Now they go one step further and "condemn" the true believers for standing firm for Christ. Some see athletic imagery in the verb, translating it "rob you of a prize" (and thus "disqualify you"), but this does not fit well here. The idea is condemnation for breaking the rules established by the leaders of the movement.

Paul describes the heretical teaching using four participles; the first two ("insisting" and "going into detail") depict the tenets of the teaching, and the last two ("puffed up" and "lost connection") depict the false teachers' mindset or attitude.

First, the heretics "insist on" their practices; this translation is better in my opinion than "delight in" because it is a basis for their condemnation more than a description of what gives them pleasure; they demand adherence to their ascetic practices. The "false humility" or "self-humiliation" alludes to rituals like fasting and self-denial ("what you eat and drink" in v. 16), noted in verse 23, below, as "false humility" and "harsh treatment of the body."

The "worship of angels" seems to point to an angel cult, but there is little evidence in Judaism of worshiping angels, which are elevated in the **Septuagint** and placed in settings like Sinai. They do seem to take on mediator-type roles in Judaism, but they are not really worshiped. This could be referring to the Jewish superstitious practice of invoking angels to help ward off evil, a kind of worship. It also could be evidence of syncretism, with angels read into the pantheon of minor pagan gods and worshiped as quasi-deities; this would have constituted idolatry, introducing a serious situation. Although the false teachers saw these beings as angels, Paul points out that they were actually *fallen* angels—cosmic spirits or demonic powers. Thus, the situation seems to reflect a combination of idolatry and occult worship. Another viable possibility is that the cult members were joining in the veneration of God performed by angels in heaven through mystical ascents to heaven via visions. Syncretism, I believe, is slightly more likely. Perhaps the two options should be combined, with the cult members evidently experiencing visions and claiming that they were joining the angels at the throne of God in heaven. Paul considered these rituals to be satanic, joining the adherents with the elemental spirits.

Second, the heretics went "into great detail about what they have seen," a definite reference to visionary experiences. The verb can be rendered more generally—"entering" into visions—or more strongly—"taking their stand" on the visions they receive. All three readings connote a religion that not only included visionary encounters but was obsessed with them, studying them closely and embracing deeply what these visions were thought to communicate. Cultic rituals might have been performed, with the idea that the initiates joined the angels and learned the secrets of the universe, but this cannot be verified. We can say for certain that the false teachers embraced and treasured visionary encounters and placed great stock in what they saw and heard through them.

Third, the heretics were "puffed up with idle notions by their unspiritual mind." This depicts an incredible arrogance with no basis in fact or reason. Such arrogance also characterized the Corinthians (1 Cor 4:6, 18, 19; 2 Cor 12:20) and is the natural product of the "carnal" or "fleshly" (*sarkos*) mind. The heretics' illogical conceit ("idle notions" is literally "conceited for no logical reason") in all its falsehood was brought about by a thought life controlled by the flesh—a mindset governed by sin and completely "unspiritual" or separated from God. The terrible irony is that they claimed to be joining the angels as they worshiped God—to be proud of their God connection—while in reality they had nothing to do with God.

Fourth, they had "lost connection with the head" (2:19). The implication is that the heretics had arisen from within the church and were probably at one time more orthodox. Yet now Christ was diminished in their system, perhaps to the level of one of the angelic powers, and their notion of salvation stemmed more from their asceticism and charismatic experiences than from the reality of Christ's death on the cross. Literally, the verb states that they had "failed to grasp firmly" or "hold fast to" Christ, the head. They had drifted away from the centrality of Christ and so had lost the solid foundation for their faith. There can be no truth in a religion that ignores Christ.

As "head of the body" (1:18) Christ is the source that provides power for all the members. As in 1 Corinthians 12:12–29, Romans 12:4–8, and Ephesians 4:14–16 (material that is replicated here), Paul develops a body-life metaphor for the relationship between Christ and the church. The Greeks believed that the head provided the life-force for the rest of the body and held the bones together—a model underlying the word-picture here of "joints and ligaments" proceeding from the head and providing both nourishment and cohesion for the rest of the body. Christ, Paul declares, is the sole authority for truth and meaning, the one means of nourishment, the uniting force that "knits the church together" (see 2:2). The metaphor conveys that, with the impetus coming from the head, the members of the body are to nourish and support one another, thereby growing together in Christ. Christ guides and feeds the church, and "God causes it to grow"—an undoubted reference to spiritual more than numerical growth (though it could include both).

Warning Against Asceticism and Legalism (2:20-23)

Apparently quite a few Colossian Christians had been sufficiently cowed by the cult leaders' pressure tactics to submit to their legalistic demands. Paul finds it necessary to challenge them on their compromise using a condition of fact: "you died with Christ" (in Greek the sentence begins with "if," which is validly translated "since" in the niv). He shows how ridiculous and dangerous it was for them to give in on so critical an issue, returning to the point he made in verse 12 ("having been buried with him"). The false teachers had created a fleshly religion stemming from the "carnal mind" (v. 18), but the true believers have "died with Christ," both to this world and to the things of this world—including the pseudo-religion of these heretics.

Specifically, Christians have died to "the elemental spirits of the world" (2:8), the very demonic powers that Christ disarmed and triumphed over (v. 15). So the beings to which the Colossians were subjecting themselves were the implacable enemies, both of themselves and of God. Yet in Christ the saints have been set free from these evil powers, and Christ has given his followers authority over these demonic spirits (Mark 3:15; 6:7). This does not mean that the forces of darkness have no weapons and cower before us. They still seek to "sift [us] as wheat" (Luke 22:31) and "devour" us like lions (1 Pet 5:8), but they can do so only by deceiving us (Rev 12:9; 20:3). Satan and the fallen angels cannot overpower us.

Paul asks how the Colossian believers can submit to beings that have already been defeated and over which they have been given power. "Why," he asks, "as though you still belonged to the world (literally, "as though you are still living in the world"), do you submit to its rules?" In fact, Paul says, followers of Christ have died to this world (see also Col 3:3). We are "foreigners and exiles" (1 Pet 2:11), for "our citizenship is in heaven" (Phil 3:20-21). And because we no longer belong to this world, we have been freed from its rules; a worldly religion has no place in our new lives.

In Colossians 2:21 Paul provides a sampling of the worldly rules from which we have been set free: "Do not handle! Do not taste! Do not touch!" The short, pithy nature of the commands and the terms he uses make it likely that these three are in one sense representative of the regulations, while in another sense they are sarcastic, mocking the shallow nature of these cultic practices. "Taste" refers to the dietary aspects of food and drink. Between "handle" and "touch," which refer to purity issues, some interpreters see "handle" as the stronger term and therefore suggest a downward spiral of progressively weaker commands. But in reality, the two verbs are virtual synonyms, and a downward progression is doubtful.

Others have suggested a sexual connotation, as in 1 Corinthians 7:1: "It is good for a man not to touch a woman" (literal translation; see also "sensual indulgence" in 2:23, below), but that imagery demands an object ("touch a woman") which is not present here. So these commands represent the cultic requirements of this false movement, summing up the food laws and issues of defilement. In some contexts—for instance, the religious worship of the Jewish Christians in Romans 14—this type of practice would have been allowed. But in the false teaching at Colossae, these injunctions had become **soteriological** and had replaced the cross as the basis for salvation. As such they had become heretical and extremely dangerous, as Paul points out in the next two verses.

In Colossians 2:22–23 Paul continues to explore the weaknesses of this legalistic, quasi-Christian movement with its endless regulations. Note the emphasis on "all these rules" (the NIV places "all" later in the sentence), alerting us that virtually every aspect of the system developed by these people was wrong. The Greek grammar of the verse is difficult to decipher. It is likely that the first half points to the material objects that were prohibited (the foods and items that were said to defile an individual), emphasizing their perishable nature, while the second half points to the rules or commands themselves, emphasizing their human origin. Paul condemns the entire system as earthly and at enmity with God.

"Destined to perish with use" stresses the purely physical root of this religious movement, which offered neither eternal value nor lasting power. The food and other material objects belonged to this world and would pass away like everything else associated with it. The false teachers' specific injunctions ("commands and teachings") were themselves "human" in origin, reiterating Isaiah 29:13: "Their hearts are far from me; their worship of me is based on merely human rules they have been taught." Isaiah was condemning the idolatry of the apostate nation, emphasizing the absence of God in both practice and teaching. Paul is here accusing these false teachers of the same thing (as also in Col 2:8, "depends on human tradition").

Verse 23 is difficult to translate. There are two major possibilities: (1) "These rules are of no value in restraining the indulgence of the flesh, even though they have the appearance of wisdom"; or (2) "Though these rules have the appearance of wisdom, this wisdom has no value, and they actually lead to fleshly indulgence." Both are viable translations of the Greek, but it is slightly better to connect "these rules" (literally, "which things") with "of no value" and then to translate the preposition *pros* as "against" rather than "for" in this context. This approach favors the first translation.

The problem was that these regulations did on the surface "have an appearance of wisdom" (v. 23) to the Colossians,

many of whom had been sucked in to the heretical movement. Asking them to re-examine its tenets, Paul cites three
here: (1) Theirs was a "self-imposed worship," or "religious
system," meaning again that it was human and fleshly rather
than from God. This was likely connected to the "worship of
angels" in verse 18 and the centrality of visions for their worship. (2) Their "false humility" also is featured in verse 8, and
Paul repeats the phrase here in reference to their asceticism.
This is closely linked to (3) "their harsh treatment of the body,"
centering on the physical results of their severe self-depriva-
tion. Since God was not behind what they were doing, it constituted not true worship but mistreatment of their bodies for
no good purpose.

They were gaining nothing positive from their efforts. These
harsh ascetic rites "lack any value for restraining sensual indulgence" (literally, "gratification of the flesh"). As stated above,
the Greek preposition *pros* is best translated "against," with the
sense of "for restraining." The false teachers were promising
the adherents that their methods would lead to absolute control over the "flesh," including material objects as well as sexual aberrations (see my comments on 3:5). Paul counters that,
far from giving the adherents control over the flesh, these practices could have the opposite effect, for denying themselves
certain foods and bodily needs would not equate to overcom-
ing fleshly impulses. Paul likely has more in mind than sexual-
ity. The impulses of the flesh, the old sin nature inherited from
Adam, also include pride and narcissism. When the centrality of Christ is replaced by self-denial and self-humiliation, the
self gains control—and that does indeed lead to fleshly indulgence. Every aspect of "sensuality" is intended here.

There are many modern parallels to this situation; examples can include the legalism in fundamentalist Christianity,
as well as the new "religion" of working out, in which the
beauty of the body becomes more important than that of the
soul. Self-indulgence can be found not only in hedonistic gluttony, but also in calorie-counting and exercise routines. All is

good in moderation. As Paul says, "physical training is of some value" so long as "godliness" is first (1 Tim 4:8). We need to be fit, but that focus should never take over our lives. We also do well to maintain our appearance, but overspending on clothes and beauty products is wrong (see Rev 3:18b).

There is, however, yet another heretical movement that is closer to the one we find in Colossians, though it does not have an ascetic component. That's the prosperity movement, which has made materialism "spiritual" and "gratification of the flesh" a true goal of the Christian. Counter to all biblical teaching, the claim is that God wants all his people to be rich and healthy. This movement teaches that God is obligated to give us whatever we want, as long as we have enough faith to demand that he do so. God is no longer sovereign; we are, and the result is every bit as "fleshly" (and unchristian) a movement as the Colossian heresy.

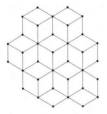

THE PREEMINENCE OF CHRIST
IN CHRISTIAN LIVING
(3:1–4:1)

In many of Paul's letters there is a shift from the theological to the practical, as at Romans 12, Galatians 5, and Ephesians 4. That is the case at Colossians 3 as well. The first two chapters have dealt with the theoretical problem of the false teachers and their tenets, responding with true theology regarding Christ and salvation. Now the final two chapters deal with the implications for the Christian life. This does not mean Paul is finished with the heretics and is simply moving on to practical living. The material here applies to the problem of the "fleshly" life already discussed in 2:18, 23 (also in 1:22, 24; 2:1, 5, 11, 13). The "old self/flesh" must be defeated; the believer has died with Christ (3:3 points back to 2:12a, 20) and has been raised to newness of life (3:1 follows up on 2:12b). That, in fact, is the theme of 3:5–11, 12–17: putting off the old and putting on the new. So the false teachers are very much in mind. Still, the emphasis is on daily Christian living, emphasized especially in 3:18–4:1, the "social code" passage that addresses practical relationships within the body of Christ. In 2:6 Paul introduced the section challenging the heretics with the exhortation to "live your lives in him," and now he expands on that theme.

BELIEVERS ARE CALLED TO A LIFE FOCUSED
ON THE THINGS ABOVE (3:1–4)

The Resurrection Life (3:1–2)

On the basis ("therefore") of all that Paul has stated in the first two chapters about the supremacy of Christ and salvation in him alone, he turns to the Christian life and personal priorities. In Colossians 2:12 he spoke of the believer's twofold union with Christ; the Christian is "buried with him" and then "raised with him" to newness of life. Now Paul explores the implications. The negative side was addressed in verses 16–23: Do not let the fleshly religion of the false teachers cause you to drift away from Christ. Now he develops the positive side: Pursue the heavenly realities in Christ.

The basis of all of this is the resurrection life, beginning with an "if" clause that assumes the reality: "since (ei, 'if') you have been raised with Christ." The people of God await the future physical resurrection at Christ's second coming (1 Thess 4:13–18), but there is first, at conversion, a spiritual resurrection in Christ that God performs (the Greek verb translated "have been raised" is a divine passive, meaning "God raised you"). So believers are part of a new creation, a new life that begins with the new birth (1 Pet 1:3–4).

The command that follows is the key to this paragraph, and clearly the two imperatives of 3:1b, 2 constitute a single command: "Set your hearts/minds on things above." If you have indeed been raised, Paul reasons, you cannot live for this world, because it is no longer your home; you have moved to a new address, and your sights have been raised. "Set your hearts" translates the Greek verb zēteite (literally, "keep seeking"), referring to motivations and priorities. We have established what is of true importance in our lives, and we will continually (present tense) "seek" these new realities rather than what used to command our attention. There is a new set of directions, and we obey a new set of paradigms.

Now that we are raised with Christ, our lives are to be dominated by "the things above," referring to our new home in heaven. Paul uses this language only here, but it is closely connected to "the Jerusalem that is above" in Galatians 4:26 and "the heavenward call" of Philippians 3:14. As Paul made clear in Colossians 2:20, we are now citizens of heaven and foreigners in this world. He expresses it well in Ephesians 1:3, 20; 3:10; 6:12, when he refers to "the heavenly realm" (literally, "heavenlies")—a part of God's final kingdom where we are already seated with Christ (Eph 2:6-7). Note the logic behind this point: We are not simply awaiting Christ's return, when we will receive our inheritance and enter our heavenly home. We *already* have entered heaven spiritually and are already a part of that new reality. Our physical environment is still earthly, but our hearts and minds are focused "above," giving us an entirely new set of priorities. There is both a spatial (above/below) and a temporal (now/not yet) distinction, for ours is a higher and greater calling. The false teachers centered on visions (2:18), believing that they provided transport to the heavenly realm. Paul is showing the error of such merely human techniques for gaining access to heaven—which is real, not something we need to "see" in a vision. The believer already dwells there.

Paul makes two points about this—Christ is there in the place "above," and he is "seated at the right hand of God." The basis of this new spatial reality is simple: This is "where Christ is." This new realm is not just a theological concept, an ephemeral, "somewhere out there" place that touches our lives only peripherally. It is a concrete reality, for Christ is there, and it is as real as he is. This is why we will orient ourselves to the heavenly realm: Our Lord is there. We already dwell there—but not alone, for we have joined him and are seated with God. In the light of this realization, why would we ever want to focus only (or mainly) on our earthly existence?

"Seated at the right hand" stems from Psalm 110:1, by far the most quoted Old Testament passage in the New Testament (more than thirty citations) because it is the Old Testament basis for the exaltation of Christ at his resurrection (e.g., Mark 12:36; Acts 2:34–35; Rom 8:34; Eph 1:20; Heb 1:3; 8:1; 1 Pet 3:22). David's coronation psalm was often understood messianically in Judaism: "The LORD says to my lord, 'Sit at my right hand until I make your enemies a footstool for your feet.'" This was fulfilled in Jesus' resurrection, ascension, and exaltation, and Paul uses this image to stress Jesus' authority, power, and glory. The "place above" is the location of God's throne, and Christ is seated there—so it must also be the center of our lives and the core of our personal aims and ambitions.

In Colossians 3:2 Paul moves from motivation to thought and will, challenging us to "think" or "set our minds on" the new heavenly realities. This includes our mindset and thought life but goes beyond them to the motivations that shape the way we live. We will determine to emulate the mind of Christ and let it guide our thoughts and their resultant actions (Rom 15:5; Phil 2:5; 1 Pet 4:1)—a transformation the Spirit will accomplish within us when we allow him to "renew our minds" (Rom 12:2) and fill us with heavenly priorities instead of mundane earthly pursuits.

Paul highlights this dichotomy by a clarifying repetition: "things above, not on earthly things." Certainly Paul is not establishing two absolutely contrasting spheres between which we must choose. We must live in both at the same time. But there is conflict between these two realms, and we must choose to make the heavenly dominant over the earthly. This is quite similar to the flesh/Spirit dualism of Romans 8. Our minds are to be filled with the Spirit-sent things of God (Eph 5:18), thereby defeating the sinful tendencies of the flesh and the world. In this Paul further corrects the heretics, who claimed to lift their adherents to the heavenly realms but in reality had developed a fleshly set of rituals that did no more than deny the body. Moreover, they were trying to minimize their bodily existence. In contrast, Paul states that by filling our minds and senses with Christ we allow him to raise our bodies higher.

THE NEW LIFE AS HIDDEN WITH CHRIST IN GOD (3:3)

Paul began this section with our being raised with Christ; now he returns (2:12, 20) to our death with Christ. How can any true believer center on the things of earth after we have "died" to them? We no longer belong to the earthly things, for we are "with Christ," meaning that we belong to him and have been freed from the things of this world, including the demonic powers (1:16; 2:8, 15, 20). Death in Christ is not an end but a beginning, not a loss but a gain—an empowerment to begin truly to live, for we have been liberated from enslavement to sin and to the things of this world. Death with Christ means power and freedom. Note that Paul has framed this section by reversing the imagery of our participation in the death (3:3) and resurrection (v. 1) of Christ. There can be no greater reality than the new life this has produced.

In the second half of verse 3 Paul further explores this new life. His metaphor provides an interesting extension of the main point of the section, as the imagery moves from death with Christ (2:20), to burial with him (v. 12) and then to the idea of hiddenness, signifying separation and protection from danger (valuables "hidden" from thieves). Often in Scripture we encounter the assurance of being hidden and kept safe in God (e.g., Ps 27:5-6; Isa 49:2). The perfect tense "hidden" stresses the ongoing state of affairs that results from our union with Christ in his death.

There is also an apocalyptic motif in this idea. As the "mystery" of God in Christ has been "hidden" and is now revealed (1:26), so the mystery of the glory of the saints is now hidden but is soon to be revealed (see 3:4). Both nuances—our safety and our hidden glory—are true entirely and only "with Christ in God." The Triune Godhead is presently at work keeping us safe and secure, and our union is with God as well as with Christ. Christ's treasures are hidden in us, and we are "kept by the power of God" (1 Pet 1:5) in the midst of the ever-present dangers in this world.

OUR FUTURE LIFE IN GLORY (3:4)

Verse 3 dealt with our present security as being "hidden" in Christ, with our glory yet to be revealed; verse 4 addresses the final revelation of that glory. As with every aspect of our salvation, this is entirely caught up with the assurance that Christ will be revealed (NIV: "appears"). This is the perfect verb, for the meaning of "apocalyptic" is the revelation of hidden mysteries (see my comments on 1:26). The motif found in 3:3-4 could be said to sum up one of the critical points of the book of Revelation, which traces how God at the end of this world will "reveal" the true glory of his Son as he returns—at the same time revealing the glory of the saints, who will triumph and be vindicated with him. In the words of 1 Peter 1:5, we are kept by the power of God "for a salvation ready to be revealed in the last time" (ESV). This is our future hope—as Paul expresses in Colossians 1:5, a "hope stored up for you in heaven." The protection of the believer is future-oriented; the goal is not just our present safety but even more our eternity with Christ after his return.

Note that Jesus does not merely give us life; he "is our life." Life is defined by and identified with him. As he states so clearly in John 14:6, "I am the way, the truth, and the life." Apart from Christ there is no life, merely existence. He alone gives life meaning and substance, not only via his work on the cross but also based on his identity as the "one and only God" (John 1:14, 18; 3:16, 18). This reality gives new depth to the "in Christ" motif, in that our union with Christ defines life itself. We can do no less than join our hearts and voices with Paul and affirm, "For to me to live is Christ" (Phil 1:21).

Christ's "revelation" is our own: "Then you also will be revealed (NIV: 'appear') with him in glory." Our present "hiddenness" has a termination point; we are meant for greater things that—due to the sinful world we inhabit and that we have fashioned—cannot be made known until the appointed time. Once again, this is possible due entirely to the reality that we experience it "with him." "Glory" is the term for the majesty and splendor of God throughout the Old Testament (e.g., the **Shekinah** glory), and here it becomes a virtual code word for the future heavenly reality the saints will enjoy. John says it well: "We know that when Christ appears (Greek: 'is revealed'), we shall be like him, for we shall see him as he is" (1 John 3:2). We will share the ultimate "glory" of Christ, both in terms of eternal life and of our resurrection body, as he "will transform our lowly bodies so that they will be like his glorious body" (Phil 3:20). As Revelation 22:5 affirms, the saints "will reign forever and ever."

BELIEVERS ARE CALLED TO REMOVE THE FILTHY CLOTHES OF THE FLESHLY LIFE (3:5-11)

THE OLD LIFE OF SIN (3:5-8)

Paul draws another conclusion (indicated by "therefore"): Since we have died with Christ, we have died with respect to our vices—those sinful actions that hinder our union with him. Furthermore, we have been raised with Christ, and this should be exemplified in newness of conduct—our triumph over these sinful impulses.

The command to put off sin (3:5)

We are to set our minds on the heavenly realities (3:1-2); since we are "dead" to this world, we will of course "put to death" everything that belongs to our "earthly nature." We do well to note the progression of the imagery here. Christ died on the cross as an atoning sacrifice so that his blood could cleanse us from sin (1:14, 20). When we turned our lives over to him, we died and were buried with him (2:12a), and then we were raised with him (v. 12b), participating in his resurrection and victory over the cosmic powers (v. 15). Since we have been "rescued" from the realm of darkness and "brought into" Christ's kingdom (1:13), we now must live in light of our new community in Christ. Note that the impetus for all of the above is the work of God and Christ in our life.

Now we must respond by doing our part, by consciously "putting to death" or "dying to" our old way of life, the characteristics and actions of our "earthly nature." This conscious relinquishment is an act of the will, a Christ-centered mindset that refuses to allow the old way of life to influence our new way of life. We have been liberated from the "old self," and it has been "nullified" or "done away with," meaning that it was "rendered powerless" by Christ (Rom 6:6; 7:6). The "earthly nature" (literally, "the members that are on the earth") pictures in Jewish fashion the parts of our body responsible for or involved in different kinds of sins; this summarizes the past pagan life of the Colossians as something that should be long dead and buried. The believers' current behavior should be the polar opposite of what it once was. So with us, our former way of life is dead and gone, and we must get on with our new life in Christ, refusing to allow our former sins to regain control.

Paul provides examples of past sinful behavior in the form of a vice list. In both Jewish and **Hellenistic** ethical exhortation it was common to provide a representative catalog of virtues or vices (e.g. Rom 1:29-32; 1 Cor 5:9-11; Gal 5:19-23; 1 Pet 4:3). The virtues are to characterize the people of God, as opposed to those of the world, while the vices, which are to be avoided at all costs, typify the non-Christian world and bring down the wrath of God on the perpetrators (3:6). Yet while this list is representative, these also are explicit sins committed by the Colossians (and by us!). Of the five listed here, the first four are sexual sins typical of their pagan past.

"Sexual immorality" (*porneia*) refers to all kinds of sexual sins that violate the marriage bond. The term also appears first in the list in Galatians 5:19 and is treated as a category in 1 Corinthians 6:18 and 1 Thessalonians 4:3; *porneia* also characterizes the immoral lifestyle of the world in Revelation (seven times, e.g., 2:21; 14:8). Here in Colossians it is likely the general category that sums up the other vices in the list, which together constitute "immorality." "Impurity" (*akatharsia*), while it denotes moral uncleanness or impurity in general

(Lev 15:30–31; Num 19:13), often refers specifically to sexual corruption and appears frequently alongside "immorality" (Gal 5:19; 1 Thess 4:3, 7). "Lust" (*pathos:* literally, "passion") could refer to strong desires in general but, as with the previous term, here refers to shameful sexual "passions" that lead to lascivious behavior. Similarly, "evil desires" (*epithumian kakēn*) can connote sinful desires of all kinds (including greed, next on the list) but most likely here refer to the same sinful sexual desires as the others. We could say that the latter two items are the carnal temptations that produce the excesses in the first two.

The final category of "greed" or "covetousness" (*pleonexian*) alludes to the desire to possess material things (Matt 6:24–34; Luke 12:15; Rom 1:29; Eph 5:3, 5)—often things that belong to another, as in the tenth commandment: "You shall not covet your neighbor's wife ... house or land, his male or female servant, his ox or donkey, or anything that belongs to your neighbor" (Deut 5:21). Note that this ends Paul's vice list in the same way it ends the Ten Commandments. The connection receives emphasis in the added phrase "which is idolatry," for the opening of the Ten Commandments centers on idolatry (no other gods, no graven image), and most of the prohibited sins deal with a preference for the things of this world over those of God. That is certainly the case with greed, which defines the human demand for material possessions over God. In recent years, a new term has arisen for this mindset: "affluenza." Indeed, affluence has become a virus that is damaging the spiritual lives not only of pagans but of countless Christians as well.

The result of sin: The wrath of God (3:6–7)

It is common in New Testament vice lists to point out that these sins bring down divine judgment on the practitioners (Rom 1:18; 1 Cor 6:9–10; 1 Pet 4:5); the emphasis here is primarily on the final judgment, though present judgment should not be entirely excluded ("is coming," though present tense, could well be a prophetic present, "is going to come"). I see here an inaugurated thrust: Judgment begins in God's present displeasure with the sinner and will consummate at the "great white throne" (Rev 20:11–15). We should remember that God is in essence a holy God and that justice and love are interdependent aspects of that holiness. As a loving God he has sent his Son to die on the cross for our sins (John 3:16), bringing salvation. As a just God, however, he must destroy evil, which is the absolute antithesis of his holy character. Sinful humanity has so rationalized the seriousness of sin that people think a loving God can do nothing less than forgive sinners. That cannot be so. Without repentance and confession there can be no forgiveness (1 John 1:9), and vices such as those in 3:5 must lead inevitably to divine wrath.

It is quite clear in the Old Testament that God does not merely lose his temper and erupt in vindictive outbursts. His wrath (Greek: *orgē* here but *thymos* elsewhere; the terms are synonymous) is part of his holy character, part of his essential nature as the enthroned Judge. He is the God of the covenant, and this involves not only blessings but also curses, for those who break covenant with him must be judged. When the Israelites fell into apostasy, a holy God had to exercise his wrath, prohibiting the wilderness generation from entering the promised land and later sending his people into exile in Assyria and Babylon.

This theme comes to fruition in the New Testament, where the grace and mercy of God (*chesed* in the Old Testament) produce the ultimate solution in the gift of his Son. Romans 2:8 states clearly that God's "wrath and anger" (note that both terms are used) fall on those who reject the truth and turn to evil, but 1 Thessalonians 1:10 declares that Jesus has arrived and that he "rescues us from the coming wrath." Romans 5:9 speaks of "his blood," by which we are "saved from God's wrath." Thus God's love has provided redemption via the atoning sacrifice of his Son, but his just wrath remains necessary for those who reject God's offer of salvation and prefer to live in sin. A righteous God *must* exercise wrath toward those who show contempt for his salvation and prefer a life of evil (some versions include "upon the sons of disobedience," but it is slightly more likely that this was added by later scribes from Ephesians 5:6 and was not originally part of Colossians 3:6).

Paul in 3:7 returns to the Colossians' former lives as pagans, reminding them that "you used to walk in these ways" during "the life you once lived." "These ways" is a clear reference to the vices of verse 5, and Paul is implicitly castigating the Colossians for falling into sin when they at times returned to their old, pagan patterns. They must completely "rid (themselves)" (v. 8) of this previous way of life, lest God's wrath fall upon them as well.

The command to get rid of sin (3:8)

There is a "once / but now" movement from verse 7 to verse 8 that shows Paul is now addressing the current situation. In "rid yourselves" or "put away" we see a metaphor of stripping off and getting rid of filthy clothes. Here and in verse 9, as well as in verses 10 and 12 ("put on"), Paul uses one of his favorite images (Rom 13:12, 14; Eph 4:22, 24; see also Jas 1:21; 1 Pet 2:1), that of throwing away the old and clothing ourselves with the new. In the ancient world—in which the average person might have owned only a single garment, and robes became a part of one's inheritance—this was a particularly strong image. Clothes would have had to be in dreadful shape to warrant their being thrown away—an apt metaphor for the terrible nature of sin's filth. Note the emphasis on "all such things"; not a single sin dare remain, for each and every sin brings about the wrath of God (see Jas 1:10–11).

In a second catalog of vices, Paul names five. The earlier list (3:5) centered on sexual sins; this one focuses on emotions and speech. It is difficult to decide whether we should divide these vices into three of emotion and two of speech or whether we should see "from your lips" as modifying all five, thus rendering all of them sins of the tongue. It is probably best to understand them in a 3-2 pattern—three sinful attitudes that easily erupt into two kinds of sinful speech.

In verse 6, Paul addressed "anger" (*orgē*) and "rage" (*thymos*) in relation to God. There God's righteous wrath was in view; here it is people's sinful, self-centered anger directed at others, stemming from animosity and resulting in hatred. Too many of us are irritable and ill-tempered—and those attitudes are sinful. Rage leading to hatred stems from the flesh (Gal 5:19-20) and will lead to divine judgment. The attitude that produces such anger is "malice" (*kakia*)—ill will that leads to a desire to hurt others.

To "slander" (*blasphēmia*) means to "speak against" or "defame" another, usually with a desire to bring them harm. When used of slandering God, the Greek term has been transliterated into "blasphemy" (e.g., Matt 12:31; Mark 14:64; John 10:33). Vilifying others is also a type of blasphemy, since they are God's children (Jas 3:9) and God's people are not to engage in such things (Titus 3:2). Instead, they are to emulate Christ, who never retaliated when insulted but entrusted himself to "him who judges justly" (1 Pet 2:23). "Filthy language" (*aischrologia*) refers both to obscene language and to slanderous speech. In Colossians 3:8 the term might combine these meanings and refer to the use of obscene, coarse language when abusing another person.

Overall, these five vices refer to the anger and malice that leads to the defamation of other people. As in James 3, such sins of attitude and speech will destroy the harmony and cohesiveness of God's community.

The New Life of Unity in Christ (3:9-11)

This section begins with another sin believers need to throw off: lying. Again it is a sin of the tongue, but with a different motivation—in this case, the desire is to deceive and get one's way. Like the others this sin deals with relationships within the community ("to one another"). God's people are to be governed by honesty and truth; followers of Christ must emulate him who is "the way, the truth, and the life" (John 14:6). There can be no place for lying or deception among the children of

God. The Triune Godhead is truth, and God's followers must be characterized by truthfulness.

This idea is anchored by the repetition in 3:8: "You have taken off your old self with its practices." The imagery of shedding unwanted clothing appears again, but this time it is the "old self" or "old man" that is cast away, an image used also in Romans 6:6 and Ephesians 4:22–24. This is an important part of Paul's anthropology (his doctrine of humankind). It has often been thought that this emphasizes the individual—our dying to self and beginning a new life. However, the current consensus is that this is a corporate, salvation-historical metaphor that pictures humanity "in Adam" under the power of sin—living within the old eon or order of existence in a fallen world. Paul adds that he is speaking of the old self "with its practices" or deeds, referring back to the vices of 3:5, 8. He is saying that such practices belong to a world long dead; they have no part in the new realm we now inhabit, and there is no longer any excuse for such deeds.

This is especially true in that we have not only "put off" or thrown away our old wardrobe but have "put on" a new set of clothes, "the new self" (v. 10)—literally, "the new man," variously called "the new nature" or "the new humanity." This describes a monumental transformation in which the old sinful nature when we were "in Adam" (Rom 5:12) has been completely removed (dead and buried) and replaced by a new creation (the result of the cross and resurrection, 2 Cor 5:17), a new person oriented to God and Christ. This doesn't mean we no longer sin or face temptation. Rather, it means our old sinful nature, which used to be an internal force controlling us, has now been relegated to an external force trying to invade our lives and regain control (a theme developed in Rom 6–7). We still have our physical bodies, but we are new persons within (see the "inner being" in Rom 7:22; 2 Cor 4:16; Eph 3:16). We must also be cognizant of the corporate dimension of "the new self." As the old self was in Adam, a part of sinful humanity, so now the new self is "in Christ," a part of regenerate humanity.

This new identity in Christ "is being renewed in knowledge in the image of its creator." There is a great deal to unpack in this. The ongoing force of "being renewed" alerts us that this is a process rather than a finished work. Our nature is made new, but we still must work continuously and grow slowly in the effects of this renewal. This is critical. We have been made a completely new person, but it takes the rest of our lives to reorient ourselves to the Christ-ward path. Spiritual growth is a lifelong process. Second Corinthians 4:16 puts it well: Our inner being is "being renewed day by day." And Romans 12:2 adds that we are "transformed by the renewal of (our) mind." Behind this is the work of the Holy Spirit, who (literally) "makes us new again and again" by reshaping our minds to think like Christ (Phil 2:5; 1 Pet 4:4).

The outworking of this renewal takes place "in knowledge"—an idea similar to those of Philippians 3:10, where Paul defines his growth in righteousness as "to know Christ," and Ephesians 4:13, where he talks about growing up spiritually "to the whole measure [of the stature] of the fullness of Christ." The basis of this (the NIV's "in" should actually be "according to" or "on the basis of") is "the image of its creator," an allusion to the creation account in Genesis 1:26–27 ("in his own image"), pointing once again to the new creation in Christ. Due to the sin of Adam that image was marred, but it has been restored in Christ, and our goal in life is to allow the Spirit to work out this new creation within us. Christ is "the image of the invisible God" (Col 1:15), and in him we are recreated in the likeness of God and of Christ.

A major result of this corporate "new humanity" is a greater depth of unity among the divergent people in God's community (3:11). In Ephesians 2:14 Paul explores this in relation to Jew-Gentile conflicts, stating that Christ has "made the two groups one and has destroyed the barrier, the dividing wall of hostility." Here he expands on the concept to cover all the racial and ethnic groups that make up fallen humanity. The new creation is corporate as well as individual, removing the sinful "barriers" that divide us from one another and forging a new humanity, united in Christ.

This verse is organized in a series of antithetical pairs, similar to the structure of Galatians 3:28. It begins with the basic biblical distinction, "no Gentile or Jew," which together with "circumcised or uncircumcised" is used often to stress the entire human race (1 Cor 1:24; 10:32), In Christ all religious and national boundaries have disappeared, replaced by the one people of God forged together by the blood of the cross. Paul may well have directed this analogy at the false teachers, who on the basis of their emphasis on the Jewish rituals were in effect strengthening these barriers.

The next two pairs also might be connected. "Barbarians" refers to those nations or tribes that did not speak Greek and thus were not considered truly civilized. "Scythians," descended from a group of tribes north of the Black Sea, were considered the lowest form of barbarians, producing a wretched class of slaves. So there is a natural, implied connection with "slave or free," the next pair. In the social code passages, Paul emphasizes that slave and master belong to the same family in Christ (Eph 6:9). In the Roman world, slaves were considered pieces of property, and their owners could deal with them however they wished. But in the church, slaves and their owners have the same Master and stand equal before God. Social and ethnic distinctions may control human interaction in the world, but in Christ unity prevails. There will always be rich and poor, male and female, corporate heads (masters) and subordinate workers (in some sense equivalent to slaves). Still, there is no such thing as superiority or inferiority among God's people; all are one in Christ, and all are to use their gifts (financial, social, and spiritual) to serve and aid other members of the body.

The section ends by reaffirming the foundation for everything Paul has just said: "Christ is all and in all." The barriers and ethnic divisions that fracture society throughout the world are abolished in Christ's community, for its unifying power is Christ himself. Herein lies the answer to racism and ethnic hatred. The "allness" of Christ means that everything in this world that has truth and value is summed up in him (see also 1 Cor 15:28 ["that God may be all in all"] and Eph 1:23 ["him who fills all in all"]). Christ is everything that matters. He is not only "all" but also "in all"—most likely meaning that he fills all people, so that the distinctions dividing humanity disappear. Diversity continues, but instead of producing barriers these differences now unite us as God's people, because we are sharing our diversity and enriching one another's lives. In the new humanity in Christ, we cherish each other's diverse heritages and look forward to seeing them enhance our lives.

BELIEVERS ARE CALLED TO LIVE IN A NEW COMMUNITY (3:12-17)

In the previous section, Paul presented the meaning and power of the Christian life in terms of negative ("put off the old") and positive ("put on the new") counterparts (3:5-10). Here (3:12-17) and in the next section (3:18-4:1), he provides details about the positive aspects. This section begins (3:12-14) by expanding on verse 10 ("put on the new self"), challenging the saints to "clothe themselves" with Christian virtues governed by love and unity. It continues (3:15-17) by reiterating the centrality of Christ, whose message of peace enables a new depth of worship. As members of the new humanity in Christ, believers are called to a life of exhorting one another and worshiping together in gratitude and thanksgiving. This theme of togetherness in Christ serves a foundation for the rest of the chapter (3:18-4:1), which explores the new social relationships that evolve from the unity of the church. Throughout these sections, Paul emphasizes the lordship of Christ (3:13, 17, 18, 20, 22, 23, 24; 4:1), who makes possible this new reconciliation and community.

CLOTHE YOURSELVES WITH CHRISTIAN VIRTUES (3:12–14)

The new clothing in Christ (3:12)

"Putting on" the new nature (v. 10) is the turning point of our transformation into becoming God's children and develops further the "put off / put on" imagery of verses 8 and 10. In verse 12 Paul once again encourages the Colossian believers to change their clothing and adorn themselves with the new spiritual garments God has given them. The new reality is further deepened by the realization that they are "the elect of God" (NIV: "chosen people"), a major Old Testament concept to describe Israel's special status among the nations as God's honored possession (Ps 105:6; 106:5; Isa 43:20; 45:4). The New Testament continues this theme, with respect first to Christ as "the Chosen One" (Luke 23:35; John 1:34) and then to the church as "the chosen race ... God's special possession" (1 Pet 2:9). Colossians 3:12 emphasizes that the Gentiles (here pointing to the Colossian church) have joined believing Jews as the new Israel, God's elect people.

In addition, they are "holy and dearly loved," which further describes what it means to be elect. Paul wants the Colossians to realize the incredible richness of the blessings God has bestowed on them. "Holy" refers to the natural result of being "God's elect." Those who are "the chosen people" are set apart by God for himself, thus becoming "holy" (living as "set apart" from this world for God). God has called them out of the world to be his "saints" or "holy people," fulfilling the imagery of Israel as "his treasured possession ... a people holy to the LORD your God" (Deut 26:18–19; also 7:6; 14:2). The basis for all of this is the love of God, which Paul affirms so clearly in Romans 5:8: "But God demonstrates his own love for us in this: While we were still sinners, Christ died for us." We as God's children are the recipients of his perfect, divine love and are categorized as "the beloved" (Rom 1:7; 1 Thess 1:4; 2 Thess 2:13).

In light of the incredible salvation blessings they have received from God and their new status as God's chosen people, the Colossian Christians are enjoined to clothe themselves with Christian virtues. The five listed here parallel the two sets of five vices each the saints are to cast off (3:5, 8). For the first virtue mentioned in verse 12, the Greek expression (*splanchna oiktirmou*; literally, "bowels of mercies") builds on the ancient view of the bowels as the seat of the emotions. Paul is referring to feelings of kindness and compassion, as well as to the actions that result from those feelings. A good translation would be "heartfelt compassion," describing the tender mercies of God and Jesus (Matt 14:14; Luke 1:78; Phil 1:8) lived out in us.

"Kindness" (*chrēstotēta*) expresses a major Old Testament concept involving God's goodness and merciful actions on behalf of his people (1 Chr 16:34; Ps 25:7; 68:10). The tender mercies in the first virtue will lead naturally to the kind actions in this one. In the New Testament this incredibly gracious mercy draws people to repentance and salvation (Rom 2:4; Eph 2:7; Titus 3:4), and we are called to emulate these loving attributes of God and Jesus in our relations with one another.

"Humility" (*tapeinophrosynē*) moves from acts of mercy and kindness to the attitude of servanthood and the giving of oneself. It is exemplified in Jesus (who "humbled himself by becoming obedient to death," Phil 2:8) and defined well by Paul in Philippians 2:3: "In humility value others better than yourselves, not looking to your own interests but each of you to the interests of the others." To the Greeks humility was a sign of weakness, not a virtue, but Christ elevated it to the apex of the godly virtues. It is the opposite of the arrogance of the false teachers; it describes people who live not to satisfy their own demands, but to serve and help others.

"Gentleness" (*praütēta*), deriving from the idea of being "made lowly" or "deprived," had come to be used for a lowly attitude—a placing of oneself beneath others in status. As such, this virtue is closely linked to humility, referring to a gentle, quiet spirit. In Zechariah 9:9 the adjective is used of the Messiah: "Your king comes to you, lowly and riding on a donkey," a prophecy fulfilled in Matthew 21:5 in Jesus' triumphal entry (see also Matt 11:29). Gentleness is thereby a sign of the strength that must be exemplified in Jesus' messianic army and a prime characteristic of servant-leadership.

"Patience" (*makrothymian*; see also 1:11) refers to the longsuffering forbearance modeled for us by God and Christ (Rom 2:4; 1 Tim 1:16; 1 Pet 3:20), which we in turn are to show to others (Gal 5:22; Eph 4:2; 2 Tim 3:10; Jas 5:10). We must learn to endure the weaknesses of others and allow them to grow alongside ourselves. As God is patient with our failures, so we are to forbear with those around us. Developing and maintaining positive relationships requires time and effort, and we must be willing to accept people's foibles.

Forgiveness and love in the new community (3:13–14)

Paul further explores the theme of relationships among the messianic people, illustrating the means by which the above virtues may bear fruit. The Greek text contains grammatical components called "instrumental participles," which here are translated as "by bearing with each other and forgiving one another." Because these participles tell us *how* to accomplish the command of verse 12, I prefer this instrumental reading over the possibility of taking the participles as imperatives (commands). Paul is saying that the way for us to put on the Christian virtues of this verse and together become God's new community is to work continually (present tense) to exercise Christian tolerance and forgiveness.

To "bear with" people exemplifies "patience" in action; the idea is to "endure" or "put up" with their foibles. We practice Christian forbearance when we empathize with others and seek to understand why people act the way they do, as opposed to criticizing and looking down on them. Note the use of "each other" and "one another"; these are virtual synonyms, stressing the importance for each of us of relating to every other member of the church. It takes only one conflict to seriously undermine a congregation's unity, as demonstrated by the enmity between Euodia and Syntyche in Philippi (Phil 4:2–3). In that situation, Paul exhorts the whole Philippian church to get involved, as the dissension is tearing apart the congregation. Underlying the positive attitudes and actions prescribed by Paul, there is a shared sense of mutual caring, involvement, and submission.

Understanding and tolerance need to be fortified by Christian forgiveness. Empathy in and of itself isn't quite enough, as it is easy to hold grudges against those with whom we differ in temperament and outlook. We human beings will invariably hurt and offend each other. Paul uses the Greek *charizomenoi*, a specific term conveying the idea of "gracious" (*charis*) forgiveness. The implication is that we will forgive even when the individual does not deserve our pardon. Paul makes this concrete by adding the qualifier "if anyone has a grievance against someone." Notice in his directive the absence of the normal human response: "But he deserves it." Our attention is to be focused not on what the offender has done to us, but rather on what we can do for them. We will often have a legitimate basis for a complaint against another person, but Paul enjoins us to ignore our rights (see 1 Cor 9:3–6, 12) and care that much more for the other person.

This is hardly a normal human reaction, for it goes against our nature. But we have put off that sinful nature (the flesh, 2:11) and have chosen to follow the model of Christ and our own experience of having been forgiven by him. Paul instructs us as God's people to "forgive as the Lord forgave you"; receiving God's forgiveness is the only and absolute foundation for our own willingness to forgive ("as the Lord ... so you also"). Paul's directive consciously builds on the Lord's Prayer in Matthew 6:12: "And forgive us our debts, as we have forgiven our debtors." Jesus took this further, stating in his expansion of the principle in Matthew 6:15, "If you do not forgive others their sins, your Father will not forgive your sins." God requires that his kingdom people be forgiving. Reconciliation is an essential commodity in the church.

All of these virtues depend entirely on the centrality of love within the community (3:14). Accordingly, Paul begins with "above all" (Greek: *epi pasan*), signifying that love is of paramount importance, that it holds together all the other virtues so that each of us may function properly among God's people. In conjunction with the metaphor of verse 12, it is likely that Paul is describing love as the garment that goes "over" or "on top of" (*epi*) the rest of the clothes and holds them in place. Love is the supreme Christian virtue, as Paul expresses in 1 Corinthians 13:13: "And now these three remain: faith, hope, and love. But the greatest of these is love."

Love is supreme among the virtues in that it "binds them all together in perfect unity" (literally, "the bond of perfection"). Pursuing the clothing imagery, we could consider love to be the thread that stitches the virtues securely into the "quilt" of the church. But there is another option: Some interpreters suggest that what join together in unity are not the virtues of verse 12 but the members of the community, as in the NLT: "binds us all together in perfect harmony." That makes a great deal of sense, for Paul had spoken earlier of "the body, supported and held together by the joints and ligaments" (2:19; see also Eph 4:3). Scholars are divided on the interpretation here, and both readings fit the context well. Still, whenever Paul discusses unity he is thinking about the church, so he probably is saying that love will perfectly "unite" (2:2, 19) God's people. This prepares us for 3:15: "As members of one body you were called to peace."

IMMERSE YOURSELVES IN CHRIST'S PEACE AND TRUTH (3:15–17)

Paul has emphasized throughout Colossians the centrality and supremacy of Christ as Lord over his creation and his followers (1:3, 10, 15–20; 2:6). In these verses this core theme is applied the church's life and worship.

Christ's peace must reign (3:15)

When love and the Spirit-enabled virtues are operative at the core of the church's life, "peace" is the natural result. There are two aspects of peace: It is a gift from Christ ("of Christ" means both that it is *his* peace and that he is its source), but the believers must still submit to and work at it. This latter point is Paul's emphasis here. He charges us to "let the peace of Christ rule in your hearts"—to surrender to the lordship of Christ and to the peace that accompanies it. Paul strongly emphasizes peace in his writings, including references at the beginning of nearly every letter (e.g., "Grace and peace to you" in Col 1:1) as well as at the end of several (see Rom 16:20; 2 Cor. 13:11; Gal 6:16; Phil 4:9; 1 Thess 5:23). In the New Testament God regularly sends his peace (Rom 15:33; 1 Cor 14:33; Phil 4:7), as does Christ (John 14:27; 16:33). Peace is a trinitarian work among God's people.

This peace is three-dimensional—vertical (peace with God, as in 1:20: reconciliation achieved by "making peace through his blood"), horizontal (peace in the church, Eph 4:3: "the unity of the Spirit through the bond of peace"), and internal (peace in the heart). In one sense all three dimensions are active here. As Christ sends his peace to rule the community, the church allows it to control its relationships, and the people experience this heartfelt peace concretely in their daily lives. Yet it is more than inner tranquility and corporate unity; peace is an **eschatological** gift, fulfilling the Old Testament promises (Ps 29:11; Isa 9:6–7; 52:7; 54:13) and providing a foretaste of the eternal peace that will be ours when the final kingdom has arrived.

The church's role with regard to this peace is clear: The believers are to "let it rule." Christ's blood has brought reconciliation and divine peace to his followers (1:20). In contrast, Rome prided itself on its *Pax Romana* (the "Roman peace"), but this was a façade for subjugation via the sword. Christ provides a lasting peace, but it is not automatic. Believers must make it operative by allowing it to "rule" their relationships—to permit it to guide and control their interactions. Interestingly, this verb is a form of the Greek word rendered "disqualify" in 2:18, where it is used negatively of the false teachers judging their followers. Paul is contrasting the two approaches: The Colossians must not let themselves be judged by others but should place themselves only under the lordship of Christ. The judgmental attitude of the false teachers will fracture the church and destroy its harmony; in contrast, Christ will unify the body and enable it to find peace.

Further, this reign of peace must take place "in your hearts"—with "heart" referring not just to the emotions but in its biblical sense to the mind and will that determine a person's actions. The entire inner being is involved in the process, and this needs to be understood both individually and corporately. The centrality of peace in the church begins in the individual and then guides each member's relationships within the community (as we will see in 3:18–4:1).

Paul wants his readers to understand that peace from Christ is much more than an option to be considered. It is an absolute mandate stemming from the very will of God: "You were called to peace" (literally, "to which also you were called in one body"). The peace of Christ, if it is allowed to rule, must produce "one body" (Rom 12:5; 1 Cor 12:12–27; Eph 2:16; 4:4, 16; Col 1:18; 2:19). The "call" of God, referring to his elect will, does not stop at the gift of salvation but encompasses his will for a church living in complete harmony. Unity in the church, the result of peace, is at the core of the divine plan, and the number of conflicts and fractured relationships in the body today is an abomination to God.

Jesus stated this powerfully in John 17:21–23: "that all of them may be one, Father, just as you are in me and I am in you. May they also be in us so that the world may believe that you have sent me. ... I in them and you in me—so that they may be brought to complete unity." The message couldn't be more direct: The unity of the church on earth is based on the unity of the Godhead in heaven, and the very mission of the church is at stake in fostering it. When each of us is reconciled to God, we also are reconciled to God's people, mandating as a prime directive that Christ's true followers do whatever it takes to make peace among their disparate groups.

Paul concludes his thoughts on this point with his fourth injunction (after 1:3, 12; 2:7) to "be thankful." He has more in mind than a grateful heart and a thankful spirit. The concept here centers on corporate thanksgiving, since the united church expresses its thankfulness in corporate worship (as will be made clear in 3:16). The letter thus far has provided a continual reminder of all that God has done, from his creation of this world and placing us in it, to the gift of his Son to provide salvation through the cross, to the defeat of the cosmic powers and the blessings poured out on his people. The community of Christ must respond with thanksgiving.

Christ's truth must indwell and produce worship (3:16)

Paul's focus on the lordship of Christ continues. From Christ's peace in verse 15 we turn to his message (Greek: *logos*; "word"). The question is whether this refers to Jesus' own words (Christ as the subject) or to the church's teachings about him (Christ as the object). There isn't a great deal here to favor a reference to the sayings of Jesus; Paul's words most likely connote the dogmatic truths about Jesus, specifically those taught in Colossians. If the church is to grow and fulfill its divinely ordained purpose, both Christ and believers' knowledge of him must be at the center of its life and ministry.

These **christological** truths must "dwell among [us] richly," with a trinitarian flavor building on the indwelling presence of God (2 Cor 6:16) and of the Spirit (John 14:17; Rom 8:11; Eph 5:18; 2 Tim 1:14) within God's people. When the church focuses on these teachings, they will work "richly" among the believers, showering upon us the riches of the Triune Godhead, as in Ephesians 1:7–8: "in accordance with the riches of God's grace that he lavished on us" (see also Col 1:27; 2:2). First Timothy 6:17 assures us that God "richly provides us with everything," and Titus 3:6 asserts that his salvation is "poured out on us generously (richly)."

This rich bestowal of divine truth is intended to be experienced "as [we] teach and admonish one another," borrowing language from 1:28 (see my comments on that verse), which enjoins the church to proclaim Christ and produce mature followers. The "riches" equate to the knowledge derived from these christological truths. The teaching ministry of the church is to be conducted "in all wisdom," building on the emphasis in 1:9, 28, and 2:3, where Paul proclaims that divinely bestowed wisdom enables these truths to flourish in the life of the church. Wisdom in this sense is the soil in which the seeds of knowledge and understanding take root and grow. This is in direct opposition to the false teachers' pretentious "appearance of wisdom" (2:23), and it demands careful attention to the deep things of God in our messages today. There is no excuse for shallow preaching and teaching. According to 2 Timothy 2:15, those who water down God's truths in his Word will stand before God in shame at the final judgment.

This issue extends especially to the worship of the church. Paul most likely did not intend for us to view the "songs, hymns, and spiritual songs" as separate categories of worship music. It is debated whether these three terms modify "teaching and admonishing" (NIV, NASB, KJV) or "singing" in the ensuing clause (NRSV, NLT, NET, ESV: "singing psalms, hymns, and spiritual songs"). The word order favors the former, and that is how I take it. The word "psalms" in the New Testament can refer to actual psalms (e.g., Luke 20:42, 44; Acts 1:20) or to praise songs (e.g., 1 Cor 14:26); hymns (also Eph 5:19) were festive anthems celebrating a deity in the Greek world and God or Christ in Scripture (as seen in Phil 2:6–11; Col 1:15–20); and "spiritual songs" probably means "songs from the Spirit" (NIV) and could refer to spontaneous, charismatic songs in the church's worship settings. Paul probably intends for these to be understood together to describe the believers' joyous singing in the context of corporate worship (1 Cor 14:15, 26).

The two clauses in the Greek text exhibit parallelism; each begins with a prepositional phrase followed by a participle ("in all wisdom teaching"; "with gratitude singing"). Obviously, this continues the idea that the church's worship anchors the people in Christ, adding the idea of thanksgiving/gratitude from 3:15. The term translated "gratitude" is itself the standard word for "grace," and Paul may intend a double meaning: our "gratitude" for the "gracious" blessings God has richly poured into our lives. "In your hearts" does not signify solitude or internal meditation but basically means "in every area of your life" (see 2 Cor 4:15; Eph 5:19).

All of our actions must be done in the name of Christ (3:17)

This is a transition verse, concluding the section on Christian ethics (3:1–17) and leading into Paul's discussion of the social codes (3:18–4:1). The way we live out the grace and love God has shown us makes a difference. Worship is not an end in itself but must lead to action—to living a life of worship and service (the Greek *latreuō* in the New Teatament carries both meanings) to the Lord. Worship is not conducted solely in the context of church services; it must infuse what we do in our daily lives as well. When we serve the church and others, we are in a real sense worshiping! Paul is forceful here, repeating "all" for emphasis—literally, "and *everything* whatever you do in word or in deed, do it *all* in the name of the Lord" (see the parallel in 1 Cor 10:31). Everything in our lives should glorify God. Our prayer each morning ought to be "Lord, may everything I do today magnify your name," as in the Lord's Prayer—"may your name be kept holy" (Matt 6:9 NLT).

"In the name of the Lord Jesus" emphasizes the lordship of Christ and the authority of his name. "Lordship," one of the primary themes of this letter (1:3, 10; 2:6; 3:13 and eight times in 3:13–24), signifies that Christ must be made sovereign over every single area of our lives. "The name of the Lord" in the Old Testament refers to Yahweh, pointing to his almighty power and control (1 Sam 6:18; 1 Chr 21:19; Ps 118:26), and in the New Testament it refers to Christ, affirming his divine status and sovereignty. The power of Christ's name is a central theme in Acts 3, where Peter heals a lame beggar "in the name of Jesus Christ" (Acts 3:6) and then tells the crowd, "By faith in the name of Jesus this man ... was made strong" (Acts 3:26). So to act and speak "in the Lord's name" means to make certain that everything we do accords with his will and magnifies his name. "In the name of," as in the baptism formula of Matthew 28:19, means "in union with" and thus refers to a Christ-oriented lifestyle.

For the fifth time (see also 1:3, 12; 2:7; 3:15) an injunction to thankfulness concludes Paul's thought. When we surrender to Christ's sovereign lordship over our lives and experience his love and grace as he guides us, we cannot help but be filled with gratitude. Note that we pour out our thanks to God "through him." Christ is not only the focus of our prayer life but also the instrument "through" whom we pray. This does not mean that Jesus is the mediator through whom we must go if we wish to speak with God. The "new covenant" promise of Jeremiah 31:31–34, repeated in Hebrews 8:8–12, states clearly that we have direct access to God and need no mediator. Rather, Paul means that Christ via his atoning sacrifice is the One through whom access to God has been made possible. The Lord Christ is the One in whom and through whom life's joy comes to full fruition, and heartfelt thanksgiving is to be a continual response on our part.

BELIEVERS ARE CALLED TO HONOR CHRIST IN THEIR HOUSEHOLDS (3:18–4:1)

Paul concludes Colossians 3:1–17 with the exhortation to "do it all in the name of the Lord Jesus." Now he builds on this, making explicit that our "all" includes every relationship in family and community. The lordship of Christ must extend into our personal interactions. Moreover, our thankfulness (3:15–16) must encompass these relationships as well. We are to thank God continually for family and friends in the community. Further, the principle of submission runs through this section— wives to husbands, children to parents, and slaves to masters. But Christians in each category must above all submit to Jesus as Lord (the term appears in 3:18, 20, 22, 23, 24; 4:1). This is especially true of those who have authority, for they will answer to God and Christ for the quality of their leadership in God's community. As Paul states clearly in Ephesians 5:21, mutual submission is at the core, as the husband submits his personal rights and desires to meet the needs of his wife. So the dominant theme is that of reciprocal relationships among God's people.

The social codes in the New Testament (Eph 5:22–6:9; 1 Tim 2:8–15; 5:1–6:2; Titus 2:2–10; 1 Pet 2:18–3:7) build on extensive examples in the surrounding world of the first century. It is generally agreed today that Hellenism is the major source for such material (sometimes called a *Haustafel*, German for "house table" or "household rules"), and these social codes generally provided the pattern for government as well. They likely were mediated through Hellenistic Judaism (similar lists appear in the works of Philo and Josephus, first-century Jewish writers), which added the theme of reciprocity by centering on the rights of the marginalized—women, children, and slaves. Paul has thoroughly modified these codes in light of Christian principles, especially the lordship of Christ. Both Paul and the early church used them to show that seeking and thinking the "things above" (3:1–2) must be reflected in concrete relationships within the community.

WIVES AND HUSBANDS (3:18–19)

As family is the core element of the church, Paul begins with wife-husband relationships. Unlike Hellenistic lists, which always centered on the male of the household, Paul addresses the wife first, demonstrating her importance to family and church and perhaps conferring on her a new status in the Christian community. The responsibility of wives is to "submit yourselves to your husbands." The Greek verb *hypotassomai* does not connote inferiority or subordination but, it is generally agreed, means to "voluntarily place yourself under" another person. It is important to remember that this injunction is not isolated and absolute but is paired with the command in verse 19 for the husband to love his wife. It is part of a reciprocal relationship. The wife submits in response to the husband's love, and vice versa. This does not mean, however, that if the husband fails to show enough love the wife is freed from her responsibility. Ephesians 5:24 makes it clear that the wife is to submit "in everything," for her submission is to the Lord, not just to her husband. We will say more about this in relation to the next verse.

The wife is to submit "as (*hōs*) is fitting in the Lord"—specifying *how* she is to do so. This continues the emphasis throughout the ethical section of chapter 3 on the lordship of Christ. As the relationship between wife and husband is an aspect of the couple's relationship with the Lord, the harmony of the marriage depends on the harmony of each spouse with Christ. Christ is both the model for their behavior and the true authority behind all they do. "Fitting" is actually the imperfect tense verb *anēken*, referring to what is at all times "proper," "expected," or "obligatory"; the term was used in Stoic circles to describe a sense of propriety in behavior. It is important for us to realize the centrality in verse 18 of "in the Lord." It is not culture that drives the propriety Paul commands but the demands of God and Christ in the new Christian community of which believers are a part. As citizens of heaven and members of the new body of Christ, they must take their expected places in it— for wives that means submission to their husbands.

The husbands, in turn, are to relate to their wives' submission with "love" (v. 19). This directive breaks Hellenistic convention (which stressed the rights and power of the husband) by showing that he is as responsible and duty bound as she to maintain harmony in the marriage. Neither Hellenistic nor Jewish discussions said much about "love," which appears to be a Christian emphasis.

It is important in this context that we define "love" carefully. I understand it as "selfless giving," a deep-seated care and concern flowing out of boundless affection and resulting in continual service of and sacrificial giving to the one who is loved. In Ephesians 5:25 such love is shown to be anchored in the love of Christ ("just as Christ loved the church and gave himself up for her"). The husband has experienced the boundless love of Christ and so both reflects and radiates the same kind of love to his wife. This love permeates every area of the relationship.

The husband's authority as "head" of the house (Eph 5:23) is mediated and controlled by his abiding love for his wife.

This love means that he is never to be harsh with her, resulting in an abrasive response. The Greek verb means "be embittered," calling to mind the taste of a bitter plant, and when used in a relational context it reflects malice and a desire to do harm (Acts 8:23; Eph 4:31); it is always the result of sin and anger. Obviously, love is the antithesis of this as well as the antidote. Love will ameliorate the anger and placate the desire to hurt the other. Looking back to 3:13, we recall that with love the husband will "bear with" his wife and "forgive" her, resulting in reconciliation.

Turning to the debate over this submission issue in our day, is there still a hierarchical order in marriage (known as the "complementarian" view), or are husband and wife equal in status (the "egalitarian" view)? We cannot resolve this question in the short space we have, but a couple of points might help. A major argument in favor of complete equality may be found in Galatians 3:28 ("nor is there male and female"). If given priority, this principle could mean that God has removed the hierarchical distinction between husband and wife he had established in Genesis 3:16 ("Your desire will be for your husband, and he will rule over you"). It may be instructive to recognize, however, that Galatians was written in AD 49, twelve years before Colossians and Ephesians (both from AD 61); I doubt Paul would still call the husband "head of the wife" in Ephesians 5:23 if Galatians 3:28 had done away with that relationship. I also see no way to work around the obvious conclusion that "headship" connotes an aspect of authority.

However, that authority must be defined with extreme care, leading to my second point: Headship is to be understood via the two-way street of submission and love. In many ways the husband has the greater responsibility, for his authority must be exercised through love. He is not to demand submission but to lovingly accept it from his wife. His every decision is to be made in love—through an unwavering desire to meet his wife's needs, rather than through manipulating his wife to meet his own. It is my conclusion that the model of mutual submission governs both the headship of the husband and the voluntary submission of the wife, and that love drives both as they live out this relationship.

CHILDREN AND PARENTS (3:20–21)

The theme of reciprocal relationships governs parent-child as well as husband-wife. The child obeys, and the parents refuse to embitter or discourage their children by misusing their authority. As with husbands and wives, implicit love is to govern both sides of the equation. Interestingly, the term "children" (Greek: *tekna*) can refer even to grown children, and Roman households often included adult children. Still, raising children is definitely in view in Ephesians 6:4 (in a parallel passage to Col 3:20–21). It is probably best to conclude that Paul has small children in mind here in Colossians, though any children in the household and thus to some extent under parental authority should be included. It is obvious that grown children under their parents' roof aren't "obedient" to the same degree as minor children, but they should follow the rules of the household.

The command itself—"obey"—is stronger than "submit," and it is followed by the equally strong "in everything," which conveys the all-encompassing nature of the children's duty. They are under the care and absolute leadership of their parents (the same injunction will be given to slaves in v. 22). The fifth commandment, "Honor your father and mother" (Exod 20:12), is implicit here; Paul's sweeping "in everything" is certainly also implied in the Exodus account. Children owe their parents complete obedience, and Exodus 20:12 (quoted in Eph 6:2) adds that the length (and no doubt the quality) of their life is at stake. In both the Jewish and Gentile worlds, the fathers held life-and-death power over their children, to the point that Exodus 21:15, 17 specifies that those who strike or curse their parents are to be put to death.

In the Christian world there are several adjustments to the severity of these codes. The ultimate authority is "the Lord," and, as with wives, the children's obedience is clearly tied in to their obedience to him. Their true goal is not just to obey their parents but also to "please the Lord." Their obedience to parents is part of their walk with Christ, and this earthly obedience is actually obedience to Christ, who mandates responsibility to parents. The term "pleasing" (*euareston*) also means "acceptable"; this is reminiscent of the burnt sacrifice with a sweet-smelling aroma that pleased God and signified that the sacrifice was acceptable to him. So the honor shown to parents both fulfills God's requirements and brings him pleasure.

The Greek text actually reads "this is pleasing *in* the Lord," which is unusual. Paul elsewhere uses the dative form, "pleasing *to* the Lord" (Rom 12:1; Eph 5:10; Phil 4:18), but here he seems to deliberately alter his phrasing. Many translations assume that Paul intends "Lord" to be understood as Christ ("pleasing [to God] in the Lord Jesus Christ"); others (like NIV, NLT, ESV) see the construction as equivalent to the dative ("this pleases the Lord"). My preference is to consider the phrase as similar to the "in Christ" motif—as in "this is pleasing to God and Christ in the community of saints, the body of Christ in which he has placed you." Paul wants his readers to realize how critical family relationships are to Christ—the very core of Christ's new messianic community.

Hellenistic discussions of family centered entirely on the authority and honor of the father, but Paul, as he did with respect to the wife, here stresses also the responsibility of parents to their children. In Colossians 3:21, he explicitly mentions only fathers (parents are addressed in verse 20) because in the Greek and Jewish worlds discipline in the home was the father's sole provenance. Fathers are not to "embitter" their children. The Greek verb Paul uses, *erethizete*, means to "irritate," "arouse," or "aggravate"; it is often translated "provoke." The reference here is to a misuse of authority that ends up frustrating and finally angering the children, with the result that they "become discouraged." This connotes not only an emotional response but also a loss of will (as in the NLT, "discouraged and quit trying"). Still today, a major error of many parents is belittling their children to the point of undermining their self-image. There are two types of child abuse—physical and psychological—and the latter can be just as devastating as the former. God charges all parents with the responsibility of helping their children develop and maintain a healthy view of themselves—to believe, as Paul says, "I can do all things through him who gives me strength" (Phil 4:13).

SLAVES AND MASTERS (3:22–4:1)

Paul's remarks to slaves and masters are more extensive than his comments about wife-husband and child-parent relationships. Although there is no hard evidence linking this passage with the rift between the slave Onesimus and his master, Philemon, many interpreters have speculated that Paul had this conflict in mind, and I think that's likely. This situation is the subject of Paul's letter to Philemon, which he wrote around the same time as his letter to the Colossians; Onesimus accompanied Tychicus in delivering both letters to Colossae (Col 4:7–9). Extensive discussion of master-slave relationships appears to have been common, as demonstrated by Ephesians 6:5–9 and 1 Peter 2:18–24, probably due to the large number of converts to Christianity from the slave ranks. Many of the names of house-church leaders in Romans 16 correspond to names known to have been used for slaves. It has been estimated that as much as one-third of the average Roman city's population consisted of slaves.

Slaves were considered part of the household, yet they also were the property of the master and in that sense part of his household goods. There were basically three kinds of slaves corresponding to where they worked—in the fields, at the house, or for the master's business holdings. Fieldworkers, who typically were prisoners of war, tended to be illiterate; other slaves performed valuable duties and often were quite educated. Slavery was normally the result of war or poverty, and in the first century large numbers of people had been forced to sell themselves into slavery. Unlike the situation in the nineteenth century, manumission (release from slavery, often through a monetary payment) was always a possibility, though this practice was not as widespread as some have suggested. Slaves also could be freed based on exemplary service or as a result of saving their money (they often were paid for services) and purchasing their freedom. That is not Paul's focus here, however; for the most part he and the early church accepted the institution of slavery as an inexorable evil. First-century Christians were not social revolutionaries (see the commentary on Philemon for more on this issue), and Paul's purpose was to help slaves and masters live within the larger social reality as brothers and sisters in Christ.

Obedience and faithfulness of slaves (3:22–25)

SINCERITY AND REVERENCE (3:22). Paul was thinking especially of household slaves, who were considered part of the family and lived in the home. Echoing his instruction to children (v. 20), he appears at the outset to affirm the institution of slavery when he tells slaves to "obey your earthly masters in everything"— a command that is surprising to us. We do well to bear in mind that there had never been a time in antiquity without slaves; by the first century, the institution was thousands of years old. Christianity was not a social movement transforming society, but a spiritual movement proclaiming the redemption of the fallen human race.

However, although Paul was not consciously trying to end the institution of slavery, he did transform the nature of its key relationships, and the principles he established did eventually help to subvert the practice. It is clear that slaves were included in early Christian worship services, sitting side by side with their masters. Within the church, slaves and masters related as brothers and sisters, demonstrating their equality in Christ. Moreover, Paul makes clear that the master is not really lord of the household (correcting pagan views); rather, Christ is Lord over slave *and* master, and both look to him as sovereign.

So Paul directs slaves (as he does everyone) to accept their place in secular society, to make the best of their situation by "obeying" their masters "in everything." Paul relegates the issue to the "earthly" situation, separating it from the heavenly reality by employing a significant play on words: In this world the owners are "masters" (Greek: *kyrios*), but in the greater reality they, together with their slaves, serve one "Lord" (also *kyrios*). While slaves "obey" their earthly *kyrios*, they "fear" only their heavenly *kyrios*, Jesus. God expects Christian slaves to be paragons of obedience in their earthly situations, thus representing their Lord. As Jesus himself was the "slave" of all (Phil 2:7), so we are to serve him faithfully "in everything."

In modern Western societies, the closest analogy to masters and slaves is employers and employees, and Paul's challenge applies in that sense to us. Employees have been placed under authority in the workplace and are to "obey in everything" they are asked to do. It is common for scholars to consider this a shallow application of Paul's words, but work and office in our day do provide (at least in part) a valid parallel to the principles Paul established here. Our situation is complicated in one sense by the addition of unions. Having belonged to a union in college, I remember the complexities: Union members were virtually required to consider management their enemy. Paul would have opposed such an attitude, demanding that management and labor respect one another and work in harmony.

Paul stipulates that slaves are to obey not just to "curry favor" with earthly masters "when their eye is on you" (in the Greek text, this expression reads more like: "not only by way of eye-service as people-pleasers"). The motivation for such practice—pleasing the authority figure to gain personal benefit—is entirely selfish. Believers are to please God, not people, and they are to serve superiors in the workplace for the glory of God rather than for personal advantage. Slaves, Paul says, are to serve in two ways: "with sincerity of heart and reverence for the Lord." The first phrase describes a focused individual who centers upon her duties and channels all her energy into successfully performing them. The second, "reverence for the Lord," is a major biblical concept with several levels of meaning. At one end is fear of punishment and at the other a deep-seated reverence for God. At the center is the idea of awe, which combines both aspects. It is likely that all these facets are part of Paul's thrust here, leading some to translate the Greek term as "reverent fear." A sense of responsibility before God does incorporate an element of fear: We know that one day we will stand before him and give account for the quality of our life and service (Rom 14:10; Heb 13:7). At the same time, service is an aspect of worship, and as we fulfill our calling we are honoring and worshiping God.

Work for the Lord and His Inheritance (3:23–24a). Verses 23–24 drive home a critical point: The slave's true master is the Lord. Slaves are to work not in a perfunctory manner but wholeheartedly, knowing they are serving their true Lord, not just their "human masters." Aware that God is the beneficiary of their endeavors, Christian slaves are to perform their duties with concerted effort and to the best of their ability. This intrinsic motivation of serving the Lord with all their hearts enables slaves even in bad situations to continue to serve well.

It is not merely the direction of their service that is to the Lord, for the true reward comes from him as well (v. 24a). The return from human masters will be sometimes good and sometimes bad, but God will repay our efforts far more richly with an eternal reward—the "inheritance" awaiting us in heaven. It is true that slaves were sometimes paid for services, and a few could even save enough to pay for their manumission, but no slave ever had an inheritance; that was reserved for the legitimate heirs in a family. The amazing reality, though, was that every Christian slave could look forward to an inheritance far greater than that of the scion of any earthly dynasty—an inheritance guaranteed by God! Slaves, then, were only such on the earthly plane. Even as they conducted themselves on a daily basis with their masters, they knew they had a far greater status and looked ahead to an eternal repayment for services rendered. Their present life was often difficult and demeaning, but they had assurance of their glorious future, and that gave them strength and courage to rise above their situation.

JESUS AS LORD AND JUDGE (3:24B–25). Paul reminds slaves that they ultimately are serving not their earthly masters but "the Lord Christ"—or, one could say, "the true Master (*kyrios*), Christ," who is Lord of all. Most scholars argue that the Greek verb should be read as a command: "Serve the Lord Christ" (*douleuete*, "serve," can be either indicative or imperative). In the context of verse 24, they are likely correct, for Paul is challenging the slaves to consciously and actively make Christ the object of their service. In a temporary human sense, of course, they serve their human owners, but the lordship of Christ is paramount. Everything slaves do in the household they do as Christians, and thus for the glory of God and Christ.

The reason (*gar*; "for") the slave can "serve" the Lord Christ is the knowledge that Christ is absolutely just and will right all wrongs, including mistreatment by a master. God, who is completely righteous, is watching out for his people. In this world injustice will occur, but the vindication of his suffering people is certain, and God will repay. The sinner will answer for his crimes at the judgment seat of God and Christ.

The referent of "anyone" in verse 25 is ambiguous, and interpreters have debated whether Paul is speaking about the master or the slave. The majority of scholars think it is the latter, since the master does not seem to be addressed until 4:1. The point, then, is that Christian slaves must be doubly concerned to do right by their owners. If they fail to fulfill their duties they will be punished not just on the earthly plane but on the heavenly plane as well, for when they refuse to do their jobs well they are failing to serve their heavenly Lord (3:24b). The Greek verb behind "wrongdoer" (*adikeō*) also occurs in Philemon 18 ("If he has done you any wrong"). Because Paul is sending the letter to Philemon along with the one to the Colossians, it makes sense for this word to have the same meaning in both letters, referring to slaves who "do wrong."

My own feeling is that Paul intended "anyone" to apply in both directions. This is a transition verse that both concludes the section on slaves (warning them not to do wrong) and introduces the next verse on masters (warning them as well). Both slave and master are required by God to take their place in his economy and to faithfully discharge their duties. Slaves must serve their earthly masters well, and owners must treat their slaves well. Both are actually serving God even more than they are their human charges, and both will answer to God for the quality of their actions.

God is the true Judge, and Paul makes two points related to this. First, God more than earthly authorities is the One who repays wrongs; the principle is **lex talionis** ("the law of retribution"), meaning that the severity of God's punishment of the wrongdoer will be equal to the gravity of the sin committed. There will be no escape or legal bargaining, so when a slave is unjustly treated there is comfort in knowing that vindication is certain (see Rev 6:9–11). Second, in divine retribution "there is no favoritism" or "partiality" (see also Rom 2:11; Eph 6:9; Jas 2:1). The Greek word Paul uses here, *prosōpolēmpsia*, literally means "receive according to face"; it indicates the human tendency to render judgments on the basis of appearance or social status. God will never do so. Both slave and master will be repaid at the judgment seat precisely on the basis of what they have done (see Rom 14:10; 2 Cor 5:10; Rev 22:12).

Once again this material applies directly to employment situations in our day. We are all part of either management or labor, and all the principles stated in this section apply directly to every one of us. Those of us hired by companies are not simply required by our labor contract to work hard at fulfilling our job description; we are obligated to God to be the best worker we can be. When someone takes advantage of us or mistreats us, we know that God will vindicate us and right the wrongs. At the same time, management is to make certain workers are treated and paid fairly. James 5:1-6 warns that wealthy owners who abuse their workers will face divine wrath for what they have done.

The fairness of masters (4:1)

Paul instructs masters (*kyrioi*) to provide justice and fairness (NIV: "what is right and fair"). They may own slaves, but they themselves answer to God as "Master" because believers are actually "slaves" of God. God will hold them to the same standards he applies to the slaves they own. The Greek word *dikaios* calls on masters to be "just" toward their slaves and treat them "right," not only in the eyes of their friends but, of infinitely greater importance, in the eyes of God. The other term Paul uses here, *isotēs*, has a double meaning, not only indicating "fair" treatment but also directing owners to consider slaves "equal" to themselves before God. In Colossians 3:11 Paul affirms that in Christ there is "neither slave nor free," and the implications should not be lost on slave owners: In Christ there is a new set of relationships, and masters must reflect that in the treatment of their slaves.

The basis is the realization that "you also have a Master in heaven." The lordship of Christ has important repercussions for the master-slave paradigm. The masters are themselves under a Master, and if they do indeed "seek and think the things above" (3:1-2) all earthly relationships will be transformed. Paul's mention of "in heaven" does not mean they can ignore the command for the time being, for believers are *already* citizens of heaven (Phil 3:20) and dwell in the "heavenlies" (Eph 1:3; 2:6-7). This is a present obligation.

No, Paul did not call for the end of slavery or the manumission of all slaves, but he did challenge owners to consider their slaves as equals before the Lord and to treat them rightly at all times. This in itself would produce a social revolution and, in time, help to undermine the institution of slavery. By extension, the principles Paul outlines in this passage apply to modern employment situations. Subordinates owe their bosses respect and obedience, and employers owe their workers justice and fairness. Too often in work relationships, there is a prevailing spirit of animosity and power politics. On both sides, such an attitude is a sin. God demands teamwork and mutual respect in the workplace.

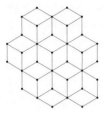

CONCLUDING THOUGHTS
(4:2–18)

There are two sets of conclusions in this section of Colossians. First, 4:2-6 closes the body of the letter itself and especially the set of basic exhortations in 3:1-4:1. Paul begins this section with a call for believers to pray, defining prayer as spiritual vigilance combined with thanksgiving for God's faithful response (v. 2). He then narrows the request to specific intercession for himself and his team as they proclaim the gospel even while imprisoned in Rome (vv. 3-4). Paul includes all of his readers in their witness to "outsiders," centering on the effectiveness of their personal evangelistic ministry (vv. 5-6).

Second, the greetings and instructions of 4:7-18 provide the formal closing of the letter. This final section has four parts: a description of the messengers who are bearing the letter (vv. 7-9); a series of greetings from coworkers (vv. 10-14); greetings and instructions about sharing the letter with those in Laodicea; and a personal greeting and signing of the letter by Paul himself (v. 18).

PAUL INSTRUCTS BELIEVERS TO PRAY AND WALK IN WISDOM (4:2-6)

The spatial movement of Paul's letter to the Colossians is informative. The opening section (1:3-2:5) looks upward and centers on the supremacy and lordship of Christ as Creator, Sustainer, and Redeemer. This is followed by two sections that look inward, first identifying the serious errors of the false teachers (2:6–23) and then addressing the needs of the Colossian believers to grow in their Christian walk (3:1–4:1). Now Paul looks outward (4:2–6), to his and the church's mission to the world.

CALL TO PRAYER AND VIGILANCE (4:2)

Paul begins this outward focus by calling the believers to a life of prayer. "Devote yourselves" (*proskartereite*) is present tense and urges an ongoing "persistence" or "perseverance" in prayer, expressed in spiritual devotion. Jesus taught the importance of corporate prayer in Matthew 18:19–20: "Where two or three gather together in my name, I am there with them." The Lord's Prayer was intended as a community prayer, and the early church thought first of corporate prayer and then of individual prayer. The early believers saw themselves primarily as a worshiping community, devoting themselves continually to prayer (Acts 1:14; 2:42; 6:4); in many cases, their prayers were accompanied by supernatural demonstrations of power and the Holy Spirit (Acts 4:31). Paul's remarks in Colossians 4:2–4 thus reflect a critical component of the Christ-centered church: persevering intercessory prayer. In the context of the church's universal mission, this refers to the need to bathe that mission in prayer.

The accompanying idea, "being watchful," is a rich concept, referring generally to "vigilance" in prayer and more specifically to "alertness" with respect to Christ's return and the end of history (see 1 Cor 16:13; 1 Thess 5:6; 1 Pet 4:7; Rev 3:3). The primary thrust here is on the former—watchfulness in prayer for God's work and for his people. However, most interpreters believe that Paul also is emphasizing readiness for the Lord's return and petition for the final coming of God's kingdom (Matt 6:10; 1 Cor 16:22). Paul wants these Christians to be "watching the times" and living in preparation for Christ's coming back. A second accompanying idea, "being thankful," has been a primary thrust of the letter (Col 1:3, 12; 2:7; 3:15, 16, 17).

A major component of true prayer is that petition must lead to thanksgiving. In response to the gift of Christ and salvation through him (1:12-14), and in light of our grounding in the faith (2:7) and worship of God (3:15-17), we are to be filled with gratitude for God's bounty in our lives.

Prayer for Paul's Gospel Ministry (4:3-4)

In 3:1-4:1 Paul's remarks had an inward focus, examining the life of the community. Here his attention shifts outward to the church's mission to the world. The central theme of prayer continues, now embracing Paul's (4:3-4) and the church's (4:5-6) proclamation of the gospel to the "outsiders," the unbelievers first in Colossae and secondarily in the rest of the world. An important aspect of true prayer is inherent here. When we pray we must get involved in fulfilling the object of our prayer. To pray for the salvation of the lost demands that we participate in God's mission to them.

First, Paul asks for ongoing (present tense) prayer for himself and his team (Timothy and Epaphras: 1:1, 7; 4:12) as they evangelize the province of Asia, one of the Roman Empire's 10 senatorial provinces and the location of Colossae. Paul deeply believed in the power of intercessory prayer undergirding his ministry (Rom 15:30-32; Eph 6:19; Phil 1:19). He desired an "open door" for the gospel—a frequent metaphor for evangelism and revival (see Acts 14:27; 1 Cor 16:9; 2 Cor 2:12; Rev 3:20), indicating receptivity and response to the "message" (*logos*). As he expresses earlier in Colossians, Paul wanted the "Word" to "bear fruit and grow throughout the whole world" (Col 1:6). Some interpreters believe he was implicitly hoping the door of his cell would open and he would be freed from imprisonment, but that is unlikely in this context (though possible, in light of the phrase "for which I am in chains" at the end of 4:3). Note that Paul is not requesting power for himself; it is "the Word" that has the power and God who will open the doors.

Paul identifies the proclaimed "message" as "the mystery of Christ." This points back to 1:26-27, where he defines "mystery" as divine truths that had been hidden from past generations but were now being revealed in Christ. In 1:27a the mystery is the riches of salvation shared with the Gentiles, but in 1:27b, 2:2-3, and 4:3 the mystery is Christ himself—or, as in 1:27, "Christ in you, the hope of glory." The best translation in 4:3 is "proclaim the mystery, which is Christ." Added to this is Paul's confession "for which I am in chains," indicating that his proclamation of the gospel of Christ has led to his arrest and imprisonment. He considered it a great privilege to experience "the fellowship of his suffering" (Phil 3:10) and to "fill up what is still lacking in regard to Christ's afflictions" (see my comments on 1:24). In Philippians 1:12-14 we read that Paul rejoiced in the results of his imprisonment for the gospel.

The second prayer request follows in 4:4—that Paul might be empowered to "proclaim it clearly," meaning that his preaching would be highly effective in making the gospel known and appealing to the pagan populace. The Greek verb *phanerōsō* (NIV: "proclaim") is unusual, but earlier in Colossians Paul uses this word to express the "revelation" of the mysteries (1:26) and of Christ in glory (3:4). It carries a strong **eschatological** connotation, probably related to the role of gospel proclamation as a significant event in salvation history. Paul's preaching is the revelation of divine truths and the turning point in the battle against sin in this world. This is also seen in his added reflection "as I should" (literally, "as it is necessary for me to speak"), alluding to the divine "must" behind his apostolic ministry. Paul realized that he was God's chosen missionary to the Gentiles, as revealed on the Damascus road (Acts 26:17; see Col 1:25; Titus 1:3), and this sense of divine necessity galvanized his every action.

CHALLENGE FOR THE COLOSSIANS' INTERACTION WITH OUTSIDERS (4:5-6)

After requesting prayer for his gospel ministry, Paul turns to the witness of the Colossians, challenging them to "be wise in the way you act toward outsiders"—that is, toward non-Christians, those outside the church. The Greek text reads "walk in wisdom," and the implication is that, as believers go about their lives in a pagan world, they need wisdom to make their encounters with unbelievers fruitful. The first two times the verb "walk" is used in this letter (1:10; 2:6) it refers to a life centered on Christ and worthy of him. This is attained through "wisdom," that God-sent, Spirit-inspired (1:9), and Christ-centered (2:3) ability to live a life that makes a difference. Paul is not instructing his readers on social relationships, advising them to avoid conflict and live in peace with pagans (that kind of instruction is found in Rom 12:14–18). Instead, his focus here is on lifestyle evangelism—living in such a way that "proclaims" Christ to the world.

This theme continues in the command to bring Christ to lost humanity: "Make the most of every opportunity" (the Greek text reads, literally, "redeeming the time"). The word Paul uses here (*exagorazomenoi*, based on the verb meaning "to buy up") is part of the redemption language in Galatians 3:13 ("Christ redeemed us") and 4:4–5 ("God sent his Son ... to redeem"). Paul's point is that Christ has "purchased" or "redeemed" humanity from the curse of the law. The thrust in Colossians 4:5 and in its sister passage, Ephesians 5:16, builds on this language. In this secular age ("because the days are evil," Eph 5:16), Paul urges believers to use their time redemptively—to take advantage of every opportunity to magnify Christ and bring glory to his name. In a world already full of evil, our task is to fill it with good. Paul could be alluding to the Greek (**Septuagint**) translation of Daniel 2:8, which describes King Nebuchadnezzar accusing his court magicians of "trying to gain (buy) time" to interpret his dream. Ultimately, the magicians failed to understand the king's "mysterious" dream, but we Christians (Paul might be saying) *do* understand God's mystery, Christ, and must use every opportunity to interpret his gospel for the world.

Bringing together the two clauses of Colossians 4:5, we use our time in a wise manner when we channel our energy toward God's mission to the lost. As in 4:2, we see a strong

eschatological emphasis here—similar to that of Hebrews 10:25, where we are enjoined to "encourage one another—and all the more as you see the Day approaching." The thought in both passages is to make wise use of the time that remains before the return of Christ (also see 1 Cor 7:29: "the time is short").

In Colossians 4:6 Paul addresses the character of the witness itself, urging the believers to "let your conversation be always full of grace." The Greek term *logos* (meaning "word," but here translated "conversation" or "speech") could refer narrowly to the proclamation of the gospel, but it also could be construed in a broader sense, meaning all conversations with unbelievers. Similarly, the phrase "always full of grace" could point specifically to the grace of God seen in gospel witness or more generally to gracious or winsome speech in general. Most likely this context calls for a combination of the two, seeking the establishment of positive, friendly relations with pagan neighbors that can become a vehicle for the spread of the gospel. Still, while Paul's thought here definitely includes the idea of healthy relationships, the primary thrust is God's grace moving out into the community through the witness of the saints. Several interpreters would add that the Greek expression behind "full of grace" (*en chariti*) also can mean "filled with gratitude" (see 3:16, where *chariti* is often translated "gratitude"). I do not see this option as Paul's main point in 4:6, but there could be some carryover from 3:16-17, in the sense of gratefulness to God being evident in believers' lives and drawing non-Christians to a life full of joy and thankfulness.

This is further clarified by the addition of "seasoned with salt," a metaphor used often in the ancient world for witty and winsome speech. Salt (as in Jesus' phrase "salt of the earth" in Matt 5:13) was widely used not just as a spice to add taste, but also as a preservative and even a purifying agent (2 Kgs 2:19-23). In Colossians 4:6 Paul's reference is to a life that makes an impact on the world, to speech that draws people to God. While the call is for rhetorical power in our proclamation, this is to be exhibited not just by preachers and teachers but by all Christians in their daily conversations. Our discussions and even our small talk with "outsiders" ought to be carefully crafted to draw people to ourselves—and through us to the God who has saved us and wants to save them too.

The purpose of this gracious, even witty, speech is to enable us to "know how to answer everyone." Paul's point here is similar to Peter's in his first letter: "Always be prepared to give an answer to everyone who asks you to give the reason for the hope that you have" (1 Pet 3:15). Although some translations (including the NIV) do not convey a sense of obligation, the Greek text of Colossians 4:6 reads literally, "to know how you *must* answer everyone"—reflecting the same sense of divine necessity Paul applies to himself in 4:4 (see above). Each of us has the same calling as Paul on the Damascus road: to engage in God's mission to the world.

Throughout verses 5-6, Paul challenges us to seek the wisdom to use every opportunity to proclaim Christ and his salvation in a winsome, grace-filled manner. We are to pray that God will enable us to answer each person based on his or her situation and need.

FINAL GREETINGS AND INSTRUCTIONS (4:7-18)

All of Paul's letters have the same traditional type of letter closing. The purpose is networking, in this case to promote a sense of unity between Paul's team and the Colossian church. Most ancient letters were framed according to the same formula—an opening greeting that contained a formal prayer and thanksgiving, and a closing farewell that conveyed personal greetings (in Paul's case from himself and his coworkers), as well as news and instructions.

THE MESSENGERS WHO BEAR THE LETTER (4:7-9)

The first person Paul mentions, Tychicus, was a resident of the province of Asia who probably spent time in Ephesus during Paul's third missionary journey. He had become a trusted associate who helped Paul at the end of that trip and, as recorded in Acts 20:4, was one of seven men representing the churches that contributed to Paul's collection for the poor in Jerusalem. He appears to have been Paul's personal envoy who was with him in Rome and then was sent to Colossae to deliver this letter and to relate "all the news" about Paul to the church—most likely details about his imprisonment. Many interpreters believe that Tychicus also delivered Paul's letters to Philemon and the Laodiceans (4:16). In a couple of years he will be sent to Crete (Titus 3:12) and later to Ephesus, possibly with the second letter to Timothy (see 2 Tim 4:12) shortly before Paul's death. So he appears to have been with Paul for the last years of the apostle's life.

Because Tychicus was Paul's personal envoy, bearing both his letter(s) and the news concerning his situation, Paul felt it necessary to relate why he had entrusted these tasks to this man. He provides a threefold description of Tychicus as a leader in the Christian movement. To Paul he is a "beloved brother." This description expresses Paul's deep affection, but there is also a semi-technical sense in which the term "brother" refers to a coworker chosen (and loved) by God for leadership in the church. In that same sense Tychicus is a "faithful servant" (*diakonos*, used of Paul in Col 1:23, 25)—a "minister" or associate of Paul who "faithfully" exercised his duties. Finally, he is a "fellow slave (*syndoulos*) in the Lord," echoing the frequent affirmation in Paul's letters that Christians have been freed from the slavery of sin to become "slaves" of God and Christ. As in 1 Peter 2:9, we belong to God as his "special possession." The key to all three descriptions of Tychicus is the final phrase in verse 7, "in the Lord"—for it is in Christ that all this is made possible. Only through his lordship can we rise above our petty selfhood to make an impact in this world.

Tychicus was sent to Colossae as the official letter-bearer for two reasons (4:8, repeated in Eph 6:22). First, he was to convey "all the news" regarding Paul and his coworkers ("our circumstances"). Paul elsewhere discusses two other team members (Timothy and Epaphras: 1:1, 7; 4:12), and Tychicus would update the Colossians not only on Paul's imprisonment but also on the team's activities in the Asian province, where they were presently ministering. Second, Tychicus was to "encourage your hearts," as Paul himself had done in 2:2. Spiritual comfort for the saints was always one of Paul's ministry goals, and he sent Tychicus to strengthen and uplift their hearts in the Lord (as in the prayer of 1:9–12 and the challenge of 3:15–17).

Moreover, Tychicus was charged with returning the slave Onesimus to his master, Philemon (4:9), who lived at Colossae and hosted a church in his home (Phlm 2). Onesimus had left his master (some think he ran away) and had met Paul in Rome, where he became a convert to Christ and "a faithful and dear brother," a trusted associate on Paul's team. It is difficult to ascertain the circumstances behind Onesimus' separation from Philemon (see the introduction to my commentary on Philemon), but Paul was sending him back to Philemon for reconciliation and reinstatement as a "dear brother" (see Phlm 16).

The language in Colossians 4:9 fits Paul's earlier comment that in Christ "there is no … slave or free" (3:11). Paul makes no mention here of Onesimus' slave status, instead promoting him to the status of "one of you"—a member of the congregation, as well as a probable coworker of Paul and member of his ministry team; those who doubt this read too much into Paul's silence on the matter. The fact that Onesimus would join Tychicus and "tell you everything" reflects his role as a representative of Paul. In Christ, social strata are nullified; both slave and free find a new calling and status in the service of the gospel. Of course, this did not mean that all secular social categories were reversed; rather, in the church slave and free served side by side and regarded one another as "brothers and sisters." This should be the case in our day as well, as business owners and menial workers serve together in the congregation. If the board of a church (or Christian organization) is made up only of wealthy people, priorities have become skewed.

GREETINGS FROM PAUL'S ASSOCIATES (4:10–14)

Six of Paul's coworkers wanted the Colossians to know that they cared deeply for them and so were sending their own greetings. Paul's "rainbow coalition" contains three Jews (vv. 10–11: Aristarchus, Mark, and Jesus Justus) and three Gentiles (vv. 12–14: Epaphras, Luke, and Demas). After Romans 16, this is the second-longest series of names in Paul's letters and reflects the close relations between his team and the Colossian church.

Aristarchus was from Thessalonica (Acts 27:2); he had been arrested with Paul in Ephesus (Acts 19:29), had accompanied the collection for the poor to Jerusalem (Acts 20:4), and had been with Paul when he sailed from Caesarea to Rome (Acts 27:2), where he presently was serving on Paul's team. Paul calls Aristarchus "my fellow prisoner," which could mean that he shared Paul's imprisonment (see Phlm 23), perhaps in Ephesus as well as in Rome. Alternatively, this description might be a metaphor, expressing that Aristarchus, like Paul, had been taken captive by Christ to serve him. Either reading is possible, and Aristarchus—along with Epaphras (Phlm 23) and perhaps others—could have voluntarily spent time with Paul in his apartment-prison (Acts 28:16, 23). I suspect Paul intends both aspects here.

Mark added his greetings. As the "cousin of Barnabas" he was the same John Mark, son of Mary in Jerusalem (Acts 12:12), who had accompanied Paul and Barnabas to Antioch (Acts 12:25) and become an assistant on the first missionary journey. He had deserted the team at Pamphylia (Acts 13:13), and when he had tried to rejoin the group at the beginning of the second missionary journey Paul had so strongly objected that he had split with Barnabas, who accompanied Mark back to their home area in Cyprus (Acts 15:38–39). There Mark apparently had matured spiritually and entered once again into ministry, this time successfully. Here and in Philemon 24, Paul presents Mark as a trusted coworker; he later asks Timothy to bring Mark to Rome, "because he is helpful to me in my ministry" (2 Tim 4:11). Elsewhere in the New Testament, the apostle

Peter calls him "my son Mark" (1 Pet 5:11). So Mark had become a cherished coworker to both Peter and Paul, and it was he who penned the second Gospel. What a wonderful model for the use of Christian discipline to reclaim a failed disciple for Christ! The Colossians had already received special instructions about welcoming Mark, possibly from Peter or Barnabas. We don't know the circumstances, but apparently Mark's earlier failure had become well known and some believers were leery of receiving him. Since Paul was sending Mark to Colossae as an official representative, it was important that he be received properly, and Paul was adding his own commendation to ensure that Mark would be reinstated and shown respect.

A third greeting came from Jesus Justus, about whom we know only his name. "Jesus" was a fairly common name among Jews (it comes from *Iēsou*, the Greek form of the Hebrew name *Yeshua*, or "Joshua"). This particular Jesus had taken the Roman (Latin) surname "Justus" (as had Joseph Barsabbas in Acts 1:23 and Titius in Acts 18:7). Many Jews adopted a Greek or Roman second name; perhaps the best known example is Paul himself, whose Jewish name was "Saul."

Some scholars interpret the rest of Colossians 4:11 as a declaration that these three men were the only Jewish Christians still involved with the mostly Gentile churches, all others having left for congregations composed primarily of Jews. This scenario is possible, but it is slightly more likely that Paul is simply distinguishing Aristarchus, Mark, and Jesus Justus as the only Jewish Christians among his "coworkers," a semiofficial title for members of his missionary team. Their work was to help establish "the kingdom of God" in this world by spreading the gospel. Paul's point is that these men had proven to be a great "comfort" to him, encouraging him both by their ministry of the gospel and through their personal fellowship with him.

Starting in verse 12, Paul relates greetings from three Gentile associates, beginning with Epaphras, a native of Colossae and the leader named in 1:7–8 as the founding pastor of the church there. His is the most extensive presentation, undoubtedly due to his importance to the Colossian believers. As in 1:7, Paul here describes Epaphras as a "slave of Jesus Christ," a description often used by Paul in reference to himself and all other Christians (e.g., 2 Cor 4:5; Eph 6:6; also see my comments on Col 4:7, above).

As a committed prayer-warrior, Epaphras was "always wrestling" in intercession for the Colossian church. The same verb is used of Paul in 1:29 (in conjunction with the noun in 2:1) regarding his rigorous "contending" on behalf of the Colossians. Obviously Epaphras and Paul were "soul brothers" in their strenuous efforts to promote the spiritual depth of the Colossian believers. Epaphras prayed that they would "stand mature and fully assured in all the will of God"; this translation reflects the Greek text better than does the NIV, and it summarizes a good deal of previous material in this letter. According to Paul, the prayer was for God (the verb is a divine passive) to enable the believers to "stand firm" in the faith (1:23, "continue in your faith, established and firm"). The aim, then, is the believers' spiritual "maturity" (1:28, "present everyone fully mature in Christ"), and the emphasis on being "fully assured" is reminiscent of 2:2, where Paul expresses his desire that the Colossians attain "all the wealth of the full assurance of understanding" (NIV: "full riches of complete understanding"). The sphere within which believers gain all of this is "the will of God," signifying that maturity and full understanding can be attained only when we live in accordance with God's will. In Romans 12:2 we see how this kind of faithfulness and maturity can be achieved—namely by living in such a way as to "prove" that God's will is indeed "good, pleasing, and perfect." So Epaphras' prayer, then, was focused on the spiritual state of the Colossian church, that its members might experience the fullness of God as they followed his will.

In 4:13 Paul adds his personal testimony on the quality of Epaphras' ministry. He wanted the church to know how tirelessly Epaphras had "labored" for the believers in Colossae, Laodicea, and Hierapolis (the three major cities in the Lycus

Valley). Hierapolis was a fairly large city about fifteen miles north of Colossae and six miles from Laodicea, and there were strong churches in all three cities (see 2:1; 4:15-16; Rev 3:14-22 on Laodicea). Most interpreters believe that Epaphras' "hard work" was in combating the heretics, and there can be no doubt that Epaphras was still desperately needed in the region. As the founder and leading pastor of these churches, he knew the false teachers better than anyone.

Finally, Paul mentions the greetings of Luke and Demas (4:14). Luke, "the beloved doctor," had accompanied Paul on his final two missionary journeys. The "we" passages of Acts 16:10-17; 20:13-15; 21:1-18; and 27:1-28:16 likely imply Luke's firsthand involvement. He probably was converted at Troas and joined Paul's team almost immediately thereafter. Many interpreters believe Luke's presence on these journeys and in Rome suggest that Paul, with his "thorn in the flesh" (2 Cor 12:7), needed Luke's medical help. Luke also was invaluable for his spiritual gifts, as evidenced in his writing of Luke and Acts—more New Testament material than all of Paul's letters combined.

We know little about Demas, who is always mentioned in the same context as Luke (Phlm 24; 2 Tim 4:10). At the time Paul wrote Colossians, Demas was a faithful member of Paul's team, but four or five years later he apparently reverted to living for himself and for worldly things. Sadly, Paul records elsewhere that during his second imprisonment Demas had "deserted" him and gone to Thessalonica because "he loved this world" (2 Tim 4:10). It is possible that the prospect of losing his life for Christ terrified Demas, who chose life in this world over death for the Lord.

FURTHER GREETINGS AND INSTRUCTIONS (4:15-17)

Paul has conveyed greetings from his coworkers and now asks the Colossians to deliver his own greetings to the Laodicean church (already noted in 2:1; 4:13). It is difficult to ascertain why he expresses a special greeting to the Laodiceans (v. 15) when, according to the next verse, he also is sending them a separate letter (v. 16). Perhaps Paul wants to strengthen the ties between these two churches. Several interpreters think that Nympha and her house-church were located in Laodicea, based on verse 15 ("Give my greetings to the brothers and sisters in Laodicea, particularly to Nympha and the church in her house there").

There is actually some debate as to whether "Nympha" is masculine or feminine; the confusion has led some translators to use masculine forms (as in the KJV: "Nymphas and the church which is in his house"). But the feminine, with slightly better manuscript support, is the more likely reading. Nympha, like Lydia at Philippi (Acts 16:14–15), is probably a wealthy widow whose home had become the meeting place for a congregation. This was the common practice during the early centuries of the church's existence (see Acts 16:15; Rom 16:5, 23; 1 Cor 16:19); separate houses of worship did not appear until the third century AD.

Colossians 4:16 (along with 1 Thess 5:27 and Rev 1:3) tells us that New Testament letters were read publicly in services (one assumes in each house-church in turn). Clearly Paul wrote this letter for all the churches of the area, and the apostolic authority from the Lord behind it is obvious. Several scholars note the parallel with the practice in Jewish synagogues, in which the Torah was read aloud in services.

Verse 16 indicates an exchange of letters between the churches: Paul specifies that, after this letter has been read at Colossae, he wants it passed along to the Laodicean church; he then asks the Colossians to "read the letter from Laodicea," which we apparently do not have. Some scholars think it refers to the letter to Philemon (but that was more private than public) or even to Ephesians (but that letter was probably written a few months after this one). Most agree that the reference is to a letter from Paul that at some point was lost. Paul's request for these letters to be widely read was probably due to the serious threat posed by the false teachers. Paul wanted to make certain the material in both letters was disseminated to every church, lest the heresy continue to grow and damage the cause of Christ in the region.

From 2 Peter 3:15–16, which indicates that Paul's letters had been distributed, it seems likely that copies were made and delivered to other churches. These two verses from Peter are immensely important for our understanding of the processes involved in the collection of Paul's letters and the formation of the canon. Paul's letters seem to have been collected from an early date—probably even before the writing of Colossians, for 2 Peter was written in the mid-60s, just a few years after this letter. Along with recognition of the four Gospels, the collection of Paul's letters marked the beginning of the formation of the New Testament canon.

Paul's final instruction is for Archippus (Col 4:17), called a "fellow soldier" in Philemon 2 and either Philemon's son or a member of his household. Paul wants him to "complete the ministry you have received in the Lord," most likely some specific task involved with the ministry of the gospel in Laodicea. Many interpreters connect this with the sending of Onesimus back to Philemon and suggest that Archippus had been tasked with overseeing the reconciliation between the two. However, the use of "complete the ministry" here indicates that Archippus had received his task earlier. The fact that he had received it "in the Lord" probably relates to his particular calling in ministry and assigned task in the Laodicean church. The general consensus is that the reference is to a preaching and teaching ministry, but we cannot know for sure. We should not surmise that Archippus was failing in this ministry or needed to be stimulated. Paul's remark here can just as easily be read as encouragement to persevere (as I prefer to see it).

PAUL'S SIGNATURE AND BENEDICTION (4:18)

Paul often added his personal signature (1 Cor 16:21; Gal 6:11; 2 Thess 3:17) to authenticate a letter (Phlm 19) and to ensure his readers that it was not a forgery falsely attributed to him (2 Thess 2:2). Authors frequently had an **amanuensis** (or secretary) pen their letters for them, and Paul had a vision problem that some scholars think was the "thorn in the flesh" (2 Cor 12:7) that required his own handwriting to be large (Gal 6:11). Thus he needed a secretary (like Tertius in Romans 16:22), though he could still sign a letter to verify that he was indeed behind its content.

Paul closes with a request that the Colossian believers "remember my chains"—that is, to pray for him, especially due to his imprisonment (as he does in Rom 15:30–32; Eph 6:18–20; see also 1 Thess 5:25). Paul would need their prayers for at least another year before his release from prison, but the intercession ultimately would succeed, and he would indeed be liberated. However, by the time Paul was freed, his ministry plans would change. Earlier, he had wanted to shift his focus to the western half of the Roman Empire and to Spain (Rom 15:24, 28), but the situation with the false teachers in the province of Asia would prompt him to send Timothy there and then to travel there himself, as the Pastoral Letters tell us. Eventually, Paul would be arrested in Asia Minor and taken back to Rome, where he would be executed (2 Tim 1:15–17; 4:6–8). (For more discussion about the end of Paul's life, see my introduction on Colossians.)

Paul closes with his customary "Grace be with you all," with which he concludes every letter. **Hellenistic** letters typically ended with some form of "Farewell; may you prosper," but Paul, as in his letter openings, Christianizes the standard form and finishes with a promise of God's grace. He always begins with "grace and peace" and closes with "grace," frequently from "our Lord Jesus Christ." Still today, the people of God need the grace of God to survive in this evil world—and that divine grace, which will guarantee our final victory and carry us home to God, is an ever-present reality in our lives.

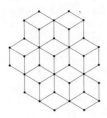

PHILEMON

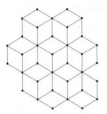

INTRODUCTION TO PHILEMON

This short letter, addressed by the apostle Paul to his friend and coworker Philemon in Colossae, has long captivated readers for its intimate tone, its model of friendship, and the way it handles the issue of slavery. At the same time, many have considered it the least important book in the New Testament and have wondered why it was included in the canon. It is rarely preached from the pulpit or taught in Bible study classes, and it contains no important doctrinal issues, focusing instead on an ethical matter regarding Paul's desire for Philemon to forgive his slave Onesimus and welcome him back. This commentary will explore and help readers understand the contribution this little letter can make to the church and to our Christian lives.

AUTHORSHIP AND DATE

Paul's authorship of this book is accepted even by the vast majority of critical scholars, so we will explore his circumstances at the time he wrote it. Paul identifies himself in verse 1 as "Paul, a prisoner of Christ Jesus," and the letter generally is included as part of the corpus of the Prison Letters (along with Colossians, Ephesians, and Philippians), those books written during a time when Paul was in prison. So we should begin there.

There were at least three occasions when Paul was in prison: in Ephesus at the end of the third missionary journey (not mentioned by Luke, but it still probably took place; Acts 19:32-41); two years in Caesarea after being arrested in Jerusalem (Acts 24:27); and two years in Rome while in a capital trial before Caesar (Acts 28:30). For the writing of Philemon, Ephesus would make sense based on its proximity to Colossae (the letter's destination), but there is no explicit mention of this episode anywhere in Paul's letters, making it unlikely as the occasion for the Prison Letters. Some have preferred the Caesarean imprisonment, but Caesarea is not mentioned anywhere in the Prison Letters, so this too is doubtful. The best option is Rome, which is reflected in Paul's remarks about his imprisonment in Philippians 1:12-26.

The letter to Philemon probably was written in AD 61 at the same time as Colossians. It is best to think of Colossians as having been written before Ephesians; the two letters share similar language and themes, and it seems likely that Ephesians (the longer letter) is expanding on Colossians (see the introductions of my commentaries on Colossians and Ephesians). Colossians and Philemon probably were written in AD 61, with Ephesians following in 61-62 and Philippians just before Paul's release from prison in 62 (see the introduction to my forthcoming Philippians volume). Based on this timeline, at the time Paul wrote Philemon he had been in his "rented house" in Rome, awaiting trial, for six months to a year (Acts 28:23, 30). This private letter was carried along with Paul's letter to the Colossian congregation by Tychicus and Onesimus (Col 4:7-9).

The church in Colossae was founded during the third missionary journey when Paul, based in Ephesus for two years, is thought to have sent mission teams throughout the province of Asia (Acts 19:10). The seven churches of Revelation 2-3 were located in that province. Epaphras founded the church at Colossae and became its first pastor (Col 1:5-7), and Philemon was a wealthy leader in the church, as well as a "coworker" of Paul (v. 1) who sponsored and led a house-church in Colossae.

THE SITUATION BEHIND THE LETTER

We know that Paul was writing to Philemon and his house-church and interceding on behalf of Onesimus, Philemon's slave. The two, master and slave, were in serious conflict over an unspecified issue, and Onesimus (whose name means "useful") had come to Rome, perhaps to seek asylum and assistance from Paul. He had been converted to Christ by Paul, who now was sending him back to Colossae to be reconciled with Philemon. The exact nature of the conflict between Philemon and Onesimus is unclear, though several scenarios have been suggested:

1. The traditional view is that Onesimus had stolen goods from Philemon (v. 18), run away (vv. 15–16), and somehow made his way to Rome. He spent several months as Paul's assistant before confessing the actual circumstances behind his journey; now Paul was sending him back to Philemon to face his legal problems and, hopefully, to be reconciled with the master he had so seriously wronged. The problem is that the details of this scenario—the theft and the runaway slave—have to be inferred from texts that do not explicitly support the thesis. Onesimus' wronging Philemon and owing him in verse 18 do not overtly denote thievery. The theory is simply too speculative.

2. An alternative view holds that Onesimus fled to Rome to seek asylum with Paul and with the Christians there, perhaps because Roman law allowed slaves to find sanctuary in temples and with religious groups. This is indeed possible, but once again there is no hard evidence in the text to back it up. Still, with Paul's indirect language it cannot be ruled out.

3. One of the best-known alternative views is that of John Knox, who argues that Archippus (v. 2) rather than Philemon was the owner of Onesimus, and that Paul wanted Onesimus to be freed from slavery and sent back

to him to continue assisting in his ministry. According to Knox, Philemon oversaw the churches of the Lycus Valley and lived in Laodicea. He is addressed first, Knox says, because Paul wanted him to use his authority and intercede with Archippus on Paul's behalf. While this intriguing twist is regularly discussed, virtually no one considers it likely, as Colossians 4:17 and Philemon 2 more naturally support Philemon as the owner of Onesimus and therefore the primary recipient of the letter.

4. A theory that is being accepted more and more in recent years is that Philemon and his church had sent his slave Onesimus to Rome to assist Paul—a scenario similar to the Philippian believers sending Epaphroditus (Phil 2:25-30). This explanation suits Paul's language in Philemon well in terms of Onesimus' "usefulness" and "help" (vv. 12, 13)and his work to "refresh" the saints and Paul (vv. 7, 20). In this theory the circumstances are entirely positive, and Paul is simply asking that Onesimus' ministry to him be extended. The one problem I have with this comes in verse 18, where Paul says, "If he has done you any wrong or owes you anything, charge it to me." This hypothesis has to take verse 18 as purely rhetorical, unrelated to any actual problems and added simply to cover all possible contingencies. I can't help but think there is more to the story than this.

5. In my opinion the most viable thesis regards Onesimus not as a runaway slave or an assistant sent by Philemon, but rather as a slave who had come into some kind of conflict with Philemon. The exact nature of the dispute is never explained in the letter, but it was highly personal and had fractured their relationship. As a result Onesimus had come to Rome specifically to ask Paul, as a close friend of Philemon, to intercede with him and mediate a reconciliation. This was not unheard of in the Roman world; if this were indeed the case, Onesimus

would not have been viewed as a runaway slave. The major problem with this scenario is that Paul is not speaking very clearly as a mediator or using language designed to effect a reconciliation.

All of the above theories are left to wrestle with the indirect language of the letter—which is only natural, since Paul was writing to someone (Philemon) who already knew the circumstances. Paul wants Philemon to make his own decision and trusts that his deep love and concern for others will guide him to the proper action. While the second and fifth scenarios above are both quite viable, I believe the fifth has the fewest difficulties. I do not envision a crime having been committed or regard Onesimus as a runaway. Also, if Philemon had sent Onesimus to help Paul, why would Paul have needed to send him back to Colossae? It would have been sufficient to ask Philemon in the letter to extend Onesimus' stay.

In light of this discussion, let's try to piece together the situation behind the letter. Philemon was a wealthy slave owner who had been converted by Paul during the third missionary journey, had become a leader in the church, had worked with Paul on many occasions, and had established a congregation in his home in Colossae, a town about 120 miles east of Ephesus in the Lycus Valley. Onesimus was one of Philemon's slaves. At some point after Paul had been arrested and was awaiting trial in Rome, living in a rented home and guarded by Roman soldiers, there had been a conflict between Philemon and Onesimus serious enough that the two had been unable to work through it.

Onesimus, who apparently had met Paul and knew of his close relationship with Philemon, had left Colossae and made his way to Rome—possibly to seek asylum with Paul and the church there but more likely to solicit Paul's help in reconciling with Philemon. This type of mediation was allowed under Roman law, so he would not have been considered a runaway slave. Soon after connecting with Paul, he had converted to

Christianity and had become a valuable assistant to the apostle and a member of his ministry team. After some time, Paul felt it necessary to send Onesimus back to Philemon for a face-to-face reconciliation, but in doing so he writes to ask Philemon not only to forgive Onesimus but to allow him return to Rome and continue his "useful" (v. 11) ministry with Paul.

THE PURPOSE AND VALUE OF THE LETTER

There is considerable debate as to whether Paul is asking for Onesimus' manumission—for Philemon to make his slave a free man. The letter does not overtly address this issue, and many have argued recently that Paul was not concerned with the legal issue of slavery, but rather wanted Onesimus to be received by Philemon as a brother in Christ before being returned to Rome to work alongside Paul. In other words, Onesimus would be both a slave (his earthly status) and a brother in Christ (his heavenly status). Many argue for this interpretation on the grounds that neither Paul nor Christians in general would have been been trying to mount a massive attack on slavery—an entrenched socioeconomic system that was the heart and soul of the Roman way of life. The focus of the early church was on proclaiming the new way of Christ, not on changing the ways of secular society.

While that may be true, Paul's request to Philemon was not an attack on an entire system; it simply reflected his desire to see one man freed for ministry. In my opinion, the language in verses 13, 15-16 and throughout the letter makes it likely that Paul *was* seeking Onesimus' freedom, albeit subtly. Since Philemon himself was evidently unable to leave Colossae and help Paul in Rome, Paul may have wanted him to consider Onesimus his surrogate. Paul is asking Philemon, at the very least, to return Onesimus to Rome and, perhaps, to make Onesimus a free man, as well. When Paul confidently states, "knowing that you will do even more than I ask" (v. 21), does that encompass only the return of Onesimus to Rome, or does it also include his manumission? I believe both aspects are included.

It is true that when Paul directs Philemon to "welcome him as you would welcome me" (v. 17) he primarily means as a brother in Christ. The central element in this letter is the conversion of Onesimus to Christ and the new reality of his "usefulness" (v. 11) to both Philemon and Paul. As part of this, Paul's hope is that Onesimus might be returned to the ministry he has started in Rome.

Many have wondered why such a private letter was included in the Bible. Yet the themes are incredibly significant for the church in every age: (1) This letter should be used in every discussion of conflict resolution, as it shows Paul's masterful handling of a potentially explosive situation. (2) The view Paul promotes here of the church as a household and family is quite rich; clearly the church is to be characterized by *koinōnia*, fellowship, and a caring atmosphere. (3) The centrality of the gospel ministry for the church is as important in our day as it was in the first century.

STRUCTURE AND OUTLINE

Paul structures his letter carefully to draw Philemon to the point of realizing the direction the Lord Christ would have him go. Here is the plan we understand Paul to follow in his organization of the letter:

I. Introduction: The love and faith of Philemon, 1–7
    a. Greetings to Philemon and his family, 1–3
    b. Commending Philemon's love and faith, 4–7
       i. Thanksgiving for Philemon's love and faith, 4–5
       ii. Prayer for Philemon to experience God's goodness, 6–7

II. Letter body, 8–20
    a. Paul's request on behalf of Onesimus, 8–14
       i.   Paul's relationship with Philemon, 8–9
       ii. Paul's appeal for his "son," Onesimus, 10
       iii. Paul's relationship with Onesimus: The reason for his return to Colossae, 11–12

   iv. Paul's desire for Onesimus to return to Rome, 13–14
  b. God's purpose: To return Onesimus to Philemon as a
   brother in Christ, 15–16
  c. The details of Paul's request, 17–20
   i. Request for Philemon to welcome back
    Onesimus, 17
   ii. Promise to repay any debt, 18–19a
   iii. Reminding Philemon of his debt to Paul, 19b
   iv. Confidence regarding Philemon's compliance, 20

 III. Final greetings and letter closing, 21–25
  a. Paul's confidence and future plan, 21–22
  b. Greetings from coworkers, 23–24
  c. Final benediction, 25

THE THEOLOGY OF THE LETTER

Every book of the Bible has a set of theological messages for
the readers, and it is the task of biblical theology to ascertain
what those points are. This is done by tracing the passages that
address certain theological issues—say, Christ or the church
or salvation—and discerning which aspects of those doctrines
are reflected in the biblical text. Even in a letter as short as
Philemon, distinct theological points are being made.

CHRIST

The central theological theme regarding Christ Jesus is his lordship. This makes a great deal of sense in a letter dealing with
the issue of slavery. Paul wants Philemon to understand that,
even though Philemon is master and owner of Onesimus in an
earthly, temporal sense, Christ is Lord and Master of Philemon
in a heavenly, eternal sense. Paul begins by having the letter's
greeting stem from "God our Father and the Lord Jesus Christ"
(v. 3). From the outset he portrays Christ as the One in charge
of the situation. Two verses later Paul refers to Philemon's faith
being anchored "in the Lord Jesus" (v. 5), reminding Philemon
again that Jesus is sovereign over every aspect of his life.

Paul ends two key sections of his letter with "in the Lord." In verses 15-16 he describes Onesimus as "better than a slave," a Christian "brother"—referring to a transition that has taken place "in the Lord." Then in verses 17-20 Paul discusses Philemon's response to Onesimus' conversion and return to Colossae as a new man. Paul is confident that, as a result of Philemon's decision, Paul himself will receive "some benefit from you in the Lord" (v. 20), probably referring to his expectation that Philemon will allow Onesimus to travel back to Paul in Rome and continue his ministry there. Again, such an anticipated outcome will be possible only "in the Lord," a reference to Paul's confidence that Jesus in his lordship has taken charge of the situation and move it to its God-ordained conclusion.

In this light it is natural that Paul would end his letter with a benediction calling for "the grace of our Lord Jesus Christ" to anoint the congregation at Colossae ("your" is plural in v. 25). Christ as Lord is the heart of the church, and our duty is to surrender to his lordship and allow him to take charge of difficult situations like the tension between Philemon and Onesimus. Only he Christ can solve such problems. As we, like Paul, seek to alleviate conflicts that endanger the peace and unity of the church, we must recognize that we are merely channels of the Lord Jesus Christ.

THE CHURCH

In Philemon, Paul presents the church as both a community and a family. This focus is reinforced in the titles he uses in the letter: God is "Father" (v. 3), Jesus is "Lord/Master" (vv. 3, 5), and the saints are "brothers" or "sisters" in the Lord—including Timothy (v. 1), Apphia (v. 2), Philemon (vv. 7, 20), and Onesimus (v. 16). These household terms portray the true nature of the church community: God is the Head of the family, Christ is its Lord, and all believers are children of God and brothers/sisters of one another. Paul's emphasis is on the bond of love and unity among the members of God's family.

When there is dysfunction—such as the conflict between
Philemon and Onesimus—the problem engages the whole
church, Paul is saying, not just the individuals directly
involved (another example is the dispute between Euodia and
Syntyche in Philippians 4:2-3). Earthly relationships, like that
between Philemon as master and Onesimus as slave, still matter but take second place to the greater reality of the one family of God. Women in the Roman world were considered sec-
ond-class citizens, but in the church Apphia is both a "sister"
(v. 2) and an official witness to the situation in the Colossian
church. In Christ there is a reordering of relationships and status. The church is part of the new creation in the Lord Jesus,
and all the earthly barriers have been broken down. Love and
communion have replaced power and self-seeking, and the
resulting in a dynamic is new peace and security for believers
of all social strata.

SALVATION

The turning point in the situation addressed in this short letter occurred when Onesimus arrived in Rome to ask Paul to
mediate his dispute with Philemon. In his ensuing interchange
with Paul, Onesimus came to realize that his greater conflict
was with Christ; repenting, he found Christ to be his Lord and
Savior. Onesimus was "adopted to sonship" (Rom 8:15) and joined
the family of God, finally living up to his name and becoming
"useful," first to God and secondarily to both Philemon and Paul
(v. 11). Reconciled to God, he can now be reconciled to Philemon,
for the two are now "brothers in the Lord" (v. 16). As part of the
new creation in Christ, the two men can experience a radical
new relationship with each other. Redemption invariably leads
to reconciliation and peace.

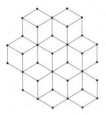

LETTER OPENING
THE LOVE AND FAITH OF PHILEMON
(1–7)

The order of this introductory section follows ancient conventions (both **Hellenistic** and Jewish), beginning with the author and the recipient and then concluding with a thanksgiving and a prayer-wish for the well-being of the addressees. In Hellenistic letters, these features tended to be perfunctory and conventional, but Paul elaborates on the standard forms, developing the thanksgiving and prayer-wish into deeply theological pieces that introduce the letter's themes. Paul commends the love and faith of Philemon, but he is doing more than praising his recipient's spiritual strengths. Paul will be asking Philemon to live up to these qualities in the way he receives Onesimus.

PAUL GREETS PHILEMON AND HIS FAMILY (1–3)

As in Colossians 1:1, Paul opens with his ordinary designation of himself is "an apostle of Christ Jesus." Here he further labels himself "a prisoner of Christ Jesus" (as in Eph 3:1), most likely with a double meaning: Not only is Paul incarcerated in a Roman prison at this time ("imprisoned *because of proclaiming* Christ Jesus"), but he also has been taken captive and "*belongs to* Christ Jesus." Paul is reminding Philemon that he has willingly suffered and sacrificed for Christ's sake, and he is asking Philemon to yield his own rights in a similar manner with respect to Onesimus. Paul's self-description also might parallel Onesimus' situation as a slave, building on the earthly and the heavenly dimensions of slavery: Paul has been taken captive and is a slave of Christ, and Onesimus is a slave both of Philemon and of Christ. Paul is challenging Philemon to realize that he too is a slave of Christ, even while he is the earthly owner of Onesimus. This is not a plea for sympathy, but a recognition of honor. Being a slave in the Roman world meant being a part of an extended household. So too all three players in this situation—Paul, Onesimus, and Philemon—are part of the same family of God and of Christ. The repetition of these themes in verses 9, 16, and 23 reinforces that this is a central motif in this letter.

Many interpreters have called Timothy a "co-author," but it is doubtful he wrote a portion of this letter. Paul could have discussed its content with him, and he may have been the **amanuensis** or secretary who wrote down Paul's dictation. The significance is that this letter is not just a private affair; it comes to Philemon and his family (and perhaps the entire Colossian church) from Paul and his ministry team in Rome. Paul's labeling of Timothy as "our brother" strengthens his emphasis on the church as a family whose members are intimately connected in Christ. In the social milieu of their world, Philemon and Onesimus may have been owner and slave, but in the greater sphere they were brothers (a point Paul expresses more strongly in v. 16).

The recipients of the letter (vv. 1b-2) comprised the family of Philemon, a wealthy believer in Colossae whose home was being used as a gathering place for one of the house-churches in that city. Colossae, one of three cities in the Lycus Valley (along with Hierapolis and Laodicea), was home to a thriving church, but it was under fire due to false teachers who were exerting influence in that region. Paul addressed this problem in a separate letter (Colossians), which he apparently dispatched at the same time as his letter to Philemon (as suggested by the mention of Onesimus in Col 4:9).

Philemon was a leader of the Christian community in Colossae and the sponsor of a major house-church. Paul calls him "our dear friend and fellow worker" (NIV); a more accurate translation is "beloved friend" (the Greek text reads "our beloved and coworker"). Paul likely has more in mind than friendship: He is reminding Philemon that God loves him, and, as Paul will go on to specify in verses 5 and 7, Philemon himself was known for his love for his fellow believers. This will be a primary theme when Paul turns to the situation with Onesimus in verses 10–18. Paul trusts that love will guide Philemon's response. The Greek word rendered "fellow worker" (*synergos,* "coworker") was a semi-technical term for a minister in the church. This suggests that Philemon had ministered alongside Paul at some stage (verse 19 makes it clear that Paul had led Philemon to Christ). Philemon would have visited Ephesus regularly on business, and he probably formed a bond with Paul there sometime during the apostle's third missionary journey (Acts 19).

Paul identifies Apphia, Philemon's wife, as "our sister," signifying that she too is a believer (much as Timothy in verse 1 is called "our brother") and likely a leader in the church. The fact that Paul mentions her is not due simply to her status as Philemon's wife; Paul does not mention the wives of Christian leaders unless they are leaders in their own right, as in the pairings of Priscila and Aquila in Romans 16:3 or Andronicus and Junia in Romans 16:7. Archippus, likely Philemon and Apphia's son, is mentioned in Colossians 4:17 as a leading minister of the church. Here Paul calls him "our fellow soldier" (used also of Epaphroditus in Phil 2:25)—a phrase describing Christian leaders as members of God's army (in the Old Testament the title "LORD of hosts" envisions God commanding an army of angels).

The additional mention of "the church that meets in your home" could indicate that this letter was addressed to the whole community of believers at Colossae, asking them to intercede

in the situation between Philemon and Onesimus. Although
that is possible it would be difficult to prove, especially since
the letter seems to address Philemon personally. Still, the presence of the plural "you/your" in verses 3, 22, and 25 probably
means the church was at least indirectly included—in that all
were aware of the situation and Paul wanted the church to help
guarantee the appropriate result. This is an important lesson
for churches today; all too often rank-and-file members prefer
to ignore problems, hoping they'll go away or feeling relieved
at not being responsible for a solution. The church is a community and a family, and problems are to be dealt with by the corporate body of Christ.

The greeting (v. 3) is the norm in Paul's letters. The double
salutation "grace" (charis) and "peace" (eirēnē, corresponding
to the Hebrew shalōm) were the normal Hellenistic and Jewish
greetings. Here they function also as theological promises, saying in essence, "What you are hoping for in your very greeting
is being offered to you in Jesus Christ." God's salvation (stemming from his grace) and eternal peace (the result of the reconciliation effected by Christ) are present realities and as such
provide a basis for this letter to Philemon. Paul also be asking Philemon to show Onesimus the same grace he himself has
received from Christ and thereby do his part in effecting peace
and reconciliation within the Christian community.

The source of this grace and peace is "God our father and the
Lord Jesus Christ"—another phrase characteristic of Paul's letters. Calling God "our father" showcases the new relationship
the believer has with God as "Abba"—the most intimate Jewish
term for the fatherhood of God, connoting a new intimacy with
the God who continuously cares for his children. The emphasis
on God as Father also considers the church a household or family; Paul expects the same intimacy enjoyed with God to perme-
ate the "brothers" and "sisters" in Christ. As God is Father, so
Christ is Lord, placing Christ at the same level as Yahweh (often
translated "Lord" in some versions of the Old Testament).

PAUL COMMENDS PHILEMON'S LOVE AND FAITH (4–7)

PAUL GIVES THANKS FOR PHILEMON'S LOVE AND FAITH (4–5)

This expression of thankfulness, found in all of Paul's letters apart from Galatians and Titus, articulates Paul's gratitude to the Lord for Philemon. As in most of Paul's writings, the verses immediately following the greeting (vv. 4–7) introduce themes that will reverberate through the body of the letter; these include Paul's love (v. 9), the fellowship of the saints (v. 17), "every good thing" (v. 14), "refreshing" God's people (v. 20), and the "hearts" of the saints (vv. 12, 20). These motifs mesh with Paul's reason for writing—to ask Philemon to live up to his reputation in handling the conflict with Onesimus.

This thanksgiving is continuous; Paul is unceasing in his gratitude, never forgetting Philemon in his prayers. Obviously Paul doesn't mean that he remembers Philemon every hour of every day but rather is saying that he invariably thinks of Philemon in his prayer time. The emphasis on "remembrance" is significant because, throughout Scripture, this term does not just apply to memory but signifies the active participation of the person in the situation. Paul ponders Philemon's dilemma and expresses that reflection in his prayer life, remembering to ask for divine blessing on Philemon for his life of faithfulness.

The basis for Paul's thanks to God are the reports he has received about the depth of Philemon's love for his fellow believers and of his great faith in Christ (v. 5). There is some debate regarding the proper translation of this verse. The Greek text reads, "your love and the faith which you have for the Lord Jesus and for all the saints." Several English translations interpret this to mean that Philemon has love and faithfulness for both Christ and the saints (NKJV, NASB, ESV). However, others present this verse as a **chiasm** (a literary device in which the inner and outer phrases are connected), as follows:

A — love
　B — and faith
　　B' — toward the Lord Jesus
A' — and toward all the saints

In this interpretation (see NIV, NRSV, NLT) Philemon's love is directed toward the saints (the "A" pair), and his faith toward Jesus (the "B" pair). This makes a great deal of sense and is being accepted by an increasing number of scholars. In light of Paul's similar statements in Colossians 1:4 and Ephesians 1:15, I prefer the chiastic reading: "because I hear about your love for all the saints and your faith in the Lord Jesus."

It is likely that Paul is commending Philemon's deep faith in Christ and the resultant love that faith produces in him for his brothers and sisters in Christ. True faith in Christ must find expression in love for his body, the church (see Gal 5:6). Note also the emphasis on "all the saints. As verse 9 shows, Paul wants Onesimus to be included in this love and is therefore asking for full reconciliation between Philemon and Onesimus.

PAUL PRAYS FOR PHILEMON TO EXPERIENCE GOD'S GOODNESS (6–7)

Verse 6 is difficult to translate. The opening (hopōs, "so that") could indicate the purpose of Philemon's faith and love (KJV), though that does not make much sense. Most interpreters take it as a reference to the content of Paul's prayer begun in verse 4 and translate: "I pray that your partnership in the faith ..." (NRSV, NASB, ESV, NET, NLT, NIV). This seems to fit better.

According to this reading Paul is lauding Philemon's "partnership (koinōnia, "fellowship") in the faith," but again it is difficult to nail down the precise meaning. The noun in the Greek text could refer to: (1) the common fellowship of Philemon and his fellow Christian believers (NJB, NET); (2) their partnership together in Christian ministry (NIV); (3) Philemon's sharing of the Christian faith with others (NKJV, NRSV); or (4) an active "generosity" that stems from his faith (NLT). The second and fourth possibilities are the better readings, for there is ample evidence that koinōnia was used to describe generous almsgiving in the first century. The second option seems stronger, as Paul later uses the related noun koinōnon to ask Philemon to be his "partner" (v. 17); furthermore, in another Prison Letter, Paul uses *koinōnia* to express "partnership in the gospel" (Phil 1:5). So Paul wants to see his Philemon's sharing in the ministry of the church (v. 1b)—both with Paul and with the believers in Colossae—extended to the situation with Onesimus. Since there is a thrust of generous giving in the concept, perhaps we should combine views 2 and 4.

Paul's prayer is that this generous participation might be "effective" (*energēs*, "working") in resolving the situation and producing the "good things" of God in Philemon's life. As in Colossians 1:9 Paul's prayer is for Philemon's "knowledge" or "understanding" (*epignōsis*, indicating a complete and experiential knowledge) to deepen, that he might realize anew all that he has in Christ. The idea behind "good things" likely moves in two directions, referring to the "good" gifts and blessings that come from God and to the "good works" Christians perform as they respond in gratitude to God's goodness.

Many interpreters connect this also with a deep understanding of the will of God, and that is probable as well (see Rom 12:2 on the "goodness" of the will of God). Paul wants a practical realization of the good will of God to be operative in Philemon's life and ministry. This understanding and the action it produces are to be pursued "for the sake of Christ"; Paul is saying that the proper goal of everything Philemon (or any of us) thinks and does is the glory of Christ. This connects closely with the "in Christ" theme in Paul's letters—the idea of believers' incorporation and participation in the body of Christ, the church.

Paul ends this opening section by declaring his personal appreciation for Philemon's love and ministry in the church (v. 7). This is a remarkable testimony of the depth of his love for God's people, and Philemon must have prized this compliment for the rest of his life. There is a second chiasm here (see v. 4), as Philemon's love and faith in verse 5 are reversed in his faith in verse 6 and love in verse 7. This practical love has given Paul "great joy and encouragement," with the second term signifying a nuance of "comfort" as well (for a parallel expression, see 2 Cor 7:4, 7, 13). Paul is clearly elated by Philemon's faithful and loving ministry at Colossae. This thought sets up the rest of the letter, where Paul will ask Philemon to demonstrate his devoted service once again in the current situation.

This love has been especially evident in the way Philemon has "refreshed the hearts of the Lord's people." The particular term for "heart" (*splanchna*, used also in vv. 12, 20) is a strong word referring to the whole person being involved in the process. Philemon was focused unreservedly on his pastoral care for the congregation. The result was a ministry of "refreshment," a term meaning "rest" used often for the inner rest of the soul, when acts of kindness produce an inner tranquility and sense of peace. This is another strong word, expressing the results of a loving concern and ministry devoted to the needs of others.

Paul's description of Philemon in these verses provides a wonderful blueprint for church ministry that should be studied by every Christian leader. If these reflections were put into practice more widely, there would be much less conflict and more contentment in our churches. Caring oversight and service are the other side of a strong teaching and preaching ministry. Pastors need to be strong preachers, but they also need to be loving people-persons who cultivate life-giving relationships within their congregations and minister to personal needs. Such a Christian leader is Philemon; as such, he serves as a beautiful example of what each of us should become.

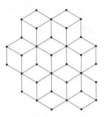

LETTER BODY
(8–20)

The introductory section (vv. 1–7) has set the scene for Paul's appeal (vv. 8–10) regarding Onesimus, a slave who is in some kind of conflict with his owner, Philemon, and has come to Paul for help. Philemon is a partner in Paul's gospel ministry and a leader in the church at Colossae. Paul lauds Philemon's faith in Christ and his love for the saints (vv. 5–7), seeking to engender a loving response from him toward Onesimus. At this point I would urge the reader to peruse the discussion of the circumstances behind this letter, which are heavily debated (see the introduction).

The majority of the letter conveys Paul's "appeal" to Philemon to reconcile with Onesimus and restore him, so he can return to Paul and resume his ministry (apparently in Rome). Having just praised Philemon's deep love for the church, Paul now explains that, since Onesimus has found Christ (v. 10), it is only natural for Philemon's love to extend to him as well (vv. 7, 9).

PAUL MAKES A REQUEST
ON BEHALF OF ONESIMUS (8-14)

PAUL REMINDS PHILEMON OF THEIR
DEEP PERSONAL RELATIONSHIP (8-9)

This section of the letter begins with an interesting claim based on Paul's apostolic authority "in Christ," undoubtedly the result of his divine commission when Christ called him into service as an apostle (1 Cor 9:1, Eph 1:1; Col 1:1) and gave him authority to guide the mission to the Gentiles. Paul therefore had *parrēsia*—"confidence" (NASB, NET) or "boldness" (NRSV, NASB, ESV, NLT, NIV)—a term often used for the freedom to speak fearlessly and boldly. Here it conveys Paul's authority to boldly command Philemon to comply with his request. This is the only place in Paul's letters where he claims to possess such a degree of authority. However, it is critical to note that he declines to actually use that authority here. Paul would never misuse his power, for Christ was the true "commander," and Paul was a team player who led his associates but never manipulated them to obedience. This is an incredibly important model for Christian leaders today, as I have seen way far too many dictators in the church and in Christian organizations. There is no place for this in the Christian community. Throughout the New Testament the demand is for servant-leaders—faithful people who lead by example and not by fiat.

Still, Paul is speaking strongly, for he states that Philemon should "do what you ought to do" (v. 8), recognizing a moral imperative to do the right thing. The term Paul uses here, *anēkon*, means "what is fitting or proper" and in this context indicates the obligation for Christian leaders to follow Christ's example and take the high ground in any situation.

Rather than order Philemon, Paul makes a request (v. 9) based on their history together and the strength of their relationship. In the Greek text "on the basis of love" begins the sentence, and this idea is strongly emphasized—paralleling verses 5 and 7, where Paul expresses the great joy he has found in Philemon's love for the saints. Philemon has consistently acted with kindness and love toward the believers at Colossae, and Paul wants him to continue this largesse with regard to Onesimus. On the grounds of Philemon's prior ministry, Paul now "appeals" to him (rather than commanding him). The verb Paul uses is *parakalō*, meaning to "exhort" or "urge." Paul's urgent request, which follows, points to an important issue affecting the entire church.

Paul then turns to his own situation as the one making the request, certainly intending to touch Philemon deeply. There is some difference of opinion as to what Paul is saying. The word he chooses, *presbytēs*, could mean "ambassador." It is used this way in Ephesians 6:20 ("ambassador in chains," RSV), referring positively to Paul's authority in Christ, but "ambassador" is an unusual meaning for the term, and most interpreters prefer to translate it here in its normal sense of "old man" (NASB, ESV, NLT, NIV). Paul moves, then, from an emphasis on his authority in verse 8 to the very opposite—his weakness. Assuming Paul was in his twenties at the time of his conversion around AD 34, he would have been close to fifty when he wrote this letter to Philemon (around AD 61–62). As an "old man," then, Paul emphasizes his weakness and dependence on others for help. This idea continues as he concludes verse 9 by describing himself again as a "prisoner of Christ Jesus" (also v. 1), here emphasizing his relative helplessness and need to rely on others. As to his physical situation he is old, and as to his societal situation he is imprisoned. For these reasons, in part, Paul is trusting Philemon to do the right thing and extend Christ's love and peace to Onesimus—and to send him back to Rome where he can continue serving Paul.

PAUL APPEALS TO PHILEMON REGARDING HIS "SON," ONESIMUS (10)

In spite of Paul's difficult situation (v. 9) there is hope, for God has sent him a "son" to provide the support he needs. Here Paul reveals for the first time the person behind his appeal—Onesimus. The language doesn't center on the request "for" Onesimus to be returned to Paul (that will come later) but simply conveys that it is being made "on behalf of" Onesimus. There is a double meaning in "son"; Paul is pointing primarily to the reality that Onesimus was converted by Paul and so became his son in the faith (see also 1 Cor 4:17; Gal 4:19). At the same time, Paul hints that he views Onesimus as the "son" he never had, sent by God to assist him in his "old age." In a sense this ups the ante for Philemon to fulfill Paul's request. The father-son relationship functions at both levels.

Paul explains that Onesimus "became my son while I was in chains"—meaning Onesimus had traveled to Rome, had somehow found Paul (perhaps to ask him to intercede with Philemon), and had become a Christian while Paul was incarcerated. The ending of Acts tells us that Paul was in prison and awaiting trial in Rome for two years (Acts 28:30) and was allowed by the Romans to live in a "rented house" and receive visitors (Acts 28:23). So it was a transformed Onesimus who returned to Colossae—no longer a pagan slave but now a brother in Christ.

Paul Conveys the Reason for Onesimus' Return to Colossae (11–12)

The name "Onesimus" means "useful," so Paul makes a play on words to highlight the altered circumstances under which he is sending the man back to Philemon. It is difficult to know how much meaning we should read into the statement, "formerly he was useless to you." This issue is closely related to the various theories about the circumstances behind the letter. If Onesimus had stolen from Philemon and become a runaway slave, that would be implied here. But if the conflict entailed a personal situation, perhaps a personality conflict or deficient work performance, that also would explain this remark. Alternatively, Paul could be alluding to Onesimus as a former unbeliever who, in that state, had been "useless" to God and his people. We must simply leave it there.

Paul's primary emphasis in verse 11 is on the second clause: "now he has become useful both to you and to me." There are several nuances here, probably all of them valid. If Onesimus is to remain a slave, he has been transformed into a model servant. Paul also may be hinting that, if Onesimus were to be returned to him, he would be greatly valuable in assisting Paul's ministry. In an overarching sense Onesimus is useful to the Lord in proclaiming Christ to the world. The emphasis on "both to you and to me" suggests all of these nuances. For a further possibility, consider that the Greek term for "useful," *euchrēstos*, sounds similar to the word for "Christ," *christos*—especially in that the letter "*ē*" was pronounced like "*i*" in the **Hellenistic** world. So it is possible, as some interpreters say, that Paul's statement highlights the transformation of Onesimus from being "non-Christ" (*achrēston*, "useless") to being a Christ-follower (*euchrēstos*). We cannot know for certain, of course, but this possibility is intriguing.

In verse 12, Paul reveals his intended action—to return Onesimus to Philemon as an incredibly "useful" and transformed person. It is possible to take the verb here (*anapempō*) in a legal manner, referring to the "sending up" of a case to a higher court for a decision (as in Acts 25:21), but there is not enough evidence here to support this reading. The simpler thrust is better: Paul is "sending him back" to Philemon, with no hint of any legal wrongdoing. Moses instructs the Israelites in Deuteronomy 23:15-16, "If a slave has taken refuge with you, do not hand them over to their master" and "do not oppress them." The same principle applied in the Roman world, as slaves were allowed sanctuary until reconciliation could be effected or a judicial decision was made. A strictly legal sense is unlikely, as there is no hint here that Onesimus had run away after committing a crime. It seems Onesimus had stayed in Rome for a time, and this letter might have been Paul's attempt to bring about the kind of reconciliation envisioned under Roman practice and by Moses. Paul was not required to send Onesimus back to Philemon, but he was expected to seek reconciliation.

Paul anchors his appeal not in legalities but in personal relationships, saying once again how much Onesimus means to him: He "is my very heart." Again there is a double nuance, for on the personal level Onesimus had become Paul's "son" and was now a part of Paul himself. Philemon should treat the returned slave in the same way he would treat Paul. At the same time, Onesimus resides in the "heart" of Christ and should now be treated with the same "love" Philemon was well known for showing God's people (vv. 5, 7). So at both the personal level and the spiritual level, Onesimus had become a different person and was to be regarded accordingly.

PAUL'S TRUE DESIRE IS FOR ONESIMUS TO RETURN TO ROME (13-14)

Note the contrast between Paul's personal preference (keeping Onesimus with himself, v. 13) and the reality of the situation (Paul needed Philemon's consent to do so, v. 14). Paul begins with "I would have liked" (or "I wish I could") to express an indirect form of his request. Paul's true desire is for Philemon to "send him back" (compare v. 12a) to Paul to continue his ministry in Rome. Reconciliation must precede ministry, and while Paul was not legally bound to return a slave to the owner, he was required to attempt reconciliation, to help Onesimus and Philemon settle their (perhaps legal) differences (see v. 12b).

Paul makes an interesting choice of words in the phrase "so that he could take your place in helping me." He uses similar language in Philippians, indicating that the Philippian church had sent Epaphroditus "to take care of my needs" (Phil 2:25); the sense here is that Epaphroditus was the believers' surrogate, to "make up for the help you yourselves could not give me" (Phil 2:30). Paul seems to be implying that Philemon would have traveled to Rome himself to aid Paul's ministry, if circumstances had allowed. Since they had not, Paul proposes that Onesimus be considered Philemon's substitute or representative. It is possible even that Onesimus ministered alongside Epaphroditus in Rome.

Paul's desire was that Onesimus be returned to "help me while I am in chains," with "help" expressed by the Greek verb *diakoneō* (meaning to "serve" or "minister"). While some believe this refers to taking care of Paul's affairs and physical needs, Paul almost certainly had in mind the ministry of the gospel. The problem was that Paul was "in chains for the gospel"—imprisoned based on his gospel proclamation. Because Paul was restricted to his guarded rental house in Rome, there was a great deal of ministry he could not do. He really needed Onesimus and the rest of his team to accomplish God's purposes for them in Rome. A further possibility is that Paul is hinting at a desire for Philemon to give Onesimus his manumission—to make him a free man to return and help Paul in Rome. There is no explicit evidence here for this possibility (though see my comments on v. 16), and this could be a request simply to send Onesimus (still a slave) to help Paul.

Instead of commanding Philemon to comply, Paul wants Philemon's voluntary consent to lie behind his decision (v. 14). To receive that consent it would first be necessary for Paul to send Onesimus back to Colossae to work out the reconciliation. There were several reasons for Paul's seeking Philemon's consent. First, Philemon was the legal owner of his slave, the only one permitted by Roman law to make decisions regarding his future. Second, since Paul and Philemon were brothers in Christ and coworkers in the kingdom task, Paul would never force any action on the basis of his own authority. Third, Christ was the one truly in charge, and both men would want to follow the Spirit's directives in the matter. Love, not compulsion, had to be behind the result. These last two factors were the primary reasons for Paul's request.

So Paul desired to make sure that Philemon's "favor" or "good thing" did not derive from coercion but was completely "voluntary." This principle of acting not out of necessity because we've been obligated to do so, as opposed to proceeding from the free will of the heart, appears often in the New Testament (see also 2 Cor 9:7; 1 Pet 5:2). Philemon needed to act based on the right thing to do under God and for the Christian community—not because of arm-twisting on Paul's part. This section of the letter is as critical in our day as it was in Paul's, and these principles should be mandatory reading for conflict-resolution in Christian circles.

GOD'S PURPOSE WAS TO RETURN ONESIMUS TO PHILEMON AS A BROTHER IN CHRIST (15-16)

Paul goes on to reflect on the possibility that, had Onesimus never come to Rome, he may never have found Christ as his Savior. Paul speculates on God's deeper purposes in effecting the separation between Onesimus and Philemon (the verb-phrase "was separated" is a divine passive, pointing to God's intervention): It was God who had brought Onesimus to Rome so he could meet Paul and be converted to Christianity. The key emphasis is the contrast between "for a little while" and "forever." In our own lives too, God's may produce a temporary separation in order to effect a new and permanent union in Christ. A short earthly loss often precedes an eternal heavenly gain.

Some have read verse 15 as hinting at a criminal action on Onesimus' part that led to him becoming a runaway slave (see also my comments on v. 18). However, this reads much more into the language than the context indicates. Paul is making a simple statement related to the time during which Onesimus and Philemon have been apart—though he does not imply that the parting was amicable. There was definitely some kind of conflict that prompted Onesimus to go to Rome (the "wrong" in v. 18), perhaps to ask Paul to intercede with Philemon. So Paul is asking Philemon to focus not on the hurts he has experienced from Onesimus in the past but on the "good things" (v. 14) that will define their future relationship. Paul never tells us what those wrongs were (Philemon, to whom the letter is addressed, would have known the details), and it does no good for us to speculate further.

Philemon will now "have him back forever." While some believe this refers to a "permanent" new earthly relationship

between the two men, it is far more likely that "eternal" connotes the new creation that both enjoy now that they share
"eternal life" in Christ. The two have been in a temporary
master-slave relationship—one that has become fractured—
but now they are in an eternal relationship in Christ.

Paul makes explicit in verse 16 what he hints at in verse 15:
Philemon is to receive back Onesimus not just as his slave but
now, much more importantly, as a "brother" in Christ. In the
phrase "no longer as a slave," several interpreters see a request
for Onesimus to be manumitted—that is, to be given his freedom. In this case, "have him back" in verse 14 would carry a
semi-technical meaning of "receive back as fully paid," the
assumption being that Onesimus would be returned to Paul a
free man. However, the majority of recent interpreters doubt
this, believing that "no longer a slave" points to a new spiritual reality that supersedes the societal reality. In other words,
Onesimus would remain a slave in terms of his earthly status
but would be considered a part of the new Christian family and
treated as such. This could be supported by the next phrase,
"better than a slave," which might indicate that Onesimus' social
status as a slave was to continue. Yet at the same time, this
social status is eclipsed by the eternal status of being a member of the family of God. Onesimus would now be "a beloved
brother," a world away from the typical status of a slave in the
Roman world. The correct explanation is difficult to determine;
we must recognize the possibility that Paul was not asking for
Onesimus' freedom but was emphasizing his new, far more significant relationship with Philemon in order to encourage the
latter to do what was right.

Still, I believe a manumission request—or at least sugges-
tion—is eminently possible. My tentative conclusion is that
Paul would have liked Onesimus to be freed but was asking for
him to be returned either way to the ministry in Rome. It may
be that Paul refrained from being explicit precisely because he
wanted Philemon to make his own decision in keeping with the
love he had shown to the saints (vv. 5, 7). Many interpreters

doubt that Paul is calling for manumission, basing their assessment on grounds that such a request would have constituted a major challenge to the Roman way of life and be viewed as a revolt against the empire (outcomes Paul would have wanted to avoid, these interpreters suggest). However, this overstates the case. Paul would not have been challenging the entire social system, but simply would have been hinting at manumission in this single situation. Many slaves were granted freedom for exemplary service, and this would have been another such instance. Throughout this letter Paul has been intimating that Philemon should exercise love and mercy in his reception of Onesimus; now this is now extended to the possibility of granting Onesimus freedom to enable his return and ongoing ministry in Rome.

Paul makes one more point here, stressing that this act will be even more beneficial to Philemon than to Paul. Due to the fractious relationship between master and slave in the past, Onesimus has heretofore been "useless" (v. 11). Now that he has been transformed by Christ, that conflict will be resolved and the tension alleviated. Onesimus has become "dear to me and even dearer to you," Paul says in verse 16, due to the healing of their relationship and even more to the fact that the two are now brothers in the Lord. Moreover, the transformation in Onesimus applies, "both as a fellow man (Greek: 'in the flesh') and as a brother in the Lord." By the use of *kyrios* here Paul stresses that, even though Philemon owns Onesimus, Christ is now the true "Master," or "Lord." Even if Onesimus' slave status is to continue (and I believe Paul is hoping it will not), his relationship with Philemon has radically and irrevocably changed. Their eternal status as "dear brothers" in Christ trumps the earthly designations and triumphs over the societal patterns. Paul emphasizes in verses 15–16 that God is involved in the decision; if Philemon fails to do the right thing he will be going against the will of God. Paul is not trying to intimidate Philemon but is making the point that this is a kingdom issue, not just an earthly one.

PAUL SHARES THE DETAILS OF HIS REQUEST (17-20)

PAUL ASKS PHILEMON TO WELCOME BACK ONESIMUS (17)

Paul here makes his request more specific, using an imperative verb form (expressing a command) for the first time in the letter: "welcome him as you would welcome me." He anchors this command in his and Philemon's "partnership" (*koinōnos*) in the gospel; the idea is that they "share" (or "have fellowship") in God's work. The term *koinōnos* (along with *koinōnia* in v. 6), referring to people who have a great deal in common, was used in the first century to describe business "partners." This adds a nuance to the concept of being "brothers" in the Lord, in the sense that the two are engaging in the same ministry for Christ. The sentence in Greek begins with a conditional particle (*ei*, "if") that assumes the statement to be true, so Paul is saying, in effect: "The reality of our relationship demands that you treat Onesimus properly before the Lord." Paul wants Philemon's ministry and the centrality of love that underlies it to be extended to Onesimus.

The command is to "welcome" or "receive/accept" Onesimus as though he were an extension of Paul himself. Paul and *Philemon* are coworkers, and at the same time Paul and *Onesimus* partner in the same ministry. Paul is asking Philemon to extend fellowship to Onesimus and so become a "partner" or coworker with him as well. The two have become not only "dear brothers" in Christ but also sharers in the kingdom ministry. On this basis Philemon is to give Onesimus exactly the same reception he would show Paul. As both a brother and a partner Onesimus is more than merely a representative of Paul; he is in a real sense *a part of* Paul himself (the Greek could be translated "receive him as *being* me") and must be treated accordingly.

PAUL PROMISES TO REPAY ANY DEBT FOR ONESIMUS (18-19A)

We are at the crux of the question regarding the circumstances behind the letter. As in verse 17, Paul uses a conditional particle (*ei*, "if") that assumes something factual behind the statement that follows. But what are the facts behind "he has done you any wrong or owes you anything"? There are four possibilities:

1. The traditional view is that Onesimus was a runaway slave who had stolen money and goods from Philemon to finance his escape—a fairly frequent occurrence.
2. Onesimus might have simply run away (perhaps due to unhappiness as a slave), and the debt could refer to his failure to accomplish the work assigned him.
3. The wrong and the debt could relate to some conflict between the two men, prompting Onesimus to ignore his obligations as a slave in the midst of the tension and while seeking Paul's intercession in the matter.
4. This verse could be rhetorical rather than relating to an actual problem—a general statement used by Paul to cover all the bases in the conflict situation.

Adjudicating among these possibilities is difficult due to the absence of hard data regarding the original situation. We know there was conflict that needed to be resolved, but the letter does not describe the nature of the dispute. As I've already indicated, I do not believe there is enough evidence for the first option; acknowledging that Onesimus has wronged Philemon does not necessarily mean that he has committed a crime. The fourth reading is in my opinion too ephemeral; there is evidence of conflict and a need for resolution. I don't see much support for the theory that Onesimus had run off to escape slavery (the second view), so I would opt for the third view and leave open the exact nature of the conflict. Philemon could have known Onesimus was traveling to Rome to see Paul in order to effect a resolution to their differences. When Onesimus met with Paul, he was converted to Christ and, for a time, served as Paul's assistant. The problem is that details are missing, and we must speculate in order to fill in the gaps.

Wanting to make certain all the bases are covered, Paul offers to "pay back" (v. 19a) any financial debts incurred by Onesimus (due to missed service, for example). How Paul would have obtained the money to do so cannot be known. We must remember, though, that he was in a "rented house" in Rome (Acts 28:23) and would have had to pay for that as well as for his Roman guards (the Roman rule for an accused lawbreaker who was allowed to live outside the prison while waiting to stand trial). Paul may have been supported by patrons, or he could have come into money in some other way (an inheritance?). We know only that he apparently had access to funds to cover any charges Onesimus may have had incurred.

Paul treats "charge it to me" almost as a binding commercial contract, adding, "I, Paul, am writing this with my own hand" as though he were acting as a signatory. In adding this detail, he essentially turns verse 18 into a formal promise to repay a debt. His purpose is undoubtedly to remove any obstacle to Philemon's appropriate reception of Onesimus. In other letters (e.g., Gal 6:11; Col 4:18) Paul's signature is used to authenticate his authorship; here it serves to substantiate his commitment to help reconcile the two men.

PAUL REMINDS PHILEMON OF HIS DEBT TO HIM (19B)

Having addressed Onesimus' debt to Philemon (vv. 18–19a), Paul now shifts the focus to Philemon's debt to Paul: "not to mention that you owe me your very self" (v. 19b). Philemon suddenly moves from the position of creditor to that of debtor. It had likely been Paul who had brought Philemon to Christ; for that Philemon "owes" Paul for his eternal life! Paul's point is that while Onesimus owes Philemon in a monetary sense, Philemon is indebted to Paul in spiritual terms. This puts even more pressure on Philemon to be merciful with Onesimus. Paul is not seeking to collect, and neither should Philemon. Both are ruled by Christian love and mercy, and all debts are to be cancelled— a Christian Jubilee!

Paul Expresses Confidence Regarding Philemon's Compliance (20)

Verse 20 concludes the body of the letter (vv. 8–20), framing Paul's words with two concepts: the relationship between Paul and Philemon as "brothers" in Christ (vv. 7, 20) and the request that Philemon "refresh" Paul's "heart" in the same way he "refreshes the hearts of the Lord's people" (once again vv. 7, 20). This culminating statement actually begins with the Greek word *nai*, "yes" or "indeed," pointing to the importance of this summation and affirmation of Paul's appeal. He implicitly looks forward to Philemon's acquiescence (seen in the NIV's translation, "I do wish").

Yet again Paul draws on his personal relationship with Philemon, asking that he (Paul) "may have some benefit from you in the Lord." On the basis of all the previous times Paul has benefitted from their friendship, he would appreciate one more favor—that Onesimus be forgiven and reinstated. All three parties will share in the "benefit": Philemon will have back his slave and new "brother," Onesimus will be reconciled both to God and to his earthly master, and Paul will hopefully receive back his new associate (perhaps as a free man) to once again help him in the ministry. Yet all of this will be possible only "in the Lord"—the One who alone can transform any difficult situation and cause all things to "work together for the good" (Rom 8:28). Neither Paul nor Philemon is the "Master" here; Christ is.

As Philemon regularly "refreshed the hearts of the Lord's people" (v. 7), Paul now asks his friend to refresh his heart by granting the request concerning Onesimus. This will be done "in Christ," stressing that Christ himself is behind the request. In verse 12 Paul calls Onesimus "my very heart," indicating that the refreshing for which Paul yearns will happen based on Philemon's willingness to "refresh" Onesimus, by reconciling and reinstating him both personally and spiritually.

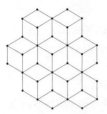

LETTER CLOSING
(21–25)

PAUL RESTATES HIS CONFIDENCE
AND TELLS HIS FUTURE PLAN (21–22)

Paul begins the letter closing with a statement of confidence related to Philemon's "obedience" to his request. The Greek verb for "being confident" carries the idea of being "completely persuaded"; Paul is saying that he is so confident in Philemon's goodness and love that he has no doubt about his friend's compliance. In light of the fact that Paul has spoken indirectly thus far, it is interesting that he now speaks of Philemon's "obedience." In verses 8–9 Paul clarifies that he is not giving an apostolic "order" but rather presenting an "appeal"; his emphasis is on Philemon voluntarily making the right decision. So why "obedience" in verse 21? Most likely the emphasis is not on obeying Paul but on obeying Christ, on whose behalf Paul is certainly speaking. In verses 3, 5, 16, and 20 Paul identifies Jesus as "Lord," and the decision regarding Onesimus centers on that lordship. Because he is confident Philemon will follow the will of God, Paul has no doubt about the outcome of his appeal.

In fact, Paul is assured that Philemon will "do even more than I ask." It is difficult to determine precisely what he means. There is the legal issue of Onesimus' slavery, the moral issue of the rift between master and slave, and the spiritual issue regarding Philemon and Onesimus having become brothers in Christ on the basis of Onesimus' conversion. At the very least

Paul's "more" involves the return of Onesimus to Paul to continue his ministry in Rome, though Paul also could have in mind the possibility that Philemon will free Onesimus from slavery. I believe both aspects are involved. Paul is certain that Philemon will go beyond his basic request to heal and forgive and thus follow the Lord's will by complying with Paul's greater hope.

Paul now turns to his plans to visit Philemon in the near future (v. 22). At first glance this seems unlikely in that Paul remains imprisoned in his rental house in Rome, facing a capital trial that could end with his being beheaded (the typical form of execution for Roman citizens; foreign peasants like those in Judea were crucified). Paul will explain below why he expects to return to Colossae, but he is convinced this trip will happen soon, and he will need a "guest room" in Philemon's home. Certainly part of this request is Paul's desire to see whether Philemon has indeed obeyed the Lord and received back Onesimus as a brother.

Paul "expect(s) to be restored to you in answer to your prayers." This is related to his belief during his imprisonment that God would indeed spare him to return to the churches in the provinces of Asia (including Colossae) and Macedonia (Phil 1:25-26). Paul is willing to die and even would prefer to "depart and be with Christ" (Phil 1:24), but he is certain that the churches still need him and that God will save him and send him to them. All the churches have been praying for Paul's release, so he is sure that it will take place. "Hope," in Paul's view, is not uncertain; it is (to borrow Peter's words in 1 Peter 1:3) "living hope"—an **eschatological** force that sees incredible results.

PAUL SENDS GREETINGS FROM COWORKERS (23-24)

Most of Paul's letters contain greetings from coworkers. The greetings in these verses of Philemon are similar to those in Colossians 4:10-15, which makes sense in light of the fact that the two letters were written and sent together. The same names are found except for the omission here of "Jesus who is called Justus" (Col 4:11). Another minor deviation is that in Colossians 4:10-14 Aristarchus is mentioned first and called "my fellow prisoner," while here in Philemon Epaphras takes the lead position. This too makes sense in that Epaphras initially brought the gospel to Colossae and was the congregation's most prominent leader (Col 1:7, 4:12). One purpose of the list here in Philemon, with Epaphras named first, may have been to exert added pressure on Philemon to do the right thing; all the leaders of Paul's team would have been awaiting his response. The use of "fellow prisoner" in Colossians 4:10 and Philemon 23, respectively, likely has a double meaning, first referring to the fact that both Aristarchus and Epaphras were assisting Paul while he was a prisoner in Rome. Second, the reference is to the spiritual reality that they, like Paul, have been taken captive by Christ to serve him.

The four men other than Epaphras who "greet" Philemon (Mark, Aristarchus, Demas, and Luke, v. 24) are also "coworkers" who served with Paul to spread the gospel in Rome and Asia. All were undoubtedly known well by Philemon, and all were watching anxiously to see whether Onesimus would be returned to Rome to take up his ministry in their midst. "Mark" is the same John Mark who had failed during the first missionary journey (Acts 13:13) but who, under the tutelage of his cousin Barnabas, overcame his shortcomings and later joined both Paul (2 Tim 4:11) and Peter (1 Pet 5:11) in ministry (in the process writing the earliest Gospel about the life of Jesus). Aristarchus, from Thessalonica, was arrested with Paul in Ephesus and accompanied him to Rome (Acts 19:29; 27:2). Demas, though a valued associate at this time, would later desert Paul and return home, because "he loved this present world" (2 Tim 4:10). Luke joined Paul's team at Troas and traveled with Paul as an associate (see the "we-passages" of Acts 16:10-17; 20:13-15; 21:1-18; 27:1-28:16), eventually writing his own Gospel of the life of Christ.

PAUL CONCLUDES WITH A BENEDICTION (25)

All of Paul's letters close with a benediction, and this one is word-for-word the same as that in Philippians 4:23. "Grace" frames this letter (vv. 3, 25), along with the theme of divine mercy—a mercy Paul wants to see extended to Onesimus—and "Lord Jesus Christ" continues the letter's emphasis on the lordship of Christ (see on v. 21). Christ is in absolute control, and in every area, on the basis of the "grace" he gives, God's people must allow him to guide their actions. The plural form of "your" shows that Paul includes Philemon's family and house-church in his benediction. "Spirit" here designates not the Holy Spirit but the human spirit. Paul wants Philemon and his family and church to experience Christ's grace to the depths of their beings.

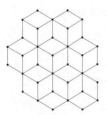

GLOSSARY

amanuensis: A scribe or secretary hired to write letters in the ancient world.

chiasm: A stylistic device used throughout Scripture that presents two sets of ideas in parallel to each other, with the order reversed in the second pair. Chiasms generally are used to emphasize the element or elements in the middle of the pattern.

christological (adj.), Christology (n.): Refers to the New Testament's presentation of the person and work of Christ, especially his identity as Messiah.

docetic (adj.), Docetism (n.): Refers to the heretical view that Jesus only *appeared* to take on a physical body and therefore did not actually die on the cross.

ecclesiological (adj.), ecclesiology (n.): Refers to the church (Greek: *ekklēsia*), especially in a theological sense.

eschatological (adj.), eschatology (n.): Refers to the last things or the end times. Within this broad category, biblical scholars and theologians have identified more specific concepts. For instance, "realized eschatology" emphasizes the present work of Christ in the world as he prepares for the end of history. In "inaugurated eschatology," the last days have already begun but have not yet been consummated at the return of Christ.

eschaton: Greek for "end" or "last," referring to the return of Christ and the end of history.

gnosis (n.), gnostic (adj.), Gnosticism (n.): Refers to special knowledge (Greek: *gnōsis*) as the basis of salvation. As a result of this heretical teaching, which developed in several forms in the early centuries AD, many gnostics held a negative view of the physical world.

Hellenistic: Relating to the spread of Greek culture after Alexander the Great (356–323 BC).

lex talionis: Latin for "law of retaliation." This is the principle that those who have done some wrong will be punished in a similar degree and kind.

parousia: The event of Christ's second coming. The Greek word *parousia* means "arrival" or "presence."

pseudonymous: Refers to a text written under a false name. In the ancient world, it was acceptable for an unknown writer to credit a famous person as the author in order to attract attention and reach a wide audience. In scholarship, pseudonymous texts are treated differently from forgeries, which reflect an intention to deceive readers.

Septuagint: An ancient Greek translation of the Old Testament that was used extensively in the early church.

Shekinah: A word derived from the Hebrew *shakan* ("to dwell"), used to describe God's personal presence taking the form of a cloud, often in the context of the tabernacle or temple (e.g., Exod 40:38; Num 9:15; 1 Kgs 8:10–11).

soteriological (adj.), soteriology (n.): Refers to the doctrine of salvation (Greek: *sōtēria*).

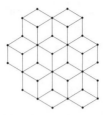

BIBLIOGRAPHY

Barclay, John M. G. *Colossians and Philemon.* Sheffield: Sheffield Academic, 1997.

Barth, Markus and Helmut Blanke. *Colossians: Translation with Introduction and Commentary.* Anchor Bible. New York: Doubleday, 1994.

Bruce, F. F. *The Epistles to the Colossians, to Philemon,and to the Ephesians.* New International Commentary on the New Testament. Grand Rapids: Eerdmans, 1984.

Dunn, James D. G. *The Epistles to the Colossians and to Philemon.* New International Greek Testament Commentary. Grand Rapids: Eerdmans, 1996.

Garland, David E. *Colossians and Philemon.* NIV Application Commentary. Grand Rapids: Zondervan, 1998.

Harris, Murray J. *Colossians and Philemon.* Exegetical Guide to the Greek New Testament. Grand Rapids: Eerdmans, 1991.

Hughes, R. Kent. *Colossians and Philemon: The Supremacy of Christ.* Preaching the Word. Wheaton, IL: Crossway, 1989.

Lightfoot, J. B. *St. Paul's Epistles to the Colossians and to Philemon.* London: Macmillan, 1897.

Lohse, Eduard. *Colossians and Philemon.* Hermeneia. Philadelphia: Fortress, 1971.

Martin, Ralph P. *Colossians and Philemon.* New Century Bible. London: Oliphants, 1974.

Moo, Douglas J. *The Letters to Colossians and Philemon.* Pillar New Testament Commentary. Grand Rapids: Eerdmans, 2008.

O'Brien, Peter. *Colossians, Philemon.* Word Biblical Commentary. Waco, TX: Word, 1982.

Schweitzer, Eduard. *The Letter to Colossians: A Commentary.* Minneapolis: Augsburg, 1982.

Thompson, Marianne Meye. *Colossians and Philemon.* Two Horizons New Testament Commentary. Grand Rapids: Eerdmans, 2005.

Witherington, Ben III. *The Letters to Philemon, the Colossians, and the Ephesians.* Grand Rapids: Eerdmans, 2007.

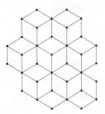

SUBJECT AND AUTHOR INDEX

A

abuse
   of children, 121
   of workers, 127
achrēston, 169
action, in Christ's name, 114–15
Adam, 35, 87, 101–02
adikeō, 125–26
adoption, of Onesimus, 156
afflictions, messianic, 52–53
affluence, and sin, 97
agōnizō, 59–61
alienation, from God, 47
allness, of Christ, 103–04
"all things," 41–43
already, vs. not yet, 14–15, 91
amanuensis, 143–44, 158
ambassador, Paul as, 167
anēkon, 117, 166
angels, 38–39, 45
   worship of, 7–8, 14, 82, 87
anthropology, 101
Antiochus III, 6–7
apekduō, 77
apokalypsis, 55

apostle, Paul as, 17, 157, 166
appeal, to Philemon, 167–68, 179
Apphia, 155–56, 159
archangels, 38
archē, 42
Archippus, 143, 149–50, 159
Aristarchus, 138–39, 181
arrogance, of the false
   teachers, 83
asceticism, 7–8, 79–88
Asia, 131, 144, 180
assurance, full, 62, 140
author
   of Colossians, 3–5, 16–18, 32
   of Philemon, 147–48, 177
authority
   of the husband, 118
   of masters, 123–24
   of Paul, 166–67, 171

B

baptism, and circumcision, 72–74
barbarians, 103
Barnabas, and Mark, 138–39, 181
believers, 28–29
   as body members, 41

and Christ, 73–76, 109–12
and reconciliation, 46–51
and the world, 84–86
benediction, 144, 155, 182
benefit, from Philemon, 178
blasphēmia, 100
blood of Christ, and
    reconciliation, 44–45, 48
body, the, 87–88, 92, 95–96
body of Christ
    the church as, 13–14, 18, 40–41,
        62, 81–84, 89
    and his death, 48, 73
    and the incarnation, 43, 71
    love for, 117, 162
    unity in, 103, 109–11
    See also head, Christ as
boldness, of Paul, 166
bowels, 106, 164
brother
    Onesimus as, 137, 152–54, 168,
        173–75, 178–80
    Philemon as, 171, 178–79
    Timothy as, 158–59
    Tychicus as, 136
building, believers as, 49–50
burial, with Christ, 73–75, 90, 95

C

Caesarea, Paul's imprisonment
    in, 4, 148
calendar observances, 79–81
cancellation, of debts, 76–77, 177
canon, New Testament, 143, 147
chains. *See* imprisonment of Paul
charis, 134, 160
charizomenoi, 108
cherubim, 38
chesed, 98

chiasm, 33–34, 38, 161–63
children, and parents, 119–21
Christ, 32–46, 70–75
    and believers, 90–95, 109–12
    as beloved Son, 29–30, 43–44
    brotherhood in, 172–74
    as the foundation, 50
    and the household, 117,
        120, 123–27
    as Lord, 66–67, 178
    redemption by, 28–31
    sufferings of, 52–54
    See also death of Christ; head:
        Christ as; "in Christ";
        lordship of Christ;
        mystery, of Christ; union
        with Christ
"Christ in you," 56–57
Christlikeness, 35, 59, 100–02,
    108, 117
Christology
    and the Colossian heresy, 8, 81
    in Colossians, 3, 12–13, 32–46
    in Philemon, 154–56
    and truth, 112–13
christos, 169
church, the, 67
    Christ's headship over, 40–41
    Colossian, 18–19
    in Colossians, 13–14
    Laodicean, 140–43
    in the Lycus Valley, 150
    as the new community, 103–09
    and Paul, 51–54, 60–61
    in Philemon, 155–56
    prayer in, 130, 180
    proclamation ministry of,
        57, 132–35
    and reconciliation, 46–51

and slavery, 122, 137, 152
See also body of Christ: the
    church as; head: Christ as
circumcision, 72–73
circumstances
    of Colossians, 5–7
    of Philemon, 149–52, 168, 175–76
citizenship, in heaven, 19, 30, 85,
    91, 117, 127
clothing, imagery of, 99–101,
    105–09
codes, social, 116
coercion, 171–72
Colossae, 6–7, 17, 60–61, 131
    and Epaphras, 140–41
    Paul in, 151, 180
    Philemon in, 147–48, 152, 158
Colossians (letter)
    introduction to, 3–15
    and Philemon, 148
commission, of Paul, 54–57
complementarianism, 118
compromise, with heresy, 84
conditional clauses, 49, 90, 175–76
conversion, of Onesimus, 151–55,
    167–68, 172, 179
covetousness, 97
coworker, Philemon as, 148, 159,
    171, 175
coworkers, of Paul, 138–41, 180–81
creation, 50
    and Christ, 32–43
    reconciliation of, 45–46
Creator, Christ as, 36

D
darkness, vs. light, 28–29, 47, 95
date
    of Colossians, 5

of Philemon, 147–48
David, 30, 36
death, and sin, 95–96
death of Christ
    and believers, 93
    and circumcision, 73
    and forgiveness, 75–77
    and reconciliation, 44–49
    and sin, 95, 98
    as victory, 77–78
debt
    of Onesimus, 175–77
    of Philemon, 177
    sin as, 76–77
deception, by the false teachers,
    64, 70
defilement, 85–86
deity, of Christ, 12–13, 35, 43–44,
    70–71
Demas, 141, 181
demons, in the Colossian heresy,
    8, 14
desires, evil, 97
diakoneō, 171
diakonos, 22–23, 54, 136
dietary restrictions, 79–81, 85–86
discipline, of children, 120–21
diversity, and unity, 104
doctor, Luke as, 141
doctrine, true, 66–68
dominion, of darkness, 29
door, open, 131
douleuete, 125
duties, of slaves, 125–26
"dwelling," of God, 13, 26, 35,
    43–44, 56, 69–71

E
earth, vs. heaven, 38, 45, 90–93

earthquake, and Colossae, 6
egalitarianism, 118
ei, 90, 175
eirēnē, 160
elect, the, 105
employers, and employees,
   123, 126–28
encouragement, 61, 137, 163–64
endurance, 27
enemies, of God, 47
energeia, 60, 74
Epaphras, 7, 20, 131, 136, 148, 181
   ministry of, 22–23, 139–41
   proclamation by, 50–51
Epaphroditus, 22, 150, 159, 170
Ephesians, and Colossians, 3–6,
   142, 148
Ephesus
   Aristarchus in, 138, 181
   and heresy, 5–6
   Paul in, 4, 148
   Philemon in, 159
   Tychicus in, 135–36
epi, 108–09
epiginōskō, vs. *ginōskō*, 22
erethizete, 120
eschatology
   final, 14–15, 134
   inaugurated, 4, 15, 30, 45
   realized, 3–4, 14–15, 20
euchrēstos, 169
exaltation, of Christ, 78, 92

F
fairness, of masters, 127–28
faith
   of the Colossians, 19, 65–68, 140
   of Philemon, 161–62
   steadfastness in, 49–51

family, the church as, 155–60, 173
fathers, and children, 120–21
feasts, Jewish, 80
firmness, of the Colossians, 65
firstborn, Christ as, 36–37, 40
flesh, the, 83, 89, 92
   and asceticism, 86–88
food, restrictions concerning,
   79–81, 85–86
forgiveness of sin, 30–31, 75–77, 98
   in the new community, 107–08
foundation, Christ as, 50
fruit
   of believers, 25
   of the gospel, 21
   of the Word, 131
fulfillment, of Paul's
   commission, 54–55
fullness
   of Christ, 59
   of God, 43–44, 70–72

G
generosity, of Philemon, 162–63
Gentiles
   in the church, 28
   vs. Jews, 72, 102–03
   mission to, 55–56
gentleness, 106–07
ginōskō, vs. *epiginōskō*, 22
glory
   future, 94–95
   of God, 26–27, 56–57
gluttony, 87
gnosis, 12, 24
Gnosticism, and the Colossian
   heresy, 8
goal, Christ as, 39–40

God
    and Christ, 34–36, 43–44
    as deserving thanks, 18–19
    as Father, 155, 160
    and knowledge, 23–26
    and Onesimus, 172
    reconciliation with, 44–45
    as the true Judge, 125–26
    as victor, 77
    wrath of, 97–99
goodness, of God, 163
gospel, 20–22
    faith in, 67–68
    partnership in, 162–63
    proclamation of, 50–54, 57,
        131–35, 139, 171
grace
    knowledge of, 21–22
    in Paul's closing, 144, 155, 182
    and peace, 18, 160
    and witness, 134–35
greed, 97
greetings
    of Colossians, 16–18, 138–43
    of Philemon, 157–60, 180–81

H

hand, right, 91–92
hands, human, 72–73
harmony, 109–11, 117
head
    Christ as, 40–41, 54, 71, 81–84
    the husband as, 118
heart, the
    circumcision of, 72–73
    gratitude in, 114
    of Paul, 170, 178
    setting of, 90
heaven, 20, 90–92, 127

vs. earth, 38, 45
Hellenism, and households,
    116–17, 120
heresy, Colossian, 6–8, 14, 24, 38,
    48, 52, 65–70, 79–88
    and Paul's letter, 142–43
hiddenness, 93–94
Hierapolis
    and Colossae, 6, 17, 60–61, 158
    and Epaphras, 140–41
holiness, of God's people, 48–49,
    105
hope, 180
    of the Colossians, 19–20, 50
    of glory, 56–57, 94–95
house-church, 142, 158–60
household, the church as, 155,
    158–60
households, and Christ, 115–28
humanity
    and the image of God, 35
    new, 14, 101–04
    redemption of, 40–42
humility, 106
    false, 82, 87
husbands, and wives, 116–19
hymn, christological, 32–46
hypotassomai, 116

I

idolatry, 82, 86, 97
image of God, 102
    Christ as, 33–36
imprisonment of Paul, 4–5, 64
    and his freedom, 131, 144, 180
    and his ministry, 131–32, 157, 167
    and others, 137–38, 168, 181
    as suffering, 52, 61
impurity, 96–97

incarnation, the, 35, 43–44, 71
"in Christ," 13, 17–19, 37, 74, 81,
    94, 163
individualism, and the body of
    Christ, 41
individuals, and peace, 110–11
inheritance, 28, 56, 91
    and slaves, 124–25
insistence, of the false
    teachers, 81–82
invisibility, of God, 34–35
invisible, vs. visible, 38
isotēs, 127
Israel, and the church, 28

J
Jesus. *See* Christ
Jesus Justus, 139, 180–81
Jews
    in Colossae, 6–7
    vs. Gentiles, 28, 72, 102–03
    among Paul's coworkers, 139
Josephus, 116
joy, 27–28, 82
Judaism, 38, 55
    and the Colossian heresy, 79–82
    and households, 116–17, 120
    and the messianic
        afflictions, 52–53
judge, Christ as, 125–27
judgment, 97–98, 126

K
kindness, 106
kingdom, of the Son, 28–30
knowledge
    and Christ, 12–13, 102, 112–13, 163
    and the Colossian heresy, 8
    of God, 25–26
    and the gospel, 21–22

Paul's prayer for, 23–25
    as riches, 62–64, 112
Knox, John, on Philemon, 149–50
koinōnia, 153, 162–63
koinōnos, 175
ktisis, 50
kyrios, 123–27, 174
kyriotēs, 39

L
labor
    of Epaphras, 140–41
    of Paul, 59–60
language, indirect, 149–51
Laodicea
    and Colossae, 6, 17, 60–61,
        141–42, 158
    Epaphras in, 140–41
    Philemon in, 150
law, and slaves, 149, 169–71, 177
legalism. *See* asceticism
letter, to Laodicea, 61, 136, 142
letters, 16, 135, 144, 157
    of Paul, 142–43
lex talionis, 126
life
    in Christ, 74–76
    eternal, 172–73, 177
    future, 94–95
    new, 90–92, 100–04
light, vs. darkness, 28–29, 47, 95
logos, 112, 131, 134
lordship of Christ, 41–43, 66–67,
        136, 154–55, 160, 178, 182
    in the church, 13–14, 104, 114–15
    and the household, 116–17, 120,
        123–25, 127, 171, 174
Lord's Prayer, 76, 108, 114, 130

love
  of the Colossians, 19, 23
  of God, 105
  of the husband, 116-18
  of Philemon, 161-67, 170, 173
  and unity, 61-62, 108-09
Luke, 141, 181
lust, 97
Lycus Valley, 6-7, 17, 60-61,
  140-41, 151, 158
lying, 100-01

M

makrothymian, 107
manumission, 122-24
  of Onesimus, 152, 171-74
Mark, 138-39, 181
marriage, 116-19
Master. *See* lordship of Christ
masters, and slaves, 121-28, 137
maturity, spiritual, 58-59, 140
mediator
  Christ as, 115
  Paul as, 150-52
mercy, of God, 106, 182
messengers, of Colossians, 135-37
Messiah, 66
  afflictions of, 52-53
  and gentleness, 106-07
Michael, 38
midrash, and the christological
  hymn, 35
mind, the, setting of, 92
minister
  Epaphras as, 22-23
  Onesimus as, 171
  Paul as, 54
  Tychicus as, 136

ministry
  of Archippus, 143
  of Onesimus, 152-55, 174
  of Paul, 50-65, 131-32, 139, 170-71
  of Philemon, 163-64, 167
mission
  of the church, 14, 19-21,
    111, 130-35
  to the Gentiles, 55-56, 166
money, of Paul, 177
mystērion, 55
mystery, of Christ, 13, 51-56,
  62-63, 66, 93-94, 131-32

N

name, of the Lord, 114-15
names, Jewish vs. Roman, 139
Nicene Creed, 35, 43
not yet, vs. already, 14-15, 91
Nympha, and a house-church, 142

O

obedience
  of children, 119-21
  of Philemon, 179
  of slaves, 122-23
obscenity, 100
Onesimus, 121, 137, 143, 147-82
  passim
orgē, 98-100
outsiders, and the church, 132-35

P

pagans, Colossians' past as, 99
parakalō, 167
parents, and children, 119-21
partnership, in the gospel,
  162-65, 175
patience, 27, 107
Paul, 144
  as an apostle, 17, 157-58, 166

as Colossians' author, 3–5,
16–18, 32
and heresy, 5–6
as knowing God, 25–26
and Mark, 138–39
ministry of, 21, 50–65, 131–32,
139, 170–71
and Onesimus and Philemon,
149–82 passim
as Philemon's author, 147–48, 177
See also imprisonment of Paul
Pax Romana, 46, 110
peace
Christ's, 109–12
and grace, 18, 160
and reconciliation, 45–46
and rest, 164
people, chosen, 105
perseverance, 49
in prayer, 130
Peter, and Mark, 138–39, 181
Philemon (believer), 137, 143,
147–82 passim
Philemon (letter)
and Colossians, 3–5, 121–22, 142
introduction to, 147–56
and Tychicus, 136
Philippians, and Colossians, 3–5
Philo, 116
philosophy, and the Colossian
heresy, 69–70
Plato, and shadows, 80–81
pleasure of God, 24–25
and the incarnation, 43–44
porneia, 96
power
of God, 26–27, 60, 74–75
of the gospel, 21

powers, cosmic/demonic, 7–8,
13–14, 38–39, 82–84
Christ's victory over, 46, 75–78
and the Colossian heresy, 69–72
praütēta, 106
prayer, 115, 129–35, 144
of Epaphras, 140
of Paul, 18–19, 23–31, 161–64
of Philemon, 180
pre-existence, of Christ, 40–42
presbytēs, 167
prisoner
Epaphras as, 22
Paul as. See imprisonment
of Paul
Prison Letters, 3–5, 147–48
proclamation, of the gospel,
50–60, 131–35, 171
propriety, 117, 166
prosōpolēmpsia, 126
purpose
of God, 172
of Philemon, 152–53

R
racism, 103–04
reconciliation
by Christ, 44–48, 110–11
between Onesimus and
Philemon, 150–52,
156, 169–71
redemption, 28–31, 40–45, 133
refreshment, by Philemon, 178
regulations, 76, 85–88
reign, of Christ's peace, 110–11
relationship
with God, 44–45
between Philemon and
Onesimus, 172–74

between Philemon and Paul,
166–67, 178
relationships, in the church,
110–11, 115–16, 156
remembrance, 161
report
of Epaphras, 18–23
about Philemon, 161
rest, 164
resurrection, of Christ, 42,
74–77, 90
revelation, of the mystery, 55,
94–95, 132
reverence, of slaves, 123–24
reward, of slaves, 124–25
riches
of the mystery, 55–57, 63
of the Trinity, 112
of understanding, 62–64,
112, 140
rituals, 79–81
Roman Empire, the gospel in, 21
Rome
Onesimus in, 149–52, 168–74
Paul's imprisonment in, 4, 148
triumph of, 78
rule, of Christ. *See* lordship
of Christ

S

Sabbaths, 80
sacrifice, Christ's death as,
48–49, 58
saints, believers as, 17–19
salt, and witness, 134–35
salvation, 28, 73–76, 85, 156
sarkos, 83
Satan
and darkness, 29

defeat of, 46, 72, 78, 84
Scripture, 57–58
self, old vs. new, 96, 101, 104
seraphim, 38
servanthood, of Paul, 54
servant-leaders, 166
service, to Christ, 125
sexual sin, 85–87, 96–97
shadow, of things to come, 80–81
shakan, 70
shalōm, 18, 160
Shekinah, 26, 56, 70–71, 95
signature, of Paul, 143–44, 177
sin, 95–104
sincerity, of slaves, 123–24
sister, Apphia as, 155–56
slander, 100
slave
Epaphras as, 140
Paul as, 158
Tychicus as, 136
See also Onesimus
slavery, 103, 121–28, 137, 147–82
passim
to heresy, 68
to sin, 30–31, 76–78, 93
soldier, Archippus as, 143, 159
sōma, 81
Son, beloved, 29–30, 43–44
son, Onesimus as, 167–68
songs, 113
sovereignty, of Christ. *See*
lordship of Christ
speech
gracious, 134–35
sinful, 99–100
spirit
human, 182
present in, 64–65

Spirit, Holy, 23–24, 92
spirits, elemental, 69–70,
     80–81, 84. *See also*
     powers, cosmic/demonic
splanchna, 106, 164
stereōma, 65
stoicheia, 69–70
Stoicism, and creation, 37
storehouse, Christ as, 63–64
"stripping off," 77–78, 99
structure
   of Colossians, 8–12, 33–34
   of Philemon, 153–54
struggle, of Paul, 59–61
submission, principle of, 115–19
suffering
   of Paul vs. Christ, 52–54
   thanksgiving in, 27–28
supremacy of Christ, 36–43
sustaining, by Christ, 39–40
syncretism, 82
synergos, 159

T
tapeinophrosynē, 106
taxis, 65
teachers, false, 64–65, 70, 81–82
teaching
   of the church, 112–13
   ministry of, 57–58
tekna, 119
temple, the church as, 67
Tertius, 144
thanksgiving, 27–28, 68, 111–15,
     130–31, 134
   of Paul, 18–23, 161–62
thelēma, 55
theology
   of Colossians, 12–15

of Philemon, 154–56
"things above," 90–91
thrones, 39
thymos, 98–100
time, redemption of, 133
Timothy, 6, 131, 136–38, 144, 155
   as co-author, 17, 158–59
toga picta, 78
tongue, the, sins of, 99–100
Torah, 76
touch, 85
tradition, human, 69, 86
treasures, of wisdom and
     knowledge, 63–64
trespasses, 75
Trinity, 43–45, 93, 100–01, 111–12
truth
   Christ's, 112–14
   and the gospel, 20–22
   vs. lying, 100–01
Tychicus, 121, 135–37, 148

U
uncircumcision, 75
understanding, 140. *See
   also* knowledge
union with Christ, 13, 18, 37,
     73–76, 90
   and new life, 93–95, 100–04
unity, 61–62, 102–04, 107–11
"useful," Onesimus as, 156,
     168–69, 174

V
vice lists, 96–100
victory, of Christ, 13–14, 77–78, 84
vigilance, in prayer, 130
vindication, 126–27
virtues, 105–09
visible, vs. invisible, 38

visions, misuse of, 81–84

W

walking, 133
  worthily, 24–28
war, spiritual, 29
weakness, of Paul, 167
welcome, of Onesimus, 175
will, of God, 23–24, 55, 163
wisdom, 23–24
  and asceticism, 86–87
  and Christ, 33, 36–38
  and teaching, 58, 113
  in witness, 132–35
witness, 132–35
wives, 116–19, 159
woes, messianic, 52–53
women, 156
Word
  of Christ, 112–13
  of God, 58–59, 131
work, 124–25
works, good, 25
world, the
  and believers, 84–86, 93
  and Demas, 141
  and the gospel, 21, 50
worship
  of angels, 7–8, 14, 82, 87
  and Christ's truth, 104, 113–14
  true vs. false, 80–81, 85–87
wrath, against sin, 97–99
wrongs, 125–27
  of Onesimus, 149–50, 169,
        172, 176

Y

Yahweh, 114

Z

zēteite, 90

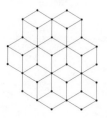

INDEX OF SCRIPTURE AND OTHER ANCIENT LITERATURE

Old Testament

Genesis
1-2.....................33, 39
1.........................33, 38
1:1.......................38, 42
1:22.......................21
1:26-27.............35, 102
1:28.......................21
3:16.......................118
5:22.......................107
13:14-17.................28
17:10-14.................72

Exodus
4:22.......................36
4:25.......................72
6:6.........................29
14:30.....................29
20:4.......................35
20:12.....................119
21:15.....................119
21:17.....................119
23:20-22.................8

31:3.........................24
33:18-23.................34
35:31.......................24

Leviticus
4:3.........................49
4:23.......................49
10:12.......................48
12:3.........................72
15:30-31.................97

Numbers
6:3-4.......................79
10:10.......................80
18:8-9.......................48
19:13.......................97
29:2.........................49
29:13.......................49

Deuteronomy
5:21.........................97
7:6.........................105
7:8.........................29

10:16.......................72
14:2.........................105
21:5.........................48
23:15-16.................169
26:18-19.................105
30:6.........................72
32:9.........................28
33:2.........................8
34:9.........................24

Joshua
19:9.........................28

1 Samuel
6:18.........................114
20:5.........................80
20:18.......................80

2 Samuel
7:11-16.................30
22:11.......................38

1 Kings
22:19.......................39

2 Kings
2:19–23 134

1 Chronicles
16:34....................106
21:19 114
23:31 80

Ezra
13:16–19 53

Psalms
2:7 36
18:10 38
23:4 68
25:7......................106
27:5–6 93
29:11 110
68:10 106
68:16 71
68:17..................... 8
87:1–2 71
89:27 36
102:25..................50
104:24...................39
105:6..................... 105
106:5..................... 105
106:20 35

110:1 91
115:3–8 35
118:26 114

Proverbs
2:2–3.....................63
3:19.......................39
8:22 36–37

Isaiah
6:2.......................38
6:6.......................38
9:6–7 110
11:2 24
29:13.................... 86
31:7........................73
40:30....................26
40:31.................26, 60
43:1......................30
43:20 105
45:4 105
46:6 73
48:20 30
49:2 93
51:11 .... 30, 50
52:7......................110
52:9 30

54:13 110
66:23 80

Jeremiah
4:4........................72
31:9......................36
31:31–34 115

Ezekiel
10:1–3 38
10:6–9 38
42:13 48
46:1 80

Daniel
2:8......................133
2:18–47 55
4:1 16
5:23......................73
7:9–10....................39
7:13......................48
10:13 38
10:21 38
12:1 53
12:4 53

Zechariah
9:9.......................106

New Testament

Matthew
5:13 134
6:9........................114
6:10 130
6:12.................76, 108
6:15.......................108
6:24–34 97
11:29 106
12:31 100
13:52 64

14:14 106
18:19–20 130
21:5.......................106
28:19......................115

Mark
1:11.................... 30, 43
2:21–22 80
3:15 .... 46, 72, 84
3:20 53
3:27 ....14, 68–70, 77–78

4:8...........................25
6:7.............. 46, 72, 84
7:3 69
12:36......................92
13:8.......................53
14:64.....................100

Luke
1:78.......................106
12:15.......................97
20:42 113

20:44 113
22:31 84
23:34 105
23:35 105
23:46 77-78

John

1:3 37
1:3-4 21
1:14 ....35, 71, 94
1:18 .... 34-35, 94
1:34 105
3:16 ....94, 98
3:18 94
3:19 47
4:24 34
10:33 100
12:36 28
14:6 .... 94, 100
14:17 112
14:27 110
15:4 21
15:8 21
16:33 ....53, 110
17:21-23 111
19:19 77
19:30 77-78

Acts

1:14 130
1:20 113
1:23 139
2:34-35 92
2:42 130
3 114
3:6 114
3:26 114
4:31 130
6:4 130
7:58 16

8:23 118
9:1 16
9:15-16 54
12:12 138-41
12:25 138-41
13:7-12 69
13:13 .... 138-41, 181
14:22 53
14:27 131
15:38-39 138-41
16:1-3 17
16:10-17 ....141, 181
16:14-15 142
16:15 142
16:19-34 4
17:19-34 69
18:7 139
19 159
19:9-10 59
19:10 .... 7, 148
19:20 22
19:29 .... 138-41, 181
19:32-41 148
19:35-41 4
20:4 ....5, 136, 138-41
20:13-15 ....141, 181
20:29 5
20:30 5
21:1-18 ....141, 181
23:23-26:32 4
24:27 148
25:21 169
26:17 132
26:17-18 54
27:1-28:16 ....141, 181
27:2 .... 138-41, 181
28:11-31 4
28:16 138-41
28:16-20 52

28:23 ....138-41, 148,
           168, 177
28:30 .... 148, 168

Romans

1:3-4 ....3, 33
1:7 105
1:12-14 28-31
1:18 97
1:20 50
1:21 47
1:22 58
1:23 35
1:29 97
1:29-32 96
2:4 106-07
2:8 98
3:21-26 44
5:8 ....44, 105
5:9 98
5:10-11 44
5:12 101
5:12-21 35
6-7 101
6 ....29-30, 68-70, 74
6:3-5 73
6:5 30
6:6 .... 96, 101
6:11 31
6:14 30
7:6 96
7:22 101
8 92
8:8 25
8:11 112
8:14-17 44
8:15 156
8:17 ....53, 76
8:18-22 ....40, 45, 50

8:26..........................28
8:28......... 27, 35–36, 178
8:34.................. 3, 92
8:38..........................3
10:4.......................... 81
10:9.....................19, 66
10:9–20.....................3
11:13.......................52
11:33..........................63
11:36 37
12 89–128
12:1............ 48, 58, 120
12:1–2.......................25
12:2..... 92, 102, 140, 163
12:4–8................41, 83
12:5....................41, 111
12:14–18.................133
13:12 ....47, 99
13:14 99
14 85
14:1–15:13 80
14:2–4...................... 80
14:5–6 80
14:10 ....124, 126
15:5.........................92
15:19 .... 21, 55
15:20..................21, 51
15:24 144
15:28 144
15:30–32........... 131, 144
15:33 110
16 .... 121, 138–41
16:3..........................159
16:5..................... 142
16:7.........................159
16:20 110
16:21 17
16:22.................... 144
16:23.................... 142

1 Corinthians
1:4 18
1:8 49
1:24...................... 103
2:6........................ 55
2:7........................ 55
3:10–15.....................50
3:11 50
3:16..........................67
4:6 83
4:17....................17, 168
4:18 83
4:19 83
5:3 64
5:9–11......................96
6:9–10 97
6:18 96
7:1..............................85
7:11 44
7:29 134
7:32 25
8:6.........................3, 37
8:9....................68–70
9:1 166
9:3–6 108
9:12.........................108
10:12 68–70
10:31 114
10:32...................... 103
12:3......................... 66
12:8..........................63
12:12–27 ....41, 111
12:12–29..................83
13:13.................. 19, 109
14:15........................ 113
14:26....................... 113
14:33 110
15:3–5.................... 66
15:24 39

15:28 104
15:32.........................4
15:45–49.................. 35
16:9 131
16:13 130
16:19 142
16:21 143
16:22.................... 130

2 Corinthians
1:11........................... 18
2:12.......................... 131
2:14–16..............77–78
3–5.......................... 51
4:4.....................29, 35
4:5 140
4:15........................114
4:16..................101–02
5:10........................ 126
5:17.........................101
5:18–20 44
6:16 ....67, 112
7:4 164
7:7 164
7:13 164
9:7..........................171
11:21–29 52
12:7................. 141, 144
12:20........................83
13:11 110

Galatians
2:8...........................52
3:13...........................133
3:28 ....103, 118
4:3 70
4:19 .... 53, 168
4:26 91
5 89–128
5:5–6...................... 19

5:6 162
5:15 68–70
5:19 96–97
5:19–20 100
5:19–23 96
5:22–23 25
6:11 ....143–44, 177
6:16 110

Ephesians

1 74
1:1 166
1:3 ....91, 127
1:7–8 ....56, 112
1:15 162
1:18 56
1:19–20 74
1:20 91–92
1:20–21 77–78
1:21 .... 39, 70
1:23 104
2:1–3 75
2:6–7 ....91, 127
2:7 106
2:11–12 75
2:12 47
2:14 102
2:16 ....44, 111
2:20 50
3:1 157
3:2 54
3:10 .... 39, 70, 91
3:16 101
4 89–128
4:2 107
4:2–5 19
4:3 109–10
4:4 111
4:12–15 59

4:13 ....49, 59, 102
4:14 6
4:14–16 83
4:15–16 41
4:16 .... 62, 111
4:18 47
4:22 99
4:22–24 101
4:24 99
4:31 118
5:3 97
5:5 .... 29, 97
5:6 99
5:10 120
5:11 47
5:16 133
5:18 .... 92, 112
5:19 113–14
5:20 18
5:21 115
5:22–6:9 116
5:23 118
5:24 116
5:25 117
6:2 119
6:4 119
6:5–9 121
6:6 140
6:9 103
6:10–12 70
6:10–17 29
6:10–18 68–70
6:11 70
6:12 ....29, 39, 91
6:18–20 144
6:19 131
6:20 167
6:22 136

Philippians

1:3 18
1:5 163
1:8 106
1:12–14 132
1:12–26 148
1:19 131
1:21 94
1:21–23 52
1:23–26 5
1:24 180
1:25–26 180
2:3 ....23, 106
2:5 ....92, 102
2:6–11 ....3, 33, 113
2:7 123
2:7–8 77–78
2:8 106
2:9–10 77–78
2:10 46
2:11 66
2:19–24 17
2:24 5
2:25 .... 22, 159, 170
2:25–30 150
2:30 170
3:10 ...... 25, 53, 102, 132
3:14 91
3:20 ....19, 30, 95, 127
3:20–21 85
4:2–3 ....107, 156
4:7 110
4:9 110
4:13 121
4:18 ....22, 120
4:23 182

Colossians

1–2 21

1 67

1:1 .... 3, 55, 66, 110,
          131, 136, 157, 166

1:1–2 16–18

1:1–14 16–32

1:2 66

1:3 .....12, 23, 27, 68, 109,
          111, 114–15, 130

1:3–5 18–20

1:3–6 65

1:3–8 18–23

1:3–14 16

1:3–2:5 129

1:4 .... 19, 23, 25, 162

1:6 .... 21, 25

1:5 .... 15, 19, 22, 50–51,
          69, 94

1:5–6 20–22

1:5–7 148

1:6 .... 23, 54, 131

1:7 ..... 19, 50–52, 68, 131,
          136, 140, 181

1:7–8 .... 7, 18, 20, 57, 139

1:8 .... 24, 65

1:9 .... 28, 53, 58, 62,
          67, 113, 133, 163

1:9–10 23–25

1:9–11 65

1:9–12 137

1:10 .... 12, 24, 62, 67,
          69, 109, 133

1:10–12 .....25–28, 66–67

1:11 .... 26–27, 107

1:12 .... 27–29, 68,
          111, 115, 130

1:12–13 28

1:12–14 131

1:13 .... 28–30, 70, 95

1:13–14 66

1:14 ..... 23–31, 29–30, 95

1:15 .... 33–37, 40, 42,
          44, 102

1:15–16 ....23, 33–34

1:15–17 ..... 34–40, 39, 66

1:15–18 34

1:15–20 .... 3, 12, 29,
          32–46, 50–51,
          66, 81, 109, 113

1:15–23 32–51

1:15–2:23 32–88

1:16 ....14, 36–40, 45, 70,
          72, 74, 93

1:16–17 63

1:17 ....33, 39–40, 42,
          45, 74

1:17–18 34

1:18 .... 13, 33, 40–43,
          53–54, 71, 83, 111

1:18–20 33–34,
          40–46, 66

1:19 .... 13, 23, 43–44, 63,
          69–70, 74

1:20 .... 4, 13, 28, 39,
          44–46, 48, 95, 110

1:20–23 5

1:21 .... 7, 13, 47

1:21–23 ....32, 46–51

1:22 ....4, 13, 15, 28,
          48–49, 58, 65,
          89–128

1:22–23 65

1:23 .... 49–51, 54, 62, 67,
          136, 140

1:24 ....13, 52–54, 59,
          89–128, 132

1:24–25 ....23, 52–54

1:24–29 52–65

1:24–2:5 51–66

1:25 .... 54, 62, 65, 67,
          132, 136

1:25–27 54–57

1:26 ....13, 62, 93–94, 132

1:26–27 .... 63, 131

1:27 ....7, 13, 15, 55,
          59, 66, 112, 132

1:28 ....4, 15, 48, 51,
          57–59, 62, 65,
          112–13, 140

1:28–29 57–60

1:29 .... 51, 59, 74, 140

1:30 114

2 .... 61, 68–71

2:1 .... 51, 60–61, 64,
          89–128, 140–41

2:1–5 .... 51, 60–65

2:2 ..... 23, 51, 56, 62, 84,
          109, 112, 137, 140

2:2–3 .... 23, 61–65, 132

2:2–4 13

2:3 ....63–64, 66, 74,
          113, 133

2:3–5 66

2:4 7

2:4–5 64–65

2:5 .... 49, 52, 64–65,
          89–128

2:6 .... 13, 66–69, 74,
          89–128, 133

2:6–7 .... 65–68, 79

2:6–23 .... 16, 29, 51,
          65–88, 130

2:7 .... 66, 74, 111, 115,
          130–31

2:8............. 7–8, 13–14,
          64–65, 68–70,
          77, 79–80, 84,
          86–87, 93
2:8–15 38
2:9............. 43–44, 74
2:9–10...... 13, 23, 70–72
2:9–15...........65, 70–79
2:10 70–72
2:10–12 28
2:11 ..... 7, 72–75, 89–128
2:11–12 72–75
2:12..... 13, 15, 72–73, 75,
          84, 89–128
2:13...... 7, 15, 31, 89–128
2:13–14...........13, 28, 77
2:13–15 .... 72, 75–78
2:14............. 46, 76–77
2:15...........7, 13–14, 46,
          70, 72, 77–78, 84,
          93, 95
2:16................. 7, 81–82
2:16–17...............79–81
2:16–18 7
2:16–23 ....65, 72,
          78–88, 90
2:17........................... 81
2:18......7, 70, 81, 84, 87,
          89–128
2:18–19 .... 79, 81–84
2:19............. 62, 81, 83,
          109, 111
2:20..... 8, 13–14, 31, 80,
          89–128
2:20–23.........79, 84–88
2:21.......................7, 85
2:22–23 86
2:23 ....7, 82, 85–86,
          89–128

2:23–24 5
3 89–128
3:1................15, 89–128
3:1–2 .... 4, 13, 90–92,
          95, 116, 127
3:1–4 90–95
3:1–17 114–15
3:1–4:1...........14, 89–131
3:2 ....90, 92
3:3 .... 85, 89–128
3:3–4...................13, 94
3:4 .... 4, 13, 15,
          93–95, 132
3:5 .... 87, 95–97, 99,
          101, 106
3:5–8................ 95–100
3:5–10 104
3:5–11................89–128
3:6 ....15, 96, 99–100
3:6–7 97–99
3:7 99
3:8 .... 99–101, 105–06
3:9 99
3:9–10 14
3:9–11............... 100–04
3:10 ......99, 101, 104–05
3:11 ....102, 127, 137
3:12 ...... 99, 105–07, 109
3:12–14 104–09
3:12–17 89–128
3:13 ....104, 114, 118
3:13–14 107–09
3:13–24...................114
3:14 .... 23, 62, 108
3:15 ...... 109–13, 115, 130
3:15–16 115
3:15–17 ....68, 104,
          109–15, 131, 137
3:16.......112–14, 130, 134

3:16–17 134
3:17 .... 18, 104,
          114–15, 130
3:18........... 104, 115, 117
3:18–19...............116–19
3:18–4:1............89–128
3:19 116–17
3:20 ....104, 115, 120, 122
3:20–21 119–21
3:21........................ 120
3:22 ....104, 115, 119,
          122–24
3:22–25 122–27
3:22–4:1 121–28
3:23 .... 104, 115
3:23–24 124–25
3:24 .... 15, 104, 115,
          124–25
3:24–25 125–27
3:25...................15, 125
4:1 ....104, 115, 125,
          127–28
4:2 ....68, 129–31, 133
4:2–4 130
4:2–6 129–35
4:2–18 129–44
4:3 131–32
4:3–4 .... 129, 131–32
4:4................... 132, 135
4:4–5.......................133
4:5 133
4:5–6 ..... 14, 129, 131–35
4:6......................134–35
4:7 ....136, 140
4:7–9 ....5, 121, 129,
          135–37, 148
4:7–18 ....129, 135–44
4:8........................ 136
4:9................... 137, 159

4:10 181
4:10–11 138–41
4:10–14 129,
138–41, 181
4:10–15 180
4:11 .... 139, 181
4:12 .... 22–23, 59, 131,
136, 139, 181
4:12–13 ....7, 22
4:12–14 138–41
4:13 .... 60–65, 140–41
4:14 141
4:15 141–42
4:15–16 141
4:15–17 141–43
4:16 .... 61, 136, 142
4:17 .... 143, 150, 159
4:18 ....17, 129,
143–44, 177

1 Thessalonians
1:2 18
1:3 19
1:4 105
1:10 98
2:4 25
2:15 25
2:17 64
4:3 96–97
4:7 97
4:13–18 90
4:16 38
5:5 28
5:6 130
5:8 19
5:23 110
5:25 144
5:27 142

2 Thessalonians
2:2 143
2:11–12 53
2:13 105
3:17 143

1 Timothy
1:16 107
2:8–15 116
3:16 33
4:8 88
5:1–6:2 116
6:17 112

2 Timothy
1:14 112
1:15–17 144
2:15 .... 57, 113
3:10 107
3:16 57
4:6–8 .... 5, 144
4:10 ....141, 181
4:11 .... 138–41, 181
4:12 136

Titus
1:3 132
1:7 54
2:2–10 116
3:2 100
3:4 106
3:6 112
3:12 136

Philemon
1 .... 147, 155, 159, 167
1–2 158
1–3 157–60
1–7 157–65
2 .... 137, 143, 149–50,
155–56
3 ....154–55, 160,
179, 182
4 ....18, 162–63
4–5 161–62
4–7 161–64
5 ....154–55, 159, 161,
163, 166, 170,
173, 179
5–7 165
6 ....162–63, 175
6–7 162–64
7 .... 150, 155, 159, 163,
165–66, 170, 173, 178
8 166–67
8–9 .... 166–67, 179
8–10 165
8–14 166–72
8–20 165–78
9 .....158, 161–62, 165–67
10 .... 165, 167–68
10–18 159
11 ....152–53, 156, 174
11–12 168–70
12 .... 150, 161, 164,
169–70, 178
13 .... 150, 152, 170
13–14 170–72
14 ....161, 170–73
15 172–73
15–16 ....149, 152, 155,
172–74
16 .... 137, 155–56, 158,
171, 173–74, 179
17 ....153, 161–62, 175
17–20 .... 155, 175–78
18 .... 125, 149–50,
172, 177
18–19 175–77

19 ....143, 159, 177
20 ...... 150, 155, 161, 164,
178–79
21 .... 152, 179, 182
21–22 179–80
21–25 179–82
22 ....160, 180
23 .... 22, 138–41,
158, 181
23–24...............180–81
24 .... 138–41, 181
25 .... 155, 160, 182

Hebrews

1:3.......35, 37–38, 40, 92
1:6 36
1:10....................50
2:2 8
3:13 61
4:12....................58
5:12 69
8:1 92
8:5 80
8:8–12.................... 115
10:1....................... 80
10:24...................... 25
11:1......................... 20
12:11...................27, 68
12:23.......................36
13:7...................... 124

James

1:2 .... 27, 52
1:10–11 99
1:21 99
3............................100

3:9 100
5:10.......................107

1 Peter

1:1...........................19
1:3............... 19, 57, 180
1:3–4 90
1:5 .... 20, 26, 60,
75, 93–94
1:6 .... 27, 52
1:17 19
1:18 69
2............................59
2:1 99
2:2–3.......................59
2:5 67
2:9...................105, 136
2:11 ....19, 85
2:18–24 121
2:18–3:7 116
2:23 100
3:15 135
3:19...................77–78
3:20 107
3:22 92
4:1 92
4:3 96
4:4 102
4:5 97
4:7 130
5:2 171
5:8 84
5:11 .... 139, 181

2 Peter

3:15–16 143

1 John

1:9 98
3:2 95
3:5 98

Jude

9..............................38

Revelation

1:3.......................... 142
1:5............................36
2–3 148
2:1–7...................... 6
2:12–29 68–70
2:21..........................96
3:3 130
3:14–22 ....60–65, 141
3:18........................ 88
3:20 131
3:14–22 17
4:4............................39
6:9 53
6:9–11 126
6:11 53
12:9..........................84
12:12 46
13:7.......................... 53
14:8 96
19:20 46
20:3..........................84
20:10 46
20:11–15 98
20:14........................46
21:1–22:5 39
22:5 95
22:12 126

Other Ancient Literature

1 Enoch

20:1–7 38

47:1–4 53

2 Enoch

20:1 39

4 Ezra

4:35–37 53

Josephus

Antiquities of the Jews

15:163 8

Jubilees

1:27 8

2:1 8